Cairo, the glory years

Harpocrates

Also from Harpocrates:

Alexandria 1860–1960: the brief life of a cosmopolitan community
Ed. Robert Ilbert & Ilios Yannakakis

Alexandria, third century BC: the knowledge of the world in a single city
Ed. Christian Jacob & François de Polignac

A Short Guide to the Græco-Roman Museum, Alexandria
Jean-Yves Empereur

A Short Guide to the Catacombs of Kom el Shoqafa, Alexandria
Jean-Yves Empereur

Siwa; the oasis
Alain Blottière

The Fayoum, a historical exploration
Pierre Gazio

Copyright © Harpocrates Publishing 2003
9, Sesostris Street, Attarine
Alexandria, Egypt
Tel: 03 486 2669

Dar el Kutub no. 18378/2003
ISBN 977-5845-08-4

Original photography by Tim Loveless
CG maps by Ismail Awad & Cécile Shaalan
Printed by BAFRA GRAPHICS, 58 Moharrem Bey Street, Alexandria.
Tel: 03 3920547/3925482
Fax: 03 4939975

Front cover: The Beyerlé Palace after its transformation into Kasr al Dubara Girls' College. Courtesy of Nelly al Alfy.

Cairo, the glory years

Who built what, when, why and for whom...

Samir Raafat

"If you ignore bad neighbourhoods, they will eventually haunt you."

Contents

7. *Appendices*   *299*

Introduction

This book began as a series of brief articles in a weekly newspaper, the *Cairo Times,* under the heading *Landmarks.* I was hoping to save the memories of districts, landmarks, buildings and their inhabitants. The information collected came primarily from personal conversations and on-site visits. At times it was like entering an archaeological dig in which the remnants of an elegant past and the accompanying stories can only be discovered by burrowing through urban debris. Along with my own memories of the city I grew up in, this is how I learned that, in contrast to its current state of crowded, crumbling gridlock, Cairo was once a world-class capital featuring the creations of some of the best architectural talents of the day.

At the same time, I observed how several fashionable new compounds and gated communities were mushrooming around the city, readily accessible via ring-roads, bridges and tunnels. Big money is moving away from downtown Cairo and the "old" suburbs to newer, more expensive enclaves in the desert, where the architecture ranges from neo-California to *faux* Luis Baragan passing through Disneyland and Mount Olympus. The centre, it would appear, is being abandoned to an already well-advanced rot.

Given the present decay, overcrowding and haphazard planning, it may sometimes be difficult to grasp that modern Cairo was once an architecturally attractive city. The period from the end of the nineteenth century up until the 1950s witnessed an architectural flowering that was unparalleled, with a variety of styles existing side by side: baroque, neo-classical, art nouveau, art deco, rococo khedivial, colonial, Bauhaus, Italian renaissance, arabesque and neo-pharaonic. Altogether this produced an eclectic riot of elegant buildings.

Much of the city's downtown was built at a time when Cairo was booming with money, taste and a sense of proportion. It was also an era when Egypt was more firmly tied into the world economy, when society was both open to and more accepting of outside influences. The architects of that period had often studied in the West when Frank Lloyd Wright was making headlines in America and Le Corbusier and Hausmann were still seriously revered in Paris. Committed to bringing back part of what they had seen, they were bent on making a difference in Cairo. A difference that would not only enrich Cairo's skyline, but also provide a lead for Egypt's home-grown architects.

Between 1960 and 1990, however, almost all new construction east and west of the Nile could be written off as void of any architectural appeal. Worse still are certain modern Cairo districts like Nasr City and Mohandiseen—ugly urban sprawls conceived in the 1960s and now ants' nests of crumbling concrete high rises.

So, what happened?

Two decades of ill-managed socialism and a host of flawed legislation regulating housing and rent control produced more long-term architectural devastation than Black Saturday, when much of central Cairo went up in flames on January 26, 1952. Attempts by the new "revolutionary" regime to create a more egalitarian society saw the sequestration and confiscation of what were viewed as "elitist" properties. These same properties were then turned to purposes for which they were most often not suited. Luxury villas became overcrowded and under-funded schools; apartment blocks were transformed into public sector offices. It is as if Cairo's buildings were all at once painted over with grime. Air-conditioning units were randomly stuck to façades and inappropriate advertisements obscured exterior detailing. One by one, the regal foyers saw their embellishments and accoutrements replaced by neon lights and cracked mirrors. And while their flower-boxes, marble fountains and oak letterboxes receded into horrific shadows, the new tenants of these buildings retreated into xenophobia. Their civic responsibilities did not get out the front door. The rest was up to the socialist state, their new and useless landlord.

The end result of the half-baked rental laws imposed during this period is that today the monthly rent for a luxury four-bedroom apartment in Zamalek's Lebon Building is considerably *less* than for a hovel in any one of the slums that encircle Cairo. And while the original owner of an entire apartment block may receive a measly LE25, the tenant can turn around and sub-lease his flat for $2,500. Does he plough back any of his gains into the building's general upkeep? Take a look around and guess...

During socialism's heyday, Egypt's rising *apparatchiks*, many of them members of a regime that had set its face hard against the old elites, unabashedly tailored decrees enabling them to lay their hands on apartments hastily vacated by the former captains and kings of Egypt's defunct industry. Many of these buildings had been passed on to state-owned insurance companies with no knowledge of real estate management, and favours were regularly hawked to the regime's favourite cronies. Curiously, few of President

Nasser's entourage and praise-writers wanted to live in his banal district of Nasr City.

Another and very contemporary part of the problem is, of course, a lack of education about and appreciation of the city's rich architectural past. Until very recently, anything associated with Egypt's *ancien regime* was viewed as irrevocably bad, and thus wished away, consigned almost literally to the famous dustbin of history. Not long ago, I asked a mid-level diplomat slotted for a posting in a major Western capital, in whose palace the Ministry of Foreign Affairs was until recently housed. He didn't know and behaved as if he couldn't care less. A bunch of schoolgirls and their bovine teacher were playing in the grounds of a magnificent villa-cum-school opposite the Semiramis Hotel. I asked them who was the martyr Ali Abdel Latif whose name is now inscribed on the building. "All we know is that our school is named after him," they giggled in chorus and ran off. And then I knew something was seriously wrong when a senior editor at Cairo's principal daily newspaper thought Kasr al Dubara was somewhere in Nasr City.

This lack of proper education and knowledge of a society's history is dangerous enough, but when combined with a blatant lack of civic pride it becomes very alarming. Nobody knows and nobody cares. Crass replaces brass, haste overtakes taste, and the word "maintenance" has gone the way of the *tarboush*. Most people if asked now would rather have an apartment in a new concrete pile in Dokki rather than in the decaying gentility of old glories downtown.

In the post-*infitah* period, much wealth has been amassed, resulting in an army of new millionaires. Along with them come the second tier rich: high fee doctors, bankers, and lawyers whose principal job these days is to keep the new rich healthy, solvent and out of jail. All are fleeing the city for the new-fangled manicured condominiums: Mirage, Dreamland, Gardenia and Utopia, just like the 1920s and 1930s when monied Cairenes and the new bourgeoisie migrated from Shubra, Helmia, Abbassia and Mounira to Heliopolis, Maadi, Zamalek and Giza, leaving behind them crumbling relics of a hastily forgotten past.

Après moi le deluge has become an endemic attitude.

Maadi, 2003

1. The east bank

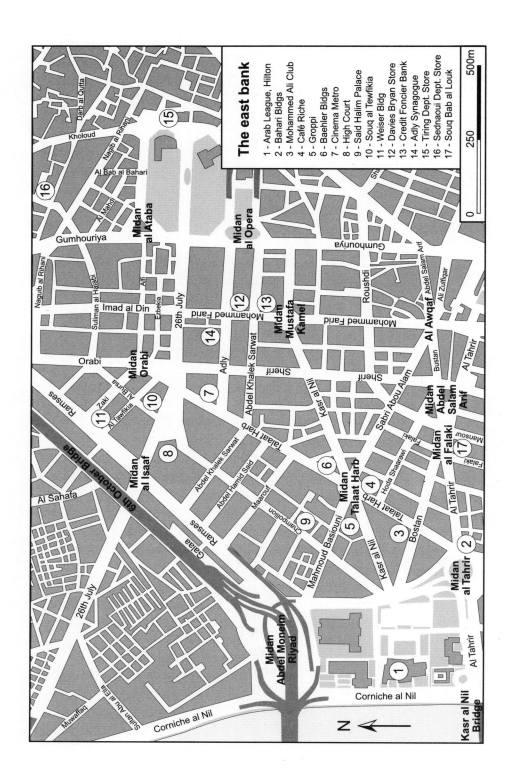

The east bank

1 - Arab League, Hilton
2 - Bahari Bldgs
3 - Mohammed Ali Club
4 - Café Riche
5 - Groppi
6 - Baehler Bldgs
7 - Cinema Metro
8 - High Court
9 - Said Halim Palace
10 - Souq al Tewfikia
11 - Weiser Bldg
12 - Davies Bryan Store
13 - Credit Foncier Bank
14 - Adly Synagogue
15 - Tiring Dept. Store
16 - Sednaoui Dept. Store
17 - Souq Bab al Louk

0   250   500m

The nation's plaza

Like ageless Cairo, Midan al Tahrir in the city centre cannot sit still. Whether reflecting the city's moods or the leadership's political agenda, the nation's most important plaza has gone from *faux* Champs de Mars to Stalinesque esplanade. Whenever a new regime feels the nation's capital needs a new look, the Midan has been the place to start.

Until the nineteenth century, the area of the present Midan al Tahrir (Liberation Square) was a large swamp faithfully replenished each summer by the Nile flood. That changed when Egypt's then ruler decided to build a Western-style city. In his obsession to create a Paris-sur-Nil, with long broad boulevards punctuated by midans and public gardens, Khedive Ismail continued an ambitious canal scheme first started by his father. One of its aims was to reclaim Cairo's western flank to make room for the famous '*kasr*' (palace) series: Kasr al Aini, Kasr al Aali, Kasr al Dubara, Kasr al Nil and Kasr al Walda, each with its own Nile-front garden.

The new palace district featured a magnificent square, called at the time, Midan Ismailia. It was the country's biggest—larger even than Alexandria's Midan Mohammed Ali, or downtown Cairo's Midan Ibrahim Pasha, named for Khedive Ismail's grandfather and father respectively.

The new surrounding area came to be known as Cairo's European Quarter, Al Kahira al Ismailia, or Ismailia for short. Likewise, the city's first modern bridge was christened *Kobri* Ismail and the avenue running towards it from the royal palace of Abdin was also *Sharia Kobri* Ismail. And just to make sure everyone was clear on who was behind it all, one of the palaces abutting the new square was Kasr al Ismailia.

With so many namesakes of Khedive Ismail among Cairo's landmarks, it would need a revolution to remove him from the face of the capital city, which, as it turned out, is what eventually happened.

Kasr al Nil was the first construction in the area and although credit for that goes to Ismail's uncle and aunt, Viceroy Said Pasha and his sister Nazli Hanem, it was Ismail who made numerous extensions and adjustments to the palace. For a while, part of the vastly expanded palace was home to Ismail's army as well as his council of ministers. It also housed his ill-fated treasury, whose coffers were nearly drained by the ambitious khedivial building schemes.

Uniquely situated, with tracks linking it to Cairo's main railway station,

Kasr al Nil was just too much of a temptation for the British, the new rulers of Egypt after 1882. It became the principle headquarters for the British Army of Occupation, where every morning beefy, red-faced soldiers paraded by the square and, whenever necessary, shot Egyptian nationalists who marched upon the highly visible palace-turned-*Ingilizi*-barracks.

The new century brought its own changes to the square and in March 1902, the Italian firm of Giuseppe Garozzo & Francesco Zaffarani completed the neo-classical Egyptian Museum, designed by Frenchman Marcel Dourgnon. The world's most prized antiquities collection moved from Ismail's riverside Giza Palace (later turned into a zoo) to its present home. Khedive Abbas Hilmi inaugurated the museum on November 15, 1902, and its first curator was French Egyptologist, Gaston Maspero Pasha.

Other fine structures fronting Midan Ismailia at the turn of the century included the palace of reigning Khedive Abbas Hilmi's sister (now owned by the Ministry of Foreign Affairs and currently undergoing restoration), and the palace of Ahmed Khairy Pasha. The latter became Nestor Gianaclis' cigarette factory, then Cairo University and is now the American University in Cairo (AUC). Also on the midan was Kasr al Ismailia, occupied for some time by Ghazi Mukhtar Pasha, the Turkish High Commissioner to Egypt.

Midan Ismailia's north-eastern flank was home to large villas, including Count Zogheb's *Okel*, a resounding example of an oriental palace. Passers-by took pleasure in admiring the neighbourhood's railed-in gardens, where proud Nubian *bowwabs* stood guard behind closed iron gates.

Not long after, these villas were overtaken by smart apartment houses belonging to affluent businessmen and merchants whose fathers and grandfathers—Messrs. Sarpakis, Zogheb, Soussa, Zaidan, Matossian and Bahari—had been lured to Egypt by Ismail's massive building schemes. It is interesting to note that during the first half of the twentieth century, only two of the buildings fronting the square were attributed to bona fide Egyptians, Abdel Malek Hanna and Ahmed Bey Ihsan. As for the surviving villa, belonging to renowned 1920s feminist Hoda Shaarawi, it understandably became an urban anachronism, a lonely testimonial of things past. It was singled out for annihilation in the 1970s. What was once a unique arabesque villa, is today a large parking lot, next door to, appropriately enough, a restaurant called *Arabesque*.

As the century moved towards its midpoint, further changes took place around the nation's largest plaza. The Kasr al Nil barracks, finally evacuated by the British on March 29, 1947, were torn down a few years later to make way for modern developments that included Africa's first Hilton Hotel, designed by Santa Monica's Wilton Becket, and the Arab League Headquarters, designed by Mahmoud Riad.

Meanwhile, on the other side of the esplanade, the mountainous governmental *Mogamaa* complex, housing offices of all manner of ministries, was inaugurated in 1952. It became the beacon of mediocrity for Egypt's rising state-run bureaucracy.

On September 2, 1954, in its effort to remove all traces of the old regime, Egypt's new leadership renamed 15 Cairo streets and squares. The emerging strongman, Gamal Abdel Nasser, decreed that all things Ismailian belonged in the doghouse, so Midan Ismailia became Midan al Tahrir.

Yet the big question remained; whose statue would be placed atop the colossal red granite pillar at the centre of Cairo's broadest traffic circle? It must surely be crowned with the statue of *Al Rais* himself, clamoured Nasser's devotees and praise writers.

The crushing June 1967 defeat removed any expectation of a Nasserite icon adorning Cairo's epicentre. Within hours of Nasser's pledge of a lightning victory, Egypt lost the entire Sinai Peninsula while the Arab nation lost Gaza, the Golan Heights, the West Bank and half of Jerusalem. Curiously, until 2003 when a statue of Sheikh Omar Makram was erected in front of the Mogamaa building, the only statue remotely overlooking Midan al Tahrir was that of French archaeologist Auguste-Edouard Mariette Pasha, designed by Denys Pierre Puesch. It stands in the garden of the Egyptian Antiquities Museum honouring the man who rendered exceptional services to Egypt's heritage.

Meanwhile, the granite pillar intended for the great leader's statue stood unadorned until the 1980s. It was finally removed when construction of the Cairo Metro began. This period can be considered the lowest point for the midan, as the whole area was torn up to install the underground tunnels. A metal pedestrian footbridge of astonishing ugliness was erected so that people could move from one side of Tahrir Square to the other. Ten years later, the metro was completed and the footbridge came down. From then on, things could only get better.

Besides the Kentucky Fried Chickens and Golden Arches, Midan al Tahrir's latest look (currently in the making) includes a massive underground garage and several palm-decked gardens, welcome developments in a city choked by cars and pollution. As alterations continue, perhaps, sometime in the not-too-distant future, a commemoration of the midan's original founder will materialise. Stranger things have happened at Midan al Tahrir— or, dare I say Ismail?

Witness to history

Khedive Ismail was quick to note that Europe boasted dozens of plazas, piazzas and squares honouring its princes and generals. Vienna and Berlin had Teutonic kaisers and V-shaped generals, Paris had someone of consequence at almost every major intersection, and perched on London's Trafalgar Square there is that admiral of Abou Kir fame.

Egypt's reply was not late in coming. Soon enough, statues of Ismail's father and grandfather—Ibrahim and Mohammed Ali—were erected in Cairo and Alexandria's main squares. Both claimed lists of victories the length of your arm. Yet a city as big as Cairo could do with more than one generalissimo.

Enter Soliman Pasha, Egypt's fabled French-born general. He proved that Mohammed Ali's arsenal was second to none in the region. Although Jean Anthelme Seve (a.k.a. Soliman Pasha al Fransawi) never made it beyond the middle ranks of Napoleon's armies, in Egypt, as Bimbashi Soliman, he made the big time.

In return for his dedication, the converted Frenchman was showered with medals, gifts and elevated positions. In 1872, a life-size statue of the soldier-pasha dressed in Zouave costume was earmarked for erection at the epicentre of Cairo's emerging European district. Its author was French sculptor, Henri Alfred Jacquemart, also responsible for the four Kasr al Nil Bridge lions, as well as the equestrian statue of Mohammed Ali (erected on August 11, 1872) at Alexandria's Place Mohammed Ali. The base of Soliman Pasha's statue is reportedly the work of Louis Louvet.

It was also Jacquemart who made Mohammed Laz-Oglou's statue that stands at the square of the same name near Parliament House. In Paris, Jacquemart sculpted the stone sphinx of the Chatelet fountain and the dragons of the St Michel fountain.

Soliman's greatest honour was awarded posthumously in 1922, when his great-granddaughter, Nazli Abdel Rehim Sabry, became the first modern-day Queen of Egypt. This ultimate recognition was to be the general's undoing. After the revolution, xenophobic Republican Officers, with not a single victory to their name, ordered the removal of Soliman Pasha's statue. In their effort to erase the preceding era, the military junta apparently proclaimed the nineteenth century conqueror 'guilty by royal association!'

As a result, General Soliman is today wallowing next to a coca cola stand in some dappled corner of the Military Museum, not far from his benefactor's final resting-place.

Yet as much as the establishment willed against it and despite four decades of his former square being named after nationalist financier Talaat Harb, Soliman's memory lives on. Neither the name-change that took place on February 12, 1964, nor the statue of Talaat Harb (by sculptor Fathi Mahmoud) that followed a month later succeeded in wiping out the memory of Egypt's old warrior. Young taxi drivers who never saw the original statue would still take you straight to Midan Soliman Pasha whenever asked.

The history of the square itself is just as rich as that of its namesake. It started out in life as Midan Karakol (a Turkish word meaning black hole), so named because of a police station that was placed there. Because of its commanding position at the intersection of three major avenues and the seven important *belle époque* buildings overlooking it, renaming it Midan Soliman Pasha befitted one of Cairo's most prominent squares. Ask any aged Cairene and he'll tell you about its glitz, glamour and gaudiness.

He will recount how history paraded under Soliman Pasha's nose whenever the funeral corteges of Egypt's greats marched by during the first half of the twentieth century, from Midan Ismail (now Tahrir) to the Kekhia Mosque, located at the end of Kasr al Nil Street. He will evoke the day when Lord Allenby strutted around the tree-lined midan at the head of his triumphant regiments, with planes flying above, celebrating the defeat of the German-backed Ottomans in Palestine and Syria. Soliman had conquered those very same adversaries a century earlier.

Others may even recount the failed December 1919 assassination attempt of Egypt's last Coptic Prime Minister, Sir Youssef Wahba Pasha. And how the Coptic would-be assassin had been waiting for his victim at the nearby Café Riche, located on the ground floor of the Tawakol Building at No. 17 Soliman Pasha Street.

According to a commercial directory, Café Riche opened sometime during 1908. Its first owner was Bernard Steinberg who also owned Carnaval de Venise, a small haberdashery in downtown Cairo. On the other hand, deeds and titles in the possession of the café's current owner, Magdi Abdel Malek, say that the first operator was Frenchman Pierre-Henri Ressigné. In any case, it was Michel Politis who, having acquired the establishment in 1916, spent a difficult period trying to obtain a license allowing him to host an orchestra since neighbourhood residents were first required to hand in their collective consent to the then chief of police Harvey Pasha. Politis belonged to the vast association of Greek café operators who had a quasi monopoly on this particular occupation up to the 1950s.

Soon, Politis' celebrated café-theatre extended from its present location all the way to the midan. Then, like now, hardly anyone recalled that most of the area south-east of the square had been where the palace of Prince Mohammed Ali Tewfik stood. However, in order to build what became Manial Palace on the island of Roda, the brother of the reigning khedive reportedly had to mortgage his downtown residence to the Egyptian Mortgage Company. Eventually the Egyptian Land Company acquired the property along with a bunch of Syrian entrepreneurs including the Pharaons, Zoghebs and Shiha families. Soon enough the palace was cleared and the land divided into smaller lots. Which is how, in an effort to expand in 1921-22, Café Riche bought the stretch of land separating it from the nearby midan. It was on this extension that Politis established a garden theatre where Mounira al Mahdia, Umm Kulthum, Zaki Murad and other well-known or rising singers performed for paltry sums.

Just as now, *fin de siècle* tourists knew Midan Soliman Pasha well. To begin with, it was home to the Savoy Hotel, where titled lords and ladies stayed before it was transformed into British Army Headquarters during the First World War. In 1924-5, Swiss hospitality czar, Charles Albert Baehler, would pull down the Savoy, replacing it with two blocks of handsome apartment buildings.

During the interwar years, Egypt's beautiful people would rendezvous at either Groppi or Locke, the city's most elegant tearooms, located by the midan. Following a savoury repast, or perhaps before high tea, they converged on the nearby French boutiques or leafed through the latest *ouvrage* at Feldman & Liebovitch's 'Au Bouquiniste Oriental', then situated on the ground floor level of No. 6-8 Midan Soliman Pasha.

Cairo's leading bookshop was domiciled in one of the city's most interesting examples of 1900s art nouveau architecture, Immeuble Michel Ayyub. It has since lost much of its grandeur along with its unique corner turrets, but in days gone by this singular building housed Cairo's best doctors, the cleverest Parisian couturiers and for some time was home to Egypt's golden youth. The latter eagerly scaled the building's three floors to attend Lucien Robert's famous ballroom dancing classes.

Meanwhile, at the abutting 1900s Gresham Court and Building (No. 20-22 Soliman Pasha Street) designed by Ariston St. John Diamant, British barristers—when Consular Courts were still around—exchanged judicial gossip. During the First World War, Gresham Court became home to a branch of the popular YMCA. It was here where British and Allied officers found welcome entertainment, relief and companionship.

Like the Savoy, several other original structures disappeared from Midan Soliman Pasha, to be replaced by newer buildings. For instance, Mazza's Immeuble Sednaoui replaced an older building, which itself had squatted on part of the former garden of Palais Aslan Cattaui.

Another newcomer on the square was the semi-circular building, designed by Desiré Wartza in 1927-8, on what had been Café Riche's short-lived garden theatre. The choice piece of land fronting the square had become the property of the sons of Jewish broker David Adda—Joseph and Leon— who sold it in 1927 to Gaston Homsy, a Syrian businessman from Aleppo. Acquired in 1946 by the Al Chams Company, the building was subsequently purchased by the French insurance company, La Paternelle. With the private sector being nationalised in July 1961, the building is today the property of Misr Insurance Company.

The story of this singular piece of property is typical of much of Cairo's other *belle époque* assets. Notwithstanding who owned the land and when, the fact remains that No. 1 Midan Soliman Pasha would forever separate Café Riche from the famous square.

Among other prominent businesses, Midan Soliman Pasha housed the prestigious Standard Life Insurance office building, then run by Sir Scott Moncrieff. Also located on the first floor of No. 14 Soliman Pasha Street, was the popular *Circolo Risotto* Italian Club, where *fascios* held rowdy meetings in the years preceding the Second World War. Decades later Air France and its associate, Air Liban, would move into the rejuvenated building's ground floor extension.

Another romantic milestone in the Midan's repertoire was the much-touted arrival in 1925 of the Mazza-designed Groppi Building, constructed on land previously owned by Antoine de Zogheb, the Honorary Consul of Portugal. The new building added yet another landmark to a city gone wildly cosmopolitan. Just as they had attracted considerable attention when they were first exhibited at an international fair in Paris, the Swiss chocolatier's unique art deco mosaics, designed by A. Castaman, were the subject of animated conversation among Groppi's international patrons. Cairo's Greeks meanwhile congregated then, as they still do today although in much smaller numbers, in the charming Greek Club, located on the building's first floor.

Cairo's baby boomers may tell you how Groppi made history again during the burning of Cairo in January 1952. This was when Midan Soliman Pasha was the venue of wild mobs circling around the fabled statue waving flags shouting "Ingilizi Out." It was on this occasion that the sweetest scent Cairo would ever know filled the air as the sugar and chocolate supplies of the celebrated teahouse were set on fire.

Not long after, Egypt's monarchy fell and streets, squares and buildings were renamed. The banishing of Soliman Pasha in order to honour Talaat Harb (father of Egypt's modern economy), not only resulted in the prejudiced removal of a cultural landmark, but also did away with a bit of precious history from the continent's oldest capital.

Egypt's premier café

Groppi, once the most celebrated tearoom this side of the Mediterranean, was the creation of Giacomo Groppi, a native of Lugano, Switzerland. Maison Groppi became chief purveyor of chocolate to monarchs and pashas throughout the Middle East. Whenever pashas, beys and resident-foreigners travelled to Europe they took cartons filled with Groppi chocolates with them. During the Second World War, it is said King Farouk freighted by air to London, via Khartoum, Entebbe, Dakar, Lisbon, and Dublin, a lacquered box emblazoned with the royal arms of Egypt and Great Britain. Inside, to the delight of Great Britain's Princesses, Elizabeth and Margaret, were100 kilos of Groppi chocolates.

After a short apprenticeship with an uncle in Lugano and brief employment in Provence in the south of France, Giacomo Groppi arrived in Egypt in the 1880s to take up employment at Maison Gianola, a popular Swiss pastry and teashop on Bawaki Street, Cairo. In 1890, 27-year-old Giacomo Groppi bought out Gianola's interests in its Alexandria Rue de France branch and proceeded to open his own pastry and dairy shop.

By 1900, Groppi was running a successful enterprise annually exporting 100,000 cartons of eggs to the United Kingdom.

At Maison Groppi's second Alexandrine branch, on Cherif Street, crème chantilly was introduced for the first time in Egypt. This was a new technological feat that Groppi acquired while touring the Exposition

Universelle in Paris. He was also the first chocolatier in Egypt to employ females. In 1906, he sold his company to a Frenchman, Auguste Baudrot, and retired. For the next 60 years, Baudrot was regarded as first amongst equals whenever compared to Alexandria's other famous tearooms such as Pastroudis, Trianon and Athineos.

Groppi, however, did not long remain in retirement. Just one year later he lost his entire savings during the economic crash of 1907. He was obliged to return to what he knew best: making chocolate. But out of deference to Baudrot, Groppi moved his activities to Cairo's Al Magrabi Street (later, Adly Pasha Street). With only La Marquise de Sévigné and Maison Mathieu (renamed Sault) as competition, Maison Groppi was ensured success in the nation's capital. The formal opening took place on December 23, 1909.

By the time the First World War broke out, Groppi's tea garden had become a favourite with the British Army of Occupation. A delicatessen was added, enhancing Groppi's image as the purveyor of quality food products.

In 1922, Maison Groppi inaugurated its own cold storage company—Industrie du Froid—employing over 120 workers and producing a daily output of 2,400 blocks of ice. Six years later, Groppi's son, Achilles, launched his famous ice cream—a technology he had imported from the United States. The names of his delicious specialities were as exceptional as they tasted. Sfogliatella, Morocco, Mau Mau, Pêche Melba, Maruska, Comtesse Marie, and Surprise Neapolitaine were some of the more famous flavours.

Cairenes were grateful to Achilles for yet another creation: the Groppi Tearoom and Rotunda situated on Midan Soliman Pasha. They were located on the ground floor of a new building designed by Giuseppe Mazza. Following the inauguration ceremony on Thursday, March 12, 1925, the next morning's papers were full of praise for the new Parisian-style café and the sumptuous reception that Achilles and Giacomo Groppi had given to mark the occasion. The description in *Egypte Nouvelle*, better left in its original French, read:

> Il serait dificile, en effet, de rever cadre plus somptueux et, en meme temps, de meilleur gout que celui dans lequel se deroula cette soirée inoubliable... Avec ses piliers gainés de marbre, sa cloture aux larges vitres garnies de brise-bise mordorés, et l'immense et splendide verrière en rosace qui forme le plafond de sa coupole tronquée, la vaste rotonde, constitue un palais féerique, le plus élégant, le plus beau qui a été, de mémoire d'homme élevé ici à Terpischore.

International celebrities visited the Rotunda whenever in town. All admired the art deco design and Castaman's exquisite mosaic display. Soon enough Cairo's top social and official functions took place there and the Rotunda became *the* rendezvous, not surprising considering Groppi's famous non-stop concert dances featured a 20-piastre set menu. Performers in those days included leading orchestras such as the Mondial Boys, court violinist Alexander Kontorowicz, and the Cherry Pickers. On Sunday mornings the Rotunda was home to concerts performed by the Small Symphony Orchestra of the Egyptian State Broadcasting (ESB).

In the interwar period, Cairo's first outdoor cinema was launched in Groppi's garden at the Soliman Pasha branch (the garden would later disappear). In her brilliant book, *Cairo in the War 1939-45*, Artemis Cooper relates how Groppi was one of the few smart places open to everyone.

> There were two, one on Midan Soliman Pasha and the other on Adly Pasha Street which boasted a garden where pashas came to sip coffee and eat cream cakes with their Levantine mistresses and where officers on leave looked out for female companionship.

A few years later, Groppi of Cairo would open a terrace café in Heliopolis overlooking Avenue des Pyramides and the legendary Heliopolis Palace Hotel (now a presidential palace). And to accommodate the less privileged, Maison Groppi launched a chain of pastry and coffee shops called A l'Americaine.

By the 1940s, Groppi owned its own farm situated outside Cairo at Gezirat al Dahab. On 1,400 feddans, Maison Groppi operated a dairy and poultry unit as well as a herb, vegetable and exotic fruit plantation. A laboratory equipped with the latest technology was imported to ensure the highest quality control. The public was invited to visit Maison Groppi's laboratories and installations on any Monday between 10am and noon.

For many decades the well-heeled catered exclusively from Groppi. All it took was a telephone call from the royal palace, a pasha's villa or an embassy and Groppi took over.

Thankfully Groppi's two main branches miraculously escaped complete destruction during the anti-British Black Saturday riots of January 1952 that ended with the burning of much of downtown Cairo. An eyewitness report states how, at around 2pm, a black Citroen entered Midan Soliman Pasha. From the car window the passengers frantically waved Egypt's crescent and three stars green flag. Suddenly, a rowdy mob came as if from nowhere and the traffic came to a complete stop. The flag-waving car made three or four more turns around Soliman Pasha's statue and disappeared. Suddenly, there was the sound of shattering glass as Groppi's display windows were stoned.

Some of the frenzied mob entered and escorted the employees safely outside while others climbed the wall reaching out for the Groppi sign in an effort to dismantle the royal emblem next to it. Sacks of sugar and flour were dragged into the square. Soon everything was blacked out because of the thick smoke that carried with it the aroma of burning sugar.

Groppi survived Black Saturday and resumed its unchallenged position as Egypt's leading chocolatier. But somehow it would shortly find itself a reluctant pawn during the squalid political machinations that followed. The story goes that in March 1954, Egypt's emerging strongman, Colonel Gamal Abdel Nasser, ordered the placing of a bomb in Groppi's patisserie. While the detonation caused widespread panic, no one was hurt.

The objective of Nasser's macabre exercise was to promote a feeling of public insecurity. The power struggle among the Free Officers had reached a new climax and the vicious smear campaign against Egypt's first president, General Mohammed Naguib, had somehow made its way to Groppi.

Groppi's premium service continued uninterrupted despite the demise of Egypt's pashas and beys and the 1961 nationalisation of Egypt's entire private sector. For a while at least, even the presidential chefs could not replace Groppi. Now, forty years later, the legend of Groppi exists in name only. The decay of the socialist 1960s took their heavy toll. By the time Egypt returned to the ways of an open economy, Groppi's descendants had abandoned the trade and left Egypt.

The Mohammed Ali Club

In 1908, Alexandre Marcel, already an acclaimed French architect, was commissioned to build a downtown club exclusively for foreign-educated pashas and other Egyptian grandees. It would be the royalists answer to the equally exclusive but understandably resented Gezira Sporting Club, where the British 'occupiers' looked down with contempt on all other races and nationalities. The contractors for the project were the

Ambron brothers, Jewish-Italian's based in Alexandria.

The plot of land on which the club would be built was located on the corner of Bostan and Soliman Pasha Streets in the budding Ismailia quarter of Cairo, not far from Kasr al Bostan (today a multi-story car park). As for the style of the one-floor-plus-basement building? Decidedly French.

In actual fact a pasha's club already existed and had been rendered famous by a Homeric altercation involving two members of the khedivial family. On 7 May 1898, in one of the Khedivial Club's halls, the Italian-educated Prince Ahmed Fouad, youngest son of Khedive Ismail, received a bullet in his throat, hereafter responsible for his incapacity to speak properly. The hand holding the gun belonged to his excitable brother-in-law Prince Ahmed Seif al Din. In a fit of sibling heroics, the latter had decided to avenge his sister on the premises that Prince Fouad had consistently mistreated her. Contemporary wags had it that the indigent Fouad was more interested in Princess Shuvikar's considerable fortune than her spare body. In any case, Fouad thought better of it and divorced his wife two weeks later.

The Khedivial was succeeded by the Mohammed Ali Club, so-named in honour of the founder of the dynasty that had ruled Egypt since 1805. It is perhaps no coincidence that the first honorary president of the club was Prince Fouad. Prince Ahmed Seif al Din meanwhile was confined to a sanatorium in the United Kingdom. His fate was further sealed when Fouad became Egypt's ruler in 1917, first as its British-backed sultan and later as its first constitutional monarch.

Sitting on the club's founding board were several other members of the khedivial family along with two future prime ministers—Adly Yeken and Ismail Sidki. The other board members included two Egyptian-Armenian pashas—Arakel Nubar and Yacoub Artin. Their respective fathers had occupied the posts of prime minister and minister of foreign affairs. Moreover, Artin Pasha had witnessed first hand the above-mentioned altercation.

Also on the board was Aziz Izzet Pasha, later to become Egypt's first ambassador to the Court of St. James, and with him were two of Egypt's leading Jewish financiers, Adolphe Aslan Cattaui and Robert Simon Rolo. Both had direct connections to the palace and all three had received a western education either in the United Kingdom, France or Austria. They knew the meaning of a club and the concomitant prestige of belonging to one.

The club's foreign board members included the future head of the Federation of Egyptian Industries, Henri Naus Bey. A Belgian national, he was the father of the Egyptian sugar industry. His compatriot on the board was leading magistrate Maitre Carton de Wiart. The third European member was Sir Alexander Byrd, a token British administrator.

The inclusion of foreigners on the board was in itself a statement by the founders of the club that, unlike the chauvinist Gezira across the Nile, the Mohammed Ali was multi-ethnic. The only requirement for membership, it seems, was that one had to be a prince, a pasha, comfortably rich and reasonably famous.

Title to the club belonged to its shareholders each holding one or more shares worth 200 Egyptian pounds each. Since the declared capital was set at LE14,000 this meant there were 70 shares in all. One such share, which is without doubt a work of art, can be found in the private collection of Ulvia Halim. Her father, Prince Abbas Ibrahim Halim, was a patron of the Mohammed Ali although decidedly more inclined towards the Royal Automobile Club, of which he was a long-time president.

With such an illustrious board it is reasonable to conclude that the Mohammed Ali was the most sought after social club in Cairo. If sporting facilities were non-existant, it more than made up in fine cuisine supervised by either French or Italian chefs. Amid the well-stocked wine cellar and amply stacked library stood a classic billiard room, a bridge room, a fumoir and a gilded banquet hall. Most definitely, the Mohammed Ali was the Athenaeum of Cairo.

Although not lacking in luxury and style, members took to donating artifacts and *objets d'arts* to the Mohammed Ali, including French orientalist paintings belonging to senate president and art connoisseur Mohammed Mahmoud Khalil Bey. Among these paintings are works by Prosper Marilhat, Louis Amable Crapelet, Jean-Leon Gérome and Louis Claude Mouchot.

As membership grew it was decided in the late 1920s to expand the club's premises. Hence in 1930, says French architectural historian Mercedes Volait, Michel Roux-Spitz was commissioned to add a third storey and a corner cupola to the original structure. The cupola was an agreeable match to the Matossian building across Bostan Street.

The Mohammed Ali continued the course as Egypt's exclusive fraternity, so much so that it was inevitably written up in countless reviews, social columns, wartime books and family memoirs. The honour of being one of the first persons to mention the club goes to Sir Ronald Storrs referring to it in passing in his book *Orientations* as the "Cercle Mahomet Ali", the word *cercle* being the French equivalent of club.

At first women were seldom seen in the Mohammed Ali. But this would change during the interwar years when the more liberal Egyptian pashas hosted evenings at the club alongside their European wives. A typically revealing social announcement in a 1931 local newspaper recounts:

> Ali Chamsi Pasha [former finance minister and Egypt's representative to the League of Nations] and Mme. Chamsi gave a luncheon party at the Mohammed Ali Club on Friday to the following guests: Sir Edward and Lady Cook, Sir Victor Harari Pasha and Lady Harari, Sir Robert Greg, Sir Otto and Lady Niemeyer, Adly Yeken Pasha, Wassef Ghali Pasha and Mme. Ghali, Henri Naus Bey and Mme. Naus, Mr. and Mrs. Ernest Trembley, Gabriel Takla Bey and Mme. Takla, Arakel Nubar Bey and Mme. Nubar, Mahmoud Khalil Bey and Mme. Khalil and Taher Bey El Lozi.

Analyzing the clipping one notes the Egyptian pashas with Egyptian wives (Yeken and Lozi) were unaccompanied. On the other hand Chamsi, Ghali and Khalil's wives attended. They were Swiss (Chamsi) and French.

Things would later change so that after Madame Chamsi unexpectedly died from pneumonia during World War II, the bereaved pasha hosted his dinners at the Mohammed Ali with Siadat Raafat by his side. His suave multilingual niece had been one of the first young ladies, along with Hoda Sharaawi, to remove the veil back in 1919.

In its overall composition, the last pre-1952 board of the Mohammed Ali Club was not unlike the first. It included members of the ruling family, the usual pasha brigade and of course, the rich and famous. The difference however was that the average age was much more advanced. Another variance is that this time around it included a Copt. Back in 1907-8 Copts had their own club situated in the Prince Halim Building. According to a latter day publication, the Ramses Club, established in 1905 by leading members of the Coptic community, aimed at reforming the ecclesiastical, social and educational affairs of the community.

After 1952 and as a result of the confiscation of all assets belonging to members of the Mohammed Ali dynasty, the state found itself in control of considerable shares in the Mohammed Ali Club. In an attempt to circumvent the new situation, the remaining shareholders elected a new board with Cherif Sabry as president, Hussein Sirry as vice president and Atta Afifi as secretary. The Club thus survived a few more years so that former pashas had a 'safe house' in which they could form hypothetical governments in the event they staged an imaginary comeback.

Regarded by the Free Officers as a stuffy refuge for royalists where the *ancien regime* held ambiguous conclaves, the Club's days were numbered. In 1963 the Mohammed Ali was seized by the state only to reopen as the Tahrir (a.k.a. Diplomatic) Club. Since the new owner was the recently purged Ministry of Foreign Affairs, it came as no surprise that the club's new board consisted of a concoction of officers-turned-ambassadors. Understandably, the new 'Excellencies' had little in common with their tarboushed predecessors who, in a sense, had now become homeless.

Last pre-1952 Mohammed Ali Club Board Members

Prince Mohammed Ali Tewfik - President (heir to the throne up to January 1952)

Cherif Sabry Pasha - VP (King Farouk's uncle)

Ismail Sidki Pasha - Honorary Secretary (former prime minister)

Atta Afifi Bey - Treasurer (landowner and MP)

Mahmoud Hassan - Secretary

Board Members:

Abdel Aziz Izzet Pasha (ex-regent)

Abdel Fattah Yehya Pasha (former prime minister)

Parrissi Belleni (wealthy contractor & head of Cairo Greek community)

Baron Louis de Benoist (French chairman of Suez Canal Company)

Aslan Cattaui Bey (Jewish CEO of several leading industrial concerns)

Sir Hussein Sirry Pasha (former prime minister)

Sir Mahmoud Chaker Pasha (former minister of transportation)

Emir Michel Lotfallah Bey (prominent Syrian landowner)

Mohammed Bahy El Din Barakat Pasha (former minister of education)

Mohammed Mahmoud Khalil Bey (senate president)

Mohammed Sultan Bey (landowner and MP)

Sir Thomas W. Russell Pasha (head of Cairo Police)

Sadek Wahba Pasha (Coptic landowner)

Victor Zagdoun (celebrated Jewish industrialist)

House of money

Built in 1903, on what was once Cairo's old hippodrome, the Credit Foncier Egyptien is by far the oldest bank in Cairo. Founded in 1880 it preceded the National Bank of Egypt by 18 years.

Credit Foncier's founders and principal shareholders were predominantly French or French-protected up until it was nationalised in the late 1950s. At any time during its first seventy years of existence you would find on its board one or more former or future prime ministers, a future speaker of the House or an ex-Senate leader. All were predisposed towards the French. On the other hand, the National Bank of Egypt was run as an exclusive British club during its first half century. In fact, the creation of the National Bank was in greater part an effort by Egypt's British occupiers to break France's hold over the country's banking system.

It was no coincidence that the Credit Foncier chose the corner plot on Manakh (later Abdel Khalek Sarwat Pasha) Street and Emad al Din on which to erect its imposing Cairo headquarters in 1903-4. Originally, the area had been part of the old hippodrome where so many races took place in the middle of the nineteenth century. In the 1860s, both the hippodrome and the outlying area were earmarked for urban development as part of Khedive Ismail's scheme to create the new Europeanised district of Ismailia. An entire block of the newly traced district was picked up by two of Cairo's biggest land speculators, Mr. Karl Heinrich Beyerlé and Mr. Raphael Menachem Suares. Both gentlemen were founding shareholders of the Credit Foncier Egyptien, which, at the time, had its main offices in Alexandria.

Most of the commercial property surrounding the bank's proposed Cairo branch (including the semi-circular *Circolo Risotto*, still standing today) belonged to Suares, hence the name Rondpoint Suares until May 14, 1940 when the midan's name changed to Mustafa Kamel. The latter's statue, designed by Leopold Savine (in co-operation with the Parisian atelier René Fulda, Fondeur d'Art), was unveiled by King Farouk. As though to indicate changing times, the name of the famous Ottoman-Egyptian nationalist replaced that of the wealthy Italian Jewish capitalist. Both men, whose paths may never have crossed, made their fame or fortune in late nineteenth century Egypt.

The site located, it was now a question of architects. Which one of the contenders was to be given the task of designing the Cairo headquarters of

Egypt's leading bank? Several names come up when researching the bank's history: Carlo Prampolini, Antonio Lasciac, Max Herz and Edward Matasek. All four were renowned architects and each had, at one time or another, worked for the Egyptian government.

His forte being neo-Islamic architecture, it is doubtful that Herz built Cairo's neo-classical Credit Foncier headquarters. All the same, his story applies to several other *fin de siècle* architects who made their way to Egypt in search of success. What actually makes Herz different is that he was primarily concerned with restoration and conservation.

Born on May 19, 1856, in the Romanian town of Otlaka, Herz was the son of a Jewish tiller of the soil. After graduating from Vienna's school of architecture, Herz came to Egypt in 1881. The following year he joined the Egyptian government service as an architect for the Department of Waqf (Religious Endowments Authority) bringing him in close contact with Islamic architecture.

In 1888, Herz was nominated to the prestigious Islamic Art Preservation Committee, and two years later he succeeded Julius Franz Pasha as its director. Herz was also responsible for putting together the Egyptian pavilion at the Chicago Universal Exhibition of 1892. That same year, he was asked to supervise the cataloguing of the contents of the National Museum for Islamic Art. The museum was re-inaugurated in 1903 with Herz at its head.

During his Egyptian career, Herz Bey was responsible for the restoration of numerous mosques including those of Sultan Hassan and Sultan Qalawun. Civil works in which he may have participated include the Zogheb Villa which became the Danish Legation and the villa of St Maurice (later the French Legation) both located in Cairo's Ismailia district, not too far from the Credit Foncier Egyptien, and both distinctly Arab in style.

Consequently if anyone knew about conservation and restoration it was Herz Bey. He would have advocated the classification of a landmark such as the Credit Foncier on Abdel Khalek Sarwat Street. He would have recommended that no additions, subtractions or defacing of the original structure be allowed. Moreover, he would have removed any additions, such as extra rooms on the roof, piping, or air condition holes. The building's shell, its façade in particular, would be minutely restored in keeping with its formal design. The magnificent gilded interior would undergo an intensive refurbishment programme bringing back this bank to its former extravagant glory.

This is a historic house and keeping it in pristine condition should be the bank's priority. Perhaps the present owner could turn the building into a plush showcase exclusively for its executive offices, flushing out the rank and file and relocating them to more modern quarters, as it is done in other world banking centres; the palace for the head office and senior executives, and the modern office buildings for the other labour-intensive departments.

Luck is on posterity's side for the present owner is the cash-rich Arab International Bank, one of the very first fruits of Sadat's *infitah* (open door) policy. The bank's chairman is Sadat's long-time confidant and prime minister, Mustafa Khalil. A refined man and a connoisseur of the arts, Khalil is sensitive enough to appreciate the special character of his headquarters. Surely he will spare no effort to restore one of Cairo's finer monuments to its former regal splendour, setting an excellent precedent. And since he is a world traveller, Khalil need only check out how other cities are coping with their grand monuments and buildings.

A restoration effort that comes immediately to mind is how New York City restored Grand Central Station, turning what has often been called a dormitory for the homeless into one of the city's most famous landmarks. Both the Arab International Bank building and Grand Central Station belong to that same generation of splendid fin de siècle buildings. Both aged badly, one from neglect in a city often on the verge of bankruptcy and the other because after nationalisation, the building endured a sucession of owners who often didn't appreciate its value.

Cinema of the stars

When, David O. Selznick's powerful *Gone with Wind* blew out of Hollywood in 1939, excited moviegoers and raucous Allied soldiers serving in the Middle East were already queuing up at the newly opened MGM Metro Theatre on Soliman Pasha Street. All wanted to savour Vivien Leigh's décolleté and take in America's steamy South.

It was with some justification that Cinema Metro sported the words 'Pride of the Orient' under its roaring lion logo. Built according to plans sent from MGM Hollywood—then home to Gable, Garland and Garbo—the new art deco theatre was the first to introduce air-conditioning in Egypt, making its 3pm screening the preferred summertime rendezvous for Cairo's white-collar professionals.

Pre-dating by some 40 years the 1980s concept of the multiplex, Cairo's MGM complex was a thriving three-storey, self-sustaining enterprise. On the ground floor was the city's first-ever *shawerma* diner, the Excelsior. Next to it was the swanky Ford car showroom. On the other side of Metro's entrance there was Eid, Cairo's leading shirt maker. The first and second floors provided fancy office space for Dominioni, Rossi & Salama Architects, the Metro's builders, while across the hallway were MGM's executive suites.

With their smart desktop lamps and art deco accoutrements, the Metro offices looked more like newsrooms out of an Edward G. Robinson movie than the regional headquarters of a leading Hollywood studio. MGM's Cairo office was also in charge of the distribution rights and the promotion of a popular rent-a-movie service. One important home-viewing customer was Gamal Abdel Nasser. Not unlike his opposite number in the White House, he had a preference for Marilyn Monroe, whose crooning of 'Happy Birthday Mr. President' in 1962 endeared her to many other world leaders besides JFK.

Another Nasser favourite, not an MGM production this time, was Elia Kazan's *Viva Zapata*. According to Madame Amira, a Syro-Lebanese who ran 20th Century Fox's distribution in Egypt, "Colonel Nasser used to watch it over and over again, fascinated with the Mexican Revolution and the peasant's uprising of 1910. Marlon Brando played the part of Emilliano Zapata."

The theatre section of the Metro was composed of an upper and lower hall, and a beautifully appointed foyer with a smoking room decorated with paintings. The imported American sanitary fixtures were the talk of the town. The pricey loge and balcony sections had upholstered chairs that reclined backwards, inducing the more tired moviegoer into a deep slumber. Despite the comfortable seats—and even before he became obese—King Farouk would have a special armchair brought in whenever he attended a gala or charity event at the Metro.

Until the 1960s, MGM dominated the Cairo cinema scene. Next in line was the Middle East Motion Pictures Co. belonging to Abdel Fattah Mansour. His company was the agent for Republic Pictures International Corp., Monogram International Corp. of New York and Associated British Pathé Ltd. of London. There was also 20th Century Fox's Cairo Palace and the older Societé Orientale du Cinema that ran 40 cinema theatres in Egypt. Societé Gaafar Frères, meanwhile, managed the Opera, Radio, Kasr al Nil, Ezbekiya and Rivoli (ex-RKO) cinema theatres. None were as innovative or as attention-getting as Cinema Metro.

The cinema-going gaiety was briefly interrupted on May 6, 1947 when, during the 3pm showing of Wallace Beery's film *Bad Man Bascombe*, a gelignite charge planted in the Metro by the outlawed Muslim Brotherhood exploded, killing and injuring a number of people. King Farouk's tenth accession anniversary was thus turned into a national tragedy. Cinema Metro was closed for several months and it was some time before Fred Astaire, Esther Williams and Tarzan lured Cairo's movie addicts back to the pictures. Once again, political unrest interfered when on Saturday, January 26, 1952, Cinema Metro, situated diagonally opposite the British-run Turf Club on Adly Street, was destroyed by fire.

When it was rebuilt with fireproof carpeting, cold-water fountains and all, the Metro's interior resembled an African savannah, dotted with African masks and shields and images of some wild animals in the background. The Free Officers Movement, led by General Mohammed Naguib, staged the reopening to create a sense of business as usual in defiance of the displacement of the monarchy. It was therefore a smiling Naguib and a retinue of officers who showed up at the Metro's re-launch, received by a beaming Maurice Dassa, who, until his death in July 1955, was Metro's representative and general manager in the Middle East.

It was around this time that MGM boss Marcus Loewe arrived in Egypt. According to architect Victor Salama, who shared office space at the Metro theatre building, Loewe promptly fired local manager Mr. Shazanz for gross incompetence, replacing him with Messrs. Gustave Zelsnick and Joseph Ventura. The deed done, the rest of the staff trooped off to the Mena House for a dinner in Loewe's honour.

The 1950s were good times for Cairo film audiences. They had their first encounter with airborne axes and knives at the Metro's 3D showings— a pair of green and red glasses were handed out with every nine piastre ticket—and there were also popular Friday and Sunday matinees and Christmas Day cartoon shows sponsored by the *Progrés Egyptien*. These featured door prizes and a costumed Tom and Jerry duo greeting wide-eyed pre-teens and toddlers as they walked in clinging to an assortment of multilingual nannies.

In 1955, Robert Taylor and Eleanor Parker attended the grand premiere of Robert Pirosh's *Valley of the Kings,* which coincided with the groundbreaking ceremony for the Nile Hilton Hotel on Midan al Tahrir. It was on that occasion that renowned Egyptian belly dancer Samia Gamal dragged Robert Taylor onto centre stage. Donning a tarboush and a hip-hugging sash, the American superstar danced before an enthralled audience. Among the amused spectators was movie star Van Johnson.

Despite its nationalisation in the 1960s, Cinema Metro still had enough clout in 1967 to make yet another first when it projected the uncensored version of Antonioni's pop culture parable *Blow Up*, featuring Vanessa Redgrave in tight Levi's and a naked torso. Even with her arms crossed over her breasts, it was considered risqué for the time. This was a far cry from what went on at Cinema Metro on certain days of the month.

According to New York teacher Viviane Curiel, formerly of Maadi, Egypt, she would occasionally join the adults who gathered once a week at the Metro to listen to Père Zohrab. "He was a film-buff friar from the Dominican Seminary in Abbassia. He would lecture on *Cinema Verité* and the *Septième Art* or invariably show a selection of little known Hungarian films. Somewhat impulsive, the edgy Dominican would stamp his foot when he felt his audience had drifted."

Then there were wonderful midnight séances when selected old movies were shown. These performances had their very own clientele who occupied the same seats at each new showing.

Cinema Metro's last hurrah was in 1978 when England's Princess Alexandra of Kent attended a special screening of Agatha Christie's *Death On The Nile*. By this time, the Egyptian cinema industry was in headlong decline. Too long ignored by the socialist state, cinema theatres had deteriorated into smelly auditoriums with stray cats meandering about and broken acoustic systems that struggled to compete with sounds of an undisciplined public that saw no need to keep quiet as long as the Arabic sub-titles could be read. With censorship becoming increasingly austere, going to the movies became more of a headache than a pleasure.

These days, things are looking up. The buzz is privatisation and cinema is seen as a good investment. Money is currently being pumped into upgrading and refurbishing Cairo's downtown theatres. Metro's neighbours, cinemas Odeon and Radio, have already benefited from being buffed up, re-fitted and re-launched. Word has it that the Metro is next.

Temple of justice

In September 1934, millennium-old Cairo was getting ready to inaugurate its first *Palais de Justice*, a colossal post-renaissance edifice designed to dwarf and awe any supplicant who walked through its massive iron portals or wandered the labyrinthine corridors that criss-crossed its interior. Observing the colonnaded Roman façade, the passing individual instantly realised he was but a mere speck in the game of life.

That was undoubtedly the objective—a giant building reducing a person to infinitesimal anonymity. Eminent judges could pass stifling sentences from their sacrosanct chambers and lofty courtrooms ensured that the ponderous surroundings would do the rest. It is worth mentioning here that most sitting judges were foreigners, for this was the new headquarters of the Mixed Tribunals, a term used to reflect the different Western jurisprudence applied therein. Under the old regime of Capitulations, foreign nationals in Egypt were outside local jurisdiction and only appeared in their respective Consular Courts. Later in the nineteenth century, these were merged together to form the Mixed Tribunals. Egyptians, meanwhile, were subject to national jurisdiction and courts.

From 1877 to 1934, Cairo's Mixed Tribunals resided in the old Daira Saneya Palace on Midan Ataba al Khadra. The building, however, was no longer able to fulfil its requirements, and also the municipality had plans to enlarge the square by building two new avenues departing from its centre to Bab al Husseinieh and to Al Azhar Mosque. It was necessary to remove the old Justice Palace.

It was decided from as early as December 1909 that the new courthouse would be built on what had been the Cairo Water Company, situated at the intersection of two of Cairo's grandest thoroughfares, King Fouad Street (now 26th of July) and Boulevard Abbas (later Queen Nazli, now Ramses Street). It would also front Rue Champollion, the name synonymous with the deciphering of hieroglyphics. The design of the proposed new courthouse would be awarded to the winner of a universal competition. All styles, concepts or ideas would be entertained.

Because of local and international upheavals, the competition was launched more than a decade later and an exclusive panel made up of lawmakers and international architects was asked to consider 35 out of 141 applicants.

Members of the jury included veteran Cairo-based architects Ernesto Verucci Bey and Antonio Lasciac. Both had served as building superintendents of the Egyptian royal palaces and both had designed several of Cairo's better-known buildings and banks, including Banque Misr and the Khedivial Buildings on Emad al Din Street. There was Monsieur Conin Pastour, the French director-general of State Buildings, who would later design the French Consulate on Al Fadl Street. It was his countryman, Chief Justice Raoul Houriet of the Mixed Courts, who made sure the blueprints were serviceable from a lawmaker's point of view. The only Egyptian on the panel was Mahmoud Fahmi Pasha, former chief architect of the Ministry of *Waqf*.

On January 15, 1924, it was announced that the first prize of LE900 would go to Messrs. Leon Azema, Max Edrei, Jacques Hardy and Victor Erlanger. Second prize went to Alexander Marcel of the French Institute in Paris. He was responsible for many of Heliopolis's architectural splendours. Third and fourth prizes went to Lionel Brandon and Michel Radoslavoff respectively.

Once an allocation of LE160,000 was set aside for the project, ground was broken on September 3, 1925. Perhaps because of the Great Depression, construction took longer than expected so that the building was still incomplete in 1931, when cracks appeared on its façade. No sooner had a commission of inquiry been convened than the front parapet was seen to be heaving. As expected, the press had a field day. With cost overruns now coming into play, the questioning moved to both the Chamber of Deputies and the Senate.

After a series of accusations and counter-accusations in which the principal designing architects Messrs. Azema and Edrei (the other two having dropped out of the project early on) were absolved, the damages, which had been much exaggerated, were successfully attended to. The building was near completion.

The first courtroom hearing took place on October 16, 1934, nine years from groundbreaking. In a matter of months the whole Mixed Courts apparatus system had successfully transplanted itself from Midan al Ataba to King Fouad Avenue.

In its early years, Cairo's new Palace of Justice functioned superbly and was considered one of the finest in the world.

Exactly 15 years after its inauguration, the Palace of Justice made history again. No longer were the resented *Al Mahkama al Mokhtalata*—Mixed

Tribunals in evidence. October 15, 1949, will always be remembered as the day in which the Mixed and Consular Courts ceased to exist in Egypt, following the long and painstaking negotiations known as the Montreux Convention of 1937. The offending sign was removed the following April.

From that day all residents in Egypt, irrespective of nationality would appear in front of the National Courts where the proceedings would be conducted in Arabic before Egyptian judges. Another logical step towards genuine independence had been achieved. From that day onwards, the courthouse would be known as Dar al Qada'a al Aali—High Court of Justice.

The Welsh connection

In the 1880s, most shoppers knew that John Davies Bryan owned one of Cairo's leading stores. What they failed to understand was why a *Taffy* from the hills of North Wales had come to Egypt.

English, Irish and Scotsmen were no strangers to colonial Egypt. Soon after Britain defeated Orabi Pasha at Tel al Kebir in 1882, St Andrews' schools and churches started to appear in Cairo and Alexandria. Next came the St Patrick's Day celebrations fuelled by a surplus of teachers and nurses from Dublin. But when it came to Wales, not much there. It was only after the British left Egypt in 1955, that we learned of Welsh rarebit, Laura Ashley's floral prints and actor Richard Burton.

The more politically minded however, recall with desolation the Welsh-born Prime Minister Lloyd George, whose government offered the Jews a homeland in Arab Palestine.

And while European Jews were anticipating a homeland, Welshmen were abandoning theirs, migrating to rural Australia and South America.

Since trade and commerce were never big in that part of the British Isles, whenever a successful shopkeeper left, it was a sad day somewhere in Wales. This was the case of John Davies Bryan. Health problems and encouragement from a cousin in Egypt brought the eldest son of Edward and Elinor Bryan of Caernarfon, to the shores of Alexandria. His cousin, Samuel Evans, was Chief of the Egyptian Coastal Service. In his spare time he dealt in the buying and selling of camels.

In Wales, John Davies Bryan, eldest of four brothers, had run a small shop at No. 12 Bridge Street, Caernarfon. Shortly after he disembarked in

Egypt, Bryan did what he knew best. He opened a shop in Cairo's Continental Hotel under the trademark name of Davies Bryan.

Bryan's shop sold an array of imported goods including men's and ladies' hats, travel gear, draperies, hosiery and shoes. His fixed price policy in a market that centred on haggling and bargaining eventually earned him his sterling reputation.

As business expanded, Bryan sent for two of his brothers, Edward and Joseph. In Alexandria they opened a large store on Cherif Pasha Street, which was second to none in terms of location. While refurbishing their building, the brothers sought the advice of architect Robert Williams. On his recommendation they redecorated the façade with polished red granite from Aberdeen and Doulting freestone from Sommerset.

In Cairo the Bryans commissioned Williams to design the St David, which was completed in 1910. Named after the patron saint of Wales, the tall redbrick building stood on a large piece of property purchased from Charles Beyerlé, a director of the Credit Foncier Bank just across the street.

Soon enough, Davies Bryan of Cairo was the pride of Emad al Din Street where most elegant shops were situated. The largest of its kind, the store occupied 1,900 square metres fronting three streets: Magrabi (now Adly), Emad al Din (now Mohammed Farid) and Al Manakh (now Abdel Khalek Sarwat). Just above eye level, the building's façades were decorated with ornate stucco motifs. One can still make out shields with roses, thistles, shamrocks and leeks. While most shields are engraved with the initials 'D', 'B', 'MGA', 'EJ' and 'AB', two of them have 'Davies Bryan 1910' written on them in Arabic and in English. A larger shield overlooking Mohammed Farid Street sports the following inscriptions:

YGWIRYN
ERBYN
YBYD

These are Welsh words for 'truth against the world.' Another shield has three lines drawn on it, one vertical and two diagonal / | \. This is the logo of the Welsh National Gorsedd of Bards (or Eisteddfod), an important annual Welsh cultural festival.

It would be another three decades before an Eisteddfod took place in Cairo. This was on September 21, 1943, when Egypt was home to thousands of Allied soldiers including several Welsh regiments.

No less than 200 Welsh servicemen, dressed in bardic robes, attended the Cairo Eisteddfod. It was held a few blocks from the St David in a cinema theatre (now a garage) off Soliman Pasha Street. Requisitioned during the Second World War, the theatre was where Lady Dorothea, wife of Cairo Police Chief Sir Thomas Russell Pasha, launched *Music for All,* a benevolent wartime organisation for the benefit of the Allied troops.

It was also at the Cairo Eisteddfod that *Enfys* was launched. At first known as *Seren y Dwyrain*, the tiny wartime Welsh-language journal became the *Yr Enfys* in Wales that today serves an expanding overseas Welsh audience.

Today's Welsh visitors may remark that several of the shields above the St David's main entrance were painted over with the inscriptions 'Chourbagui.' In order to explain this aberration one must go back in time and follow the sequence of events that transferred the St David from the Bryans to the present owner.

First to go was John Davies Bryan who died of typhoid at age 33 on November 13, 1888. During his relatively short Egyptian sojourn, John kept up a prolific correspondence with the folks back home, most of it in Welsh. These contained his impressions of Egypt, some of which were published in *Genedl* and later appeared in book form, a copy of which can be found at the Welsh National Library under *O'r Aifft* (From Egypt).

On the morning of May 13, 1920, it was the youngest brother, Robert Bryan, 61, who passed away while in residence at the St David. Never directly involved in the family business, he was the family's educated poet and musician, which explains why he bequeathed to his alma mater, the University of Aberystwyth, the sum of 2,000 pounds sterling for the establishment of a music scholarship. While in Egypt, Robert translated proverbs and pharaonic poems, one of which originated in an ancient tomb belonging to King Tehwiti-mes of the 18th Dynasty.

Edward Bryan, the second of the four brothers, died in Alexandria in 1929, leaving a large sum for the Young Men's Christian Association. It is no coincidence that Cairo's YMCA branch was located in the St David, a few floors above Pension Wales.

Last to go was Joseph Bryan. He died in 1935, aged 71, leaving the sum of 5,000 pounds sterling to the Library of Wales at Aberystwyth. Back in 1928, he had donated 85 acres on a hill above the town for the erection of new educational buildings. Between 1923-4, Joseph Bryan was president of both the Alexandria British Association and the British Chamber of Commerce. In his spare time he wrote several articles including 'The Victory of Islam' (*Buddugoliaeth Gyntaf Islam*); 'Mohammed and the Jews and Christians' (*Mohammed a'r Iddewon a'r Cristnogion*); and 'The Fate of the Jews of Medina' (*Tynged Iddewon Medina*).

After Joseph's death, Davies Bryan & Co. gradually wound up its activities in Egypt so that by the time the Welsh regiments arrived in the Second World War, they found a downsized version of what their predecessors had seen in the previous war. Another Welshman, this time from Coedpoeth, ran the store. Fred Purslow had been chief accountant for the Bryan brothers before buying a share in the business in 1929. It was mostly thanks to him and his associate, Moise Meriems, that the trade name of Davies Bryan & Co. lived on until the 1950s.

What had once been a mega-store had slowly imploded into several smaller shops and boutiques including Stephenson's Pharmacy, and Librairie Barbier. In 1957 or thereabouts, four prosperous Syrian brothers—the Chourbaguis, purchased the St David along with sundry relics left behind by their four Welsh predecessors.

In 1961 the St David was taken over by a state-owned insurance company. From then on the building slipped into steady decline, its main halls and entrances acquiring their Gothamesque character. Thus ended Egypt's Welsh connection.

The Grand Vizier's palace

A few minutes walk from the High Court you might find yourself in front of Cairo's trendy Townhouse Gallery on Mimaar Hussein Pasha Street (Sheikh al Maarouf district). The derelict palace that stands nearby often bewilders visitors. Occupying an entire block, it looks like a set from Roman Polanski's remake of *The Vampire's Ball*.

But what is such a once-magnificent edifice doing in the middle of a district cluttered with garages, coffee shops and mounds of rubbish? Who designed it and who lived there? More importantly, why is it in such a sorry state?

To begin with, the architect was Antonio Lasciac, Egypt's renowned palace builder. Italian by culture and an Austro-Hungarian citizen by accident of birth, his clients included members of the khedivial family, Cairene notables and trusted institutions. Among his more visible works are Banque Misr on Mohammed Farid Street and the Palace of Princess Nimet Kamal al Din, currently being restored across from the Arab League.

The architect's client in the case of this particular palace can be divined by the 'SH' monogram found on the many decorative pillars. He is none other than Prince Said Halim Pasha, a grandson of modern Egypt's founder, Mohammed Ali.

Born in the Palace of Shubra in 1865, history has it that Prince Halim's father could have been the ruler of Egypt had it not been for an ambitious nephew upstaging him at every level, all the way up to the sultan's inner court in Istanbul. Disregarding tradition and using lavish gifts and bribes, Khedive Ismail made sure it would be his own son, Tewfik, and not his older 'Turkish' cousins, who would succeed him.

The two cousins most likely to have succeeded Ismail, prior to the *firman* of 1873 establishing primogeniture, lived in Istanbul and had at one time or another, occupied senior military and cabinet posts in the Turkish government. Having grown up on the Bosphorus, they were familiar with and probably inspired by the palaces of Topkapi, Dolmabahce and Beylerbey.

One of the cousins, Said Halim Pasha, was enamoured with Rome and all things Italian. His choice of architect and style for his Cairo palace was therefore decidedly Roman. Moreover, Halim, a man of luxurious taste, made sure most of the material used in the construction and decoration was imported directly from Italy. *A tout prix, il fallait épaté les cousins!* This was 1900, the beginning of a new era.

It is said that Prince Halim's wife, Amina Indji Toussoun, herself a great-granddaughter of Viceroy Mohammed Ali, did not particularly like the palace. Her preferences lay with the Bosphorus, where she would eventually die in 1915.

When Mahmud Shevket Pasha, Prime Minister of the Ottoman Empire, was shot on June 11, 1913 while crossing Istanbul's Bayazid Square, he was replaced by Prince Said Halim Pasha. For the next few years, Halim was the illustrious boss of the Sublime Porte—official seat of the Ottoman government. In his capacity as *Al Sadr al Aazam* (Grand Vizier), Halim Pasha was the highest official in the empire. Yet it was no secret, both at home and abroad, that Halim was a pawn in the hands of the Young Turks, that powerful movement that had taken over the country's political stage. Wanting among other things to introduce a constitutional government in an ailing autocratic empire ruled by Sultan Mehmed V, the Young Turks instead brought the empire to an accelerated demise.

One can say that Halim's standing in British-controlled Egypt was doomed on August 2, 1914, when Turkey signed a secret alliance with Germany committing itself against the United Kingdom.

Three months later to the day, Britain, France and Russia declared war on Turkey. Although he threatened to resign, Prime Minister Halim Pasha was reluctant as ever to give up the sybaritic pleasures of his post. As a result he witnessed first-hand the final scene to a 300-year Ottoman presence in Egypt, now officially declared a British Protectorate.

In Cairo, all of Halim's assets were confiscated. These included large landholdings, several properties and bank accounts and, of course, the Halim Palace in Cairo's Ismailia district.

Following Turkey's defeat, Prince Halim was arrested by order of the British and subsequently deported from Istanbul to Malta in May, 1919. Before his departure, the pan-Islamist ex-grand vizier offered his large estate on the Bosphorus for the purpose of founding an Islamic University. The offer was not taken.

While imprisoned in the British colony of Malta, Said Halim Pasha claimed he had received a communication from the Nationalist Party in Cairo offering him the throne of Egypt once its independence was a fait accompli. That offer didn't work out either. Ultimately, he would be assassinated in Rome, falling prey to an Armenian terrorist, Arshavir Shiragian, on December 6, 1921.

Meanwhile, the Halim palace in Cairo was turned into Al Nasriya School for Boys. Many a future senator, deputy and cabinet minister received his primary education there. At first the school occupied the entire palace property. That is why the address given in 1920 was still No. 9 Antikhana al Masreya Street. A few years later the palace park disappeared, and where royal palms, fountain and garden had once been, came new apartment houses fronting Antikhana Street. The school's address was changed to No. 6 Rue Champollion (ex-Wabour al Maya; ex-Mouillard).

For a long time Al Nasriya Primary was considered together with Al Saidiya Preparatory across the river, as the leading educational establishment for sons of pashas and beys, a reputation that would later earn Halim Palace its ultimate death sentence. With the extinction of titles and Egypt's old bourgeoisie, the palace became the unlucky ward of the Ministry of Education. Thereafter, the deterioration came in steady increments fuelled by ignorance and greed. A dispensary here, an office for the Ruling Party there, plus the indiscriminate building of brick walls on the balustrades and the pilfering of the priceless pink marble and other historical rarities. The rest is shameful history.

But this state-run school was not always as dismal and inadequate. A former Nasriya student, Engineer Kamal Nabih, provides the following written description of his alma mater.

> I was in Nasriya Primary from 1936 to 1939. But I must say the crumbled down palace of today has absolutely nothing to do with our school or with today's Maarouf neighbourhood. I still reminisce the happy years I spent there. I remember the teachers, Fathi Effendi: English, Fouad Effendi: Arabic, Fawzi Effendi: Mathematics and the famous headmaster Badrawi Bey. I also remember my class, with Ahmed Ramzi (famous actor), Khorshid Sakib, the Mouro brothers, Hashem and Hisham, and Cherif Zulfikar (Queen Farida's brother). The classrooms, they were wide, clean and well lit. The restaurant (Yamak-khana) was spotless serving our daily three-course lunch plus dessert. During the lunch break (the big *foss-ha*) we played in a beautiful garden. The building was spic and span and so were the large stained glass windows. The school had a German (maybe Swiss) matron to oversee I can't remember what.

Retired diplomat Adel Zaki recalls how Dr. Rashad Roushdy was his English language teacher at Nasriya. He would later become Chair of the English Department at Cairo University as well as a prominent writer. Also teaching at Nasriya was Saad al Khadem, a prominent artist in his own right. "My mathematics teacher" recalls Zaki "obtained a PhD in pure mathematics and joined the UN Atomic Research Organisation in Vienna, Austria."

Indeed, truth is often stranger than fiction. One wonders if Messrs. Nabih and Zaki are talking about the same school, the one that is today squatting on those sad, crumbling premises.

Gates of heaven

In his copious memoirs, Sir Ronald Storrs describes a relatively new edifice in downtown Cairo; the then-young British diplomat talks of a "self-respecting but architecturally painful Sephardic synagogue." It was 1904 and Cairo's newest Jewish place of worship, Chaar Hachamaim (the Gates of Heaven) was barely five years old.

Storrs, T. E. Lawrence and others of their genus could not have missed noticing the neo-pharaonic temple. Not only was it the biggest structure on Magrabi (now Adly) Street, it was also contiguous to that most sacred of colonial sanctuaries, the Turf Club. Later the club, a brazen symbol of British imperialism in the Middle East, would move westwards down the street before being torched to the ground during the anti-British riots of January 1952. The synagogue, on the other hand, survived several bloody Arab-Israeli wars and is still intact and operating today.

Inside Chaar Hachamaim are two large marble tablets on either side of the central nave. On them are engraved in Hebrew the names of men who contributed to the synagogue's construction and helped maintain it for several decades thereafter.

The tablets are in a way, a roll-call of the Jewish financial elite of the time. The more than 100 names are historically linked with the country's first privatisation of 1898-1906. Those unable to read Hebrew can consult the tiny brass nameplates appended to the benches in the synagogue's main hall. Here, in Latin script, are the Mosseris, Suareses, Cattauis, Rolos, Adesses, Hararis, Naggars, Cicurels, Curiels, Luzzatos, and others—all of them pillars of Egypt's once powerful Sephardic community.

Collectively, these families accounted for many of Egypt's banks, department stores, transport companies, and urban and suburban housing developments. In their debt also are two important museums: Bab al Khalq's Islamic Museum and the Museum of Modern Art. Both were beneficiaries of large private collections, such as the one donated by financier Sir Robert Rolo. His name is No. 18 on the synagogue's marble tablets. It is also no small coincidence that Egypt's first modern art museum was located in the former Nessim Mosseri townhouse, abutting the synagogue's rear, at the corner of Mohammed Farid and 26th of July Streets. King Fouad officially inaugurated the museum on February 8, 1931.

A plaque on the synagogue's outer wall, facing the inner courtyard, states that Vita 'Victor' Mosseri spearheaded the campaign to erect a synagogue in Cairo's new European district of Ismailia. Missing, however, is an inscription acknowledging that it was his Cattaui relation who designed it.

Together with his Austrian partner, Eduard Matasek (a Roman Catholic), Maurice Youssef Cattaui designed the Gates of Heaven in 1899. In all likelihood, Matasek and Cattaui wanted to remind visitors that Moses had been a Prince of Egypt long before he became a prophet. Whether inside or outside the temple, you cannot fail to note the persuasive Ancient Egyptian style. Perhaps the design was a reminder that Judaism not only has its origins in the Nile valley, but that Egypt was also once home to one of the oldest Jewish communities in the world.

But if not everyone grasped the temple's historical nuances, other visitors were quick to deride it as some form of hybrid-kitsch and, later, as the perfect set for the remake of Cecil B. DeMille's *Cleopatra*.

Another scrap of information gleaned from the synagogue's wall-mounted plaques is that although it was considered a Sephardic temple of worship, several Ashkenazim contributed to its construction and upkeep. Among them was Phillip Back. His family had founded the famous department store Orosdi-Back (now Omar Effendi) in Egypt. Listed as well are Leon Heller, Maurice Schlezenger and Hermann Hornstein, names not usually associated with Oriental or Mediterranean Jews.

Other plaques on exhibit in the main hall and in the central courtyard declare that Moise Cattaui Pasha was commended "for 40 years of noble service as president of the Cairo Jewish community and a promoter of Chaar Hachamaim." Two more recent plaques state that in September 1935 Elie Curiel donated funds for the creation of an 'oratoire' and that five years later, Nathan Raphael Najar and his wife, Leonie Jabes, contributed towards the temple's restoration.

In fact, the temple's 1940 restoration was not the first. From the *Egyptian Gazette* we learn how an in-house fire in 1922 resulted in the partial destruction of the synagogue. As the president of the community showed up to inspect the damage, a charred beam fell on Cattaui Pasha, gravely injuring his shoulder.

Thanks to some aggressive fundraising by Geneva's Nessim Gaon, the temple's last restoration took place just over a decade ago, coinciding with the January 24, 1989 opening of an adjacent Historical Jewish Studies library. The library is in what had previously been the temple's wedding and celebration hall.

Notwithstanding a plaque proclaiming that a certain Zaki Mory was *gabbay* (temple functionary) between 1957-65, no mention is made anywhere of the highly respected Ottoman-born Grand Rabbi, Haim Nahum Effendi. He officiated at Chaar Hachamaim from 1922 until his death in 1960.

Also missing is a plaque explaining that for the first 50 years of its existence, the most common designation for the synagogue was 'Temple Ismailia', a reference to the district in which it stood. "Since the 40s however, people started to refer to it as Adly Synagogue," says Carmen Weinstein, the incumbent president of the Cairo Jewish community. Rightly so, for by that time most Cairenes had stopped using the term Ismailia when referring to downtown Cairo. A sleepy town on the banks of the Suez Canal had definitively hijacked the name, for it too was the creation of Khedive Ismail.

Today, the Gates of Heaven remains the last fully operating synagogue in Egypt where local and visiting Jews can congregate and worship. The synagogue was particularly active in the late 1990s when two foreign ambassadors occasionally met there on Shabbat and High Holidays. Zvi Mazel and Daniel Kurtzer, of Israel and the United States respectively, were unwitting observers of a much-ignored chapter of Egypt's modern history.

From time to time expatriate Jews write to find out about their Cairo synagogue. For instance, in September 2001, Albert Bivas inquires from the USA whether a plaque donated by his parents, Daniel and Dora, in memory of his grandmother Victoria Bivas is still in the front of the *Teva*:

> From where the hazanim—the officiants— lead the prayers. My father Daniel Bivas, was one of the main Gabbaiims of this synagogue with Mr. Joseph Farhi, Mr. Moise Farhi, Mr. Richard Mosseri and Mr. Mory. These gentlemen were among the top leaders of the Jewish Community of Cairo and Egypt. A couple of them, along with my father, served also the great synagogue Eliahou Hanavi of Alexandria and its entire community. My maternal grandfather, Youssef Haffif, officiated often at the prayer services at Shaar Hashamaim. He had a good singing voice and knew how to do it superbly. As a matter of fact that is how I was told he met my grandmother. She was the daughter of the Rishon Le Zion's Chief Rabbi of Palestine, Haiim Moshe Eliachar.

Didier Frenkel in Europe wants to know if the lacquer wooden pulpit created in 1934 by his grandfather is still in the synagogue. It was from there that the Grand Rabbi preached his Friday night sermons.

Je brule naturellement de savoir si le pupitre réalisé par mon grand-père et ses trois fils s'y trouve toujours. Je ne manquerai pas, lors d'un prochain voyage au Caire pour la réalisation d'un documentaire, de faire le pélerinage dans ce saint édifice. Mon grand-père, Betzalel Frenkel a été avec ses fils, Harry, David et Salomon, des artistes renommés du cinéma égyptien en ce qu'ils ont été les pionniers du dessin animé dans ce pays. Ils ont réalisé entre 1935 et 1950 douze films récemment redécouverts, restaurés par les Archives du cinéma de France. De nombreux hommages leur ont été rendus dans différents festivals, notamment au second festival national du cinéma du Caire en mai 1996.

The pulpit is still there, a museum piece standing at the corner of the synagogue's altar. It remains unused since there has been no resident rabbi in Cairo since the 1970s. The ebbing Jewish community, consisting mostly of elderly women, is desperately held together by its vigorous president, Ms. Carmen Weinstein.

The Baelher skyline

Baehler Passage, Baehler Buildings and Baehler Mansions remain part of Cairo's urban lexicon, yet few today recognise the origins of this Swiss name. Not many remember that when Charles Baehler died on September 12, 1937, from appendicitis complications in Lucerne, not only did Egypt's tourist and hotel sector suffer a setback, but that Cairo's metropolitan skyline would never be the same again.

Among Baehler's last creations were the downtown Baehler Buildings that overlooked Midan Soliman Pasha (now Midan Talaat Harb). Built between 1927-29, these deluxe tenements replaced the Savoy Hotel and its attachments, which included the Savoy Chambers. For a long time the Savoy had been a colonial business and residential address.

The Savoy complex was barely three decades old when it was pulled down in 1924. Its new owner, Charles Baehler cleared the site for his own conception of what an interdisciplinary urban construction should be. Nothing of that scale had ever been seen in downtown Cairo. And if the city centre lost one of its leading hotels, the father of Egypt's hospitality industry superseded the Savoy with the neo-classical Metropolitan Hotel, just around the corner, off Kasr al Nil Street. After a lifetime dedicated to hotels, the Metropolitan was Baehler's last contribution to Cairo's cityscape. Perhaps to reflect the character of Cairo at the time, Baehler re-named it the Cosmopolitan Hotel.

Baehler's downtown plaza consisted of six semi-detached buildings (blocks A through F) each with its own entrance. In total, the buildings contained 130 deluxe apartments, some conceived as offices, the rest residential. The ground floors were partitioned into 72 shops each with a separate basement. The general style was *fin de siècle* Parisian. E. Vogt and Leon Nafilyan were the principal architects of this project with the assistance of Antoine Selim Nahas. The two buildings standing on the north-western blocks (a.k.a. Chaldijian Buildings) still have a plaque with the name of Leon Nafilyan, "architecte Paris 1934". The other two eschewed mention on the buildings themselves.

The Baehler Arcade (or passage, as it soon came to be called) as almost a miniature version of Rue de Rivoli in Paris. Crawling with premium boutiques, the arcade sheltered the best haberdasheries, the finest lingerie, the smartest men's wear and the trendiest art galleries in town. It was also at No.1 Baehler Passage that foremost Cairo decorator, Jansen, kept a gallery. As for the showrooms fronting Soliman Pasha or Kasr al Nil Streets, these were only available to the highest bidder.

Baehler knew something or two about proportions, harmony and streetscape. Which is perhaps why his commercial lease contracts spelt out in the clearest of terms the dos and don'ts regarding storefront merchandising, promotional lighting and window displays. There was no thought yet that someone would append a garish medical signpost to his balcony grill or pockmark the façade with leaking air-conditioners. Baehler would surely have had multiple coronaries had he foreseen the chaos that would replace his rigid *cahier des charges*.

To Baehler's ultimate credit, his downtown building features on the cover of Cynthia Mynti's *Paris Along The Nile*, a well-illustrated book presenting some of the best of Cairo's *belle époque* architecture.

Preceding Baehler's downtown buildings, were two of the handsomest structures on Zamalek's 26th of July Street. Everyone by now has had a pizza at Maison Thomas or purchased beer from the nearby Stella depot. Welcome to the mutilated Baehler Mansions, built early last century on land carved out from the former khedivial palace gardens.

Realising Cairo was expanding westwards towards the Nile, Charles

Baehler, owner of the Gezira Palace Hotel (today Marriott Hotel) took up his option to buy more of the island's agricultural land enabling him to form an urban development company.

To attract an appropriate white-collar clientele, Baehler instructed his architects, Skynder & Skynder, to build him two grand buildings separated by a circular landing or outer court. Here too we find the splendiferous elevator cages, the lofty vaults, the ornate brickwork and the decorative details. Note also the endless foyers conceived in the days when capitalists weren't preoccupied with returns per square metre.

Here again Baehler would be aghast at the vulgar additions forced upon Zamalek's mansion blocks, with no consideration whatsoever to the existing totality. Once more, time has been unkind to Cairo's *belle époque* architecture but Monsieur Baehler may find some comfort in learning that Cairo's most photographed interior is domiciled right there at Baehler Mansions, home to Egypt's contemporary decorator, Ihab Shafik.

Zamalek's Gezira House (a.k.a. Emarat al Yemeni thus re-named after a latter-day owner) can rightly claim to be the island's first apartment house. Designed in 1907-8 by Ernest Jaspar of Heliopolis fame for the account of Baehler and the Anglo-Belgian Company of Egypt, the building reverted to the company the following year as noted in the minutes of the December 1909 board meeting:

> During the year it became necessary that the company should acquire the interest of its associate, and this it was able to do on very favourable terms; so it was now the sole proprietor of what was regarded a very favourable property.

If, for half a century, Gezira House overlooked an attachment to the Gezira Palace Hotel, today it stands on Michel Lotfallah Street opposite All Saint's Cathedral in an advanced stage of rigor mortis. True, there is the usual evidence here and there of individual and uncoordinated initiatives to bring it back to life, yet not enough to give comfort to Baehler or his like-minded kith.

It would not hurt if Gezira House's present owner, a well-known Cairo millionaire-plutocrat, took a leaf out of the Swiss man's book so that someone, somewhere, 100 years from now may remember him as warmly as one does the great Charles Baehler.

In view of his active role in the urbanisation of Gezira-Zamalek, it is not surprising that Baehler was one of its first residents. His colonial villa on

Hassan Sabry Street was known as 'Red Court'. While it isn't exactly clear why he subsequently moved from Gezira to 'Villa Lotus' in Garden City, we do know, however, that the Hassan Shaarawi Pasha family purchased Red Court and its one-acre garden and that they lived there for several decades up until the 1970s.

Although no one seemed to mind when Red Court was torn down in the early 1970s and replaced with seven high-rises situated next to the ramshackle Gezira police station, it was no less than the deputy governor of Cairo who lost his job when Villa Lotus came down in 1996. Was this unprecedented action a measure of sympathy for one of Garden City's endangered species? Not really, for it just so happens that living across from Baehler's former villa is the daunting minister in charge of parliamentary affairs; certainly not a man to cross.

The titans of Ataba

In the 1997 Egyptian movie *Al Tofaha*, a voluptuous, lustful newlywed, played by Laila Elwi, is in awe of the four Herculean statues on whose lithe shoulders rests the Tiring department store glass cupola. Each morning, to the astonishment of her adoring husband and neighbours, Elwi addresses, implores and cajoles the statues from her one-room shack atop a neighbouring building on Midan al Ataba. Glaring back at her are six faded letters written in Latin script: TIRING.

As seen in the movie, Midan al Ataba, once the nexus of Cairo's commercial district, is an area where low-income dwellers live precariously among unlimited debris, ragtag shops and wholesale warehouses. The Tiring Building is itself the home of hundreds of squatters and sweatshops. Yet ask anyone about the history of the building, and the most you will get today is a shrug of the shoulders. One or two will tell you it used to belong to some distant *khawagas* with unpronounceable names.

Despite the grotesque realities lurking inside and outside the Tiring Building, much of it mirroring the urban neglect that characterised the 1960s and 1970s, in its heyday, Tiring's architecture rivalled its Parisian contemporary Aux Galleries Lafayette, which still stands proudly on Boulevard Hausmann, a shrine to capitalistic enterprise.

Tiring's original owner was the Constantinople-born Victor Tiring, considered by many as the César Ritz of department stores. When, in 1910, he chose Ataba for the site of his Cairo emporium, the famous square stood as a gateway between the Cairo of yesterday and the Cairo of tomorrow. To Tiring's east was the bustling Mousky district, an overpopulated Egyptian *kasbah,* filled with winding *haras* (alleys) spewing oriental fragrances and exotic sounds. To its west were the plush French gardens of Ezbekiya and the modern boulevard-decked European quarters of Ismailia with imposing squares, fancy hotels, European-style apartment houses and the Cairo Opera. A tabernacle for Cairo's growing bourgeois culture, Tiring dominated the whole scene, its globe-shaped glass dome shining brightly into the night.

Designed by Oscar Horowitz, the Tiring building was completed in 1912-13. Its elegant open vistas by far outpaced its older but lesser rival— Stein's Oriental Stores—situated on the opposite side of Ataba al Khadra Street. Sadly, only the steel carcass of the latter remains today. Tiring's luxurious four floors offered everything in terms of Parisian *haute couture* and perfumes, English cloth, Austrian textiles and German houseware.

In his book on Austro-Hungarians in Egypt, historian-diplomat Dr. Rudolf Agstner of Vienna provides interesting input on the Tirings.

> Victor Tiring and his brothers, Gustav and Konrad, joined the leaders of their trade in 1882 when they opened their head office on Praterstrasse 11 in Vienna's Second District. Soon after, the firm Victor Tiring & Brothers Tailors & Exporters branched out all over their adopted city and across the Austro-Hungarian Empire. Unluckily for them, just as they set out to open branches overseas, the First World War interrupted their expanding activities.

Agstner believes that had they consolidated their shopping empire in London instead of Vienna, there could well have been a Tiring on Oxford Street today.

In 1915, Tiring of Cairo, under the management of Carlo Menasce, was temporarily listed as enemy property. The British, who governed Egypt at the time, had imposed martial law and all properties belonging to enemy aliens were sequestered. Tiring was eventually granted a conditional license "to trade in Egypt with the British Empire and with the Allies of Great Britain." But due to the loss of its supply sources the sequestered store liquidated its activities in 1920.

Stripped of its original owners, Tiring was in time outstripped by its newer rivals: Cicurel, Sednaoui and Orosdi-Back. But in the interlude, and even as the store passed from one hand to another, it was lovingly kept alive by its successive owners. Old-time clients found in Tiring a reassuring continuity where shopping remained a form of entertainment and ladies could continue to celebrate the rites of unhindered, hassle-free consumption.

By the Second World War Tiring had become home to an assortment of small shops, warehouses and offices, some of them quite seedy. Yet, on certain days of the month, a group of white-collar professionals in uncanny attire could be seen entering the building. They were the members of the Osiris Masonic Lodge presided over by William Feldstein and B. Goldenberg. Tiring had most certainly changed directions.

Today, as one drives towards downtown Cairo on the Mousky flyover one cannot miss Tiring lurking in the confused skyline to the right. "Look, it's the *Al Tofaha* building," shouted several youths on a speeding public bus. Evidently they had just seen the movie. Like the rest of the clamorous passengers, whose average age was below 40, they had never heard of a Victor Tiring or of his department store. The six bold letters below Laila Elwi's four Olympian heroes meant absolutely nothing.

Souq al Tewfikia

When Cairo's new European quarter of Ismailia was divided up into several sub-districts, the triangular precinct of Tewfikia was by no means the largest, but it possessed one of the most colourful *souqs* in the city. Today it is delineated to the south by 26th of July Street, to the west by the three kilometre long, 120 metres wide Ramses Avenue, and to the east by Gomhouriya Street. It was conceived as a semi-residential, semi-commercial and diplomatic locale. With the neighbourhood's only square and main thoroughfare both named Tewfikia (since renamed Orabi—Khedive Tewfik's nemesis), it was only natural that an emerging fruit and vegetable market was soon also named Souq al Tewfikia. Was it coincidence or was it a lack of viable names that accounted for this prolific Tewfik series? Neither, for Tewfik just happened to be the name of Khedive Ismail's eldest son and heir.

Now, 100 and some years later, Souq al Tewfikia is one of the few surviving original names in a cityscape altered by republican sensibilities.

Not unlike malls today, Cairo's open-air souqs were more than just commercially designated areas where people bought, sold, haggled and bargained. In more ways than one, they were a 'living' threshold between East and West, traditional and modern. They were places where, over the years, a cross-cultural spirit prevailed, where many a new product or fashion was passed on to the general public.

Souq al Tewfikia was no different. It was there that *galabiya*-clad peasants laden with fresh produce arrived early morning by foot, *felucca* or donkey from nearby rural areas. Having paid the required toll at the narrow Kasr al Nil Bridge or at the entrance of the nearby Ismailia Canal, they converged like locusts, settling atop tiny straw mats or perching themselves on rickety carts. Thus commenced a chaotic human cacophony only souqs know how to create.

It would be decades before *mom 'n' pop* corner grocery stores—and later supermarkets—took over from traditional souqs so that if oranges, lemons and mangoes still fought for colourful shelf space, home improvement tools, auto parts and plastic toys gradually replaced fresh onions, legumes and veggies. But these were not the first changes to insinuate themselves into Souq al Tewfikia and its parochial entourage.

First to go was the nearby Ismailia Canal that was filled up and replaced by Boulevard Abbas. This was then, as now, one of Cairo's busiest and largest avenue and was subsequently renamed Queen Nazli Avenue and later Ramses. And before noisy Belgian streetcars were swapped for Africa's first French-built Metro, there were in the interim silent Hungarian-made trolley buses.

Another loss was the celebrated Tewfikia Tennis Club with its red clay courts and swimming pool. It gave way to government edifices, including the massive neo-classical Telegraph and Telephone Headquarters on Ramses Street. A fast disappearing landmark is what had once been the red and beige Kyriazi mansion and its adjoining garden. Together they occupied 3,000 square metres in 1896. These became the Matossian cigarette factory and much later a print shop. Today parasitic boutiques and shops that front Souq al Tewfikia Street and the perpendicular Chawarby Pasha lane leach on to the ex-Kyriazi mansion. And last to check out from the crowded landscape was the souq's popular Cecil Bar and its Greek owners.

Despite these changes, Souq al Tewfikia is alive and well and still worth a visit, at the very least for its three landmark buildings which stand guard at its east-west approaches. At the Midan Orabi end are the Green and Homsy buildings. Built for Moise Solomon Green by architect Garo Balian in 1910, the massive Neapolitan building (Nos. 2-4 Souq al Tewfikia) was tenanted by leading dentists, lawyers and architects with names like Bromberger, Aladjem and Balian. The building boasts a unique passage-turned-patio linking 26th of July Street to the souq. Once a demi-monde hideaway, this bustling fresco-splattered enclosure is a favourite hangout for pony-tailed backpackers, con artists, backgammon champions and *shisha* regulars. They dub it Serenity Alley.

Across the street from Serenity Alley stands a fanciful 1925 *immeuble de rapport* (No. 1 Souq al Tewfikia) designed for the Homsy family by Marco Olivetti. If the neo-baroque façades on Souq al Tewfikia and Midan Orabi froth with Venetian gargoyles, the two other façades are by contrast plain and simple, with the fallen plaster acknowledging Olivetti's covert reliance on cheaper building techniques. Abandoned by its rent control-shackled owner, the schizophrenic building's cavernous entrance would make an ideal backdrop for the next Batman movie.

At Souq al Tewfikia's western entrance stands the modern Weiser Building (No. 19), designed *circa* 1934 by Mario Rossi for pharmacist Gaston Weiser. From New Rochelle in New York State, André Weiser writes about his grandfather:

> A pharmacology graduate, my grandfather, born in 1889, was accustomed to produce only the very best, using the purest chemicals, which he imported directly from Merck AG, Germany. He became known for the quality of his prescription work and for his own specialities. In 1925 he participated in three industrial expos, Paris, Brussels and Rome where he earned first prize—three enormous gold medals. What pride for an Egyptian pharmacist!

Egypt's long jump champion of the 1930s is alive and well in Connecticut. He too recalls Souq al Tewfikia for he is none other than the pharmacist's son, Erwin Weiser:

> Street vendors were as active and noisy as ever. Everyone shouting as they advertised their wares from early morning till late at night, making a wonderful cacophony. We were at the corner of Souq al Tewfikia and Sharia al Malika Nazli. At the other corner was an oasis of tranquility, the Matossian Cigarette manufacturer with its delightful gardens. In the middle of the Souq there was a room, which was used as a mosque. At first there were just a few adherents. The mosque grew, grew and grew so that on Fridays the street was blocked by hundreds and hundreds of worshippers.

To this day grandpa Weiser's skin irritation treatment, Poudre Suisse, is regarded the best of its time. That is perhaps why the building's subsequent owner thought better of changing the name on the building's ground floor laboratory. Also domiciled in the building is an antiquated lab created by Adolphe Del'Mar. It was Del'Mar (a.k.a. Mr. Boots of Egypt) who launched the Societé Anonyme des Drogueries d'Egypte that became the country's leading drug company.

Whereas Del'Mar, Weiser and the Cecil Bar are gone, the place is just as lively today as it was during Kyriazi Pasha's days. Anyone planning to buy children's undies, a large spanner, or a kilo of *Hindi* mangoes, should do so at Souq al Tewfikia. And remember a bubbling *shisha* awaits you at Serenity Alley. Better hurry though. Government plans for urban renewal and clean up have rung the death knell for several historic souqs in the city and there are rumours that Souq al Tewfikia may soon be the next to go.

Palace of commerce

The odd man out among Cairo's department stores was Sednaoui. While all the others belonged to Jews, the owners of Sednaoui were Nazarenes from the Syrian villages of Sednaya and Maaloula where Aramaic is still spoken. Newly arrived in Egypt by way of Damascus, the Sednaoui brothers, Samaan and Selim, opened their first haberdashery in the late nineteenth century in the district of Hamzaoui before moving to Mousky Street near Al Azhar.

The brothers' fortune took a turn for the better when employees of the khedivial harem shopping with the Sednaouis had either overpaid or forgotten to take back the correct change. When *Khawaga* Samaan ran after them, pointing out what happened, the much-obliged shoppers returned to the palace and related their exceptional encounter with an honest Shami (Syrian). From that day onwards Sednaoui was a favourite among the court ladies.

As Cairo expanded into the new European quarter of Ismailia, so did the city's great retailing names. Chemla, Cicurel and Ades were clustered on or near King Fouad Avenue (26th of July), considered by many to be Cairo's Oxford Street. Orosdi-Back (later Omar Effendi) was within walking distance on Abdel Aziz Street. Tiring, Stein and Morums had already opened on nearby Midan al Ataba, the nexus of Cairo's commercial hub.

The Sednaoui brothers kept their distance from the rest of the department stores by setting up shop in the more confined Midan Khazindar. It was there, on November 1, 1913, that they inaugurated their grand three-storey emporium near Al Bawaki, opposite the Services Club. In no time the Sednaoui store at Khazindar became the flagship of a retail chain with branches in Alexandria, Port Said, Tanta, Mansoura, Fayoum and Assiut.

With its classical *fin de siècle* architecture, Sednaoui could have been transplanted from any one of the great European capitals. In his quest to emulate Galleries Lafayette on Boulevard Hausmann in Paris, architect Georges Parcq spared nothing in terms of layout, metalwork, and general amenities. Even the flag-flying cupolas were there. Yet despite all this, it was no secret that Sednaoui played second fiddle to the classier Cicurel.

Ultimately, Cicurel set the trends of consumer culture in Cairo, though Sednaoui was not too far behind. And if there were handsome and formidably attired Circassian guards flanking Cicurel's grand entrance on Avenue Fouad, the Cairo ladies were still extremely flattered whenever Monsieur Sednaoui greeted them personally as they marched through the portals of his emporium—something which he did fairly regularly. The clever merchant-turned-bey (not to mention papal count in view of his extensive charities) promoted the idea that any *sitt* who bought from Sednaoui was a *hanem*. Sednaoui knew only too well how the enunciation of a woman's title could influence shopping habits citywide.

Samaan Sednaoui or one of his heirs was always there before the store opened to oversee the arrival of their well-mannered, dandified male and female employees, inspecting them as they drifted to their stations. Once all was shipshape, the store opened for business. As they entered Sednaoui, shoppers were immediately taken in by the grandiose atrium. Once inside, they would gape at the jewellery and cosmetic counters while the more courageous would try out the latest Parisian hats and accessories. Men, too, stopped at Sednaoui's, purchasing bolts of imported English cloth or Far Eastern fabrics for their wives or sweethearts. Sednaoui's was also the preferred location for a fleeting flirtation because its multiple entrances made for quick getaways.

There was also the toy department where the wide-eyed little ones thought they had discovered heaven.

Masters of the retail universe, the Sednaouis made it seem like there was a special event every day of the year—and perhaps more importantly, everything could be bought on credit. Through their extensive purchasing agents in Paris, London and New York and with the assistance of Sednaoui Shipping Co. Ltd. of Princess Street, Manchester (later, Selfridges of London served as buyers for the company), nothing was beyond Sednaoui's reach. Catalogues were bursting with seasonal selections whether for Christmas, Easter, Bairam or back-to-school.

Then there were those popular annual low-end sales! These were fervently anticipated by the modest and lower middle-income shoppers, who, normally intimidated by Cicurel's sophistication, boldly showed up at Place Khazindar armed with the one-page newspaper advertisement listing the various Sednaoui discounts. For some it would be their only exposure ever to an in-store fashion show, an auction, Santa Claus or Christmas in July.

For the big spenders, shopping at Sednaoui was more for pleasure than satisfying basic needs. Furthermore, pianist Selim Sednaoui, a grandson of the department store's co-founder, recalls that on certain Sundays in the late 1950s, when the rest of commercial Cairo was shut down, Sednaoui opened by special arrangement to accommodate wealthy shop-till-you-drop clients from the Gulf. These arrived by the planeload with an extra plane in reserve for the fully laden return trip.

In July 1961, Egypt's major department stores were nationalised. Mr. Elie Sednaoui, the then-director of S&S Sednaoui et Fils, was given an indefinite leave of absence. An army officer replaced him and the age of drab counters and khaki-coloured co-operatives began.

Ramses returns home

At precisely noon on Thursday, February 24, 1955, just before mid-day prayers, large crowds watched in bewilderment as a colossal pharaoh—most did not know which one—painstakingly inched his way by special convoy towards Midan Bab al Hadid next to the central railway station. Those who had read the morning papers were aware that this was no ordinary ruler of ancient Egypt. He was the grandson of a man, not of royal descent himself, who had taken over the reins of power from the 18th Dynasty, whose best-known pharaohs included erratic monotheist Akhenaton and his teenage successor Tutankhamun. Once settled on Egypt's gilded throne, this pharaoh made of the 19th Dynasty one of the most illustrious in Egyptian history. High priests and the general public alike were submissive to him and to his successors.

The implicit parallel between the pharaoh rumbling through Cairo and Egypt's current strongman, Gamal Abdel Nasser, could not be missed. Nasser too was of humble descent with a military background and had toppled a ruling dynasty. Small wonder that one of the first decisions regarding the remodelling of Cairo was to place the larger-than-life statue in the capital's busiest square. Perhaps one day, that other famous square, Midan al Tahrir, would host the statue of Egypt's latest pharaoh, Nasser the First!

The statue being moved to the centre of Africa's oldest capital was that of Ramses the Great, who reigned from 1279 to 1213 BC—the second-longest reigning monarch in Egyptian history. If one were to believe the propaganda machine of his time, he had conquered and subdued the rebellious princes of Palestine and southern Syria, and had waged war on the powerful Hittites of Anatolia.

Ever since it was sculpted out of red granite, the statue of Ramses had laid on its back watching history go by. As centuries turned into millennia the statue blended in with the surrounding scenery, eventually being buried beneath it. It was discovered in 1820 and then, inexplicably, reburied for another 67 years—the same number of years Ramses ruled Egypt.

Uncovered for a second time, the great pharaoh was now being transferred from his original temple near the ancient capital of Memphis to the nearby metropolis of Cairo. A modern day pharaoh was resurrecting Ramses.

The statue's twentieth century journey started from its lonely habitat at Mit Rahina at 5am. The made-to-order stretch trailer was preceded by outriders and tracked by a heavy security detail. Buses bursting with media men were in hot pursuit of this unprecedented motorcade as it threaded along narrow country roads in between palm trees and water buffaloes turning listlessly around waterwheels. The scenery had not changed much since pharaoh had last visited.

As the convoy crawled northward across rickety rural bridges leading out of Sakkara and towards the Giza plateau, it was as though the distant pyramids, shimmering in the first morning light, were beckoning. Ramses' crown, weighing three tons, travelled on a separate truck, as did his injured right leg. By the time the convoy reached Pyramids Avenue, the media men were running amok in order to catch the historic moment: Ramses the Great sightseeing at the monuments of his noble ancestors Cheops, Chefren and Mykerinos. Pharaohs were making history again!

After a brief stop, the procession resumed its journey. Since it was unlikely that the trailers could handle the Giza underpass, a special crossing was improvised across the Upper Egypt railway line. The rest was easy navigating. First, the drive by the Giza Zoo, then across the newly renamed Galaa (Evacuation) Bridge, under the watchful eyes of the statue of slain Prime Minister Ahmed Maher Pasha. A small stretch later and Ramses passed under the imposing statue of nationalist leader Saad Zaghloul Pasha, whose great feats and charisma had mobilised an entire nation. After Zaghloul came the legendary Kasr al Nil Bridge lions. The kings of the jungle looked on in bewilderment. Was not this pharaoh a distant cousin of the sphinx, who thought he was a lion?

Ramses then crossed onto the Nile's east bank where pharaohs had never been buried. Sacrilege!

The procession moved on towards Midan Ismail Pasha (renamed Tahrir) and went down Queen Nazli Avenue henceforth known as Ramses Street. Bab al Hadid was within sight! It was 11:53am.

At Bab al Hadid, the statue was transferred to a temporary concrete and steel bed. It lay in state until a granite base with a water fountain was ready to receive it, and the statue would stand upright for the first time in three millennia. Meanwhile, the original inhabitant of Bab al Hadid, Mokhtar's 'Egypt's Awakening', was hurriedly moved to its new location in Giza in front of Cairo University.

The unveiling ceremony of the revamped Midan Ramses was scheduled for July 23, 1955, to coincide with the third anniversary of the 1952 coup. It was only fitting that its principal beneficiary, whom modern-day scribes were already describing as "The greatest Egyptian ruler since Ramses", did the honours. Little did they realise then that while Ramses had added huge territories to his ever-expanding realm, Nasser would instead part with the Sudan and, a few years later, lose Gaza and the entire peninsula of Sinai during the June 1967 war with Israel.

On July 23 the statue of Ramses was not yet in place. "A technical hitch," claimed the cringeing contractor. The much-publicised ceremony was cancelled and *Al Rais*, with the American ambassador in tow, celebrated the groundbreaking of the Nile Hilton Hotel instead.

Today, Ramses is scheduled to return to his original home at Mit Rahina. It is as though the 51-year lapse since Nasser promised his adulatory subjects prosperity and a representative government had never taken place. Through twists and turns, timeless Egypt corrects itself so that the sanctification of our pharaohs, both ancient and modern, continues.

The modern souq

An infectious time bomb is just waiting to explode in Umm al Dunya's nerve centre. Welcome to the octogenarian Bab al Louk market, home to fetid odours, radiation-immune cockroaches, killer rats, venereal house cats, pre-teen sweat shops, rent-a-wreck garages and—brace yourself—very possibly your next dinner's vegetable soup.

Strategically situated midway between Midan al Tahrir and Abdin Palace, the gubernatorial motorcade whizzes past each morning on its way to City Hall. You would think by now Cairo's esteemed governor would recognise the hazards of upholding such a misplaced enterprise. It is entirely possible that His Excellency may have realised by now the potential worth of this unique building's adaptive re-use, but in case he hasn't, let's dig up some titbits surrounding the souq's history and the visionary capitalists who conceived it. Without a doubt, today they must be turning in their graves.

Before the First World War, Cairo already boasted an opera house, a central railway station, a khedivial library, a national museum, an observatory and the world's fourth largest zoo. The time had come for the city to introduce modern wholesale markets thus displacing traditional all-purpose *wekalas* (bazaars) and their snarled open-air versions.

If Cairo's souqs had once served their purpose, they were now considered breeding grounds for epidemics and plagues. With recent ravages of cholera still on the public's mind, improved hygiene had become a civic goal in February 1911. The covered market project first began with the backing of two French banks, represented by Messrs. David Adda and Rosenberg and a declared capital of LE30,000. It was not long thereafter that Messrs. Finzi, Mondolfo and Cattaui (Adolphe and Joseph) announced the creation of Societé des Halles Centrales d'Egypte, modelled on the one of Paris fame.

Quick to capitalise on the growing need for cold storage, one-stop purchasing and sanitary conveniences, the company drew plans for a huge complex where retailer and wholesaler alike could purchase the freshest, germ-free produce right here in the centre of Cairo. Since the populated areas surrounding Midan al Ataba and Cairo Station Square (today Midan Ramses) were already spoken for, each with its own covered market—courtesy of the municipality and a private company respectively—Les Halles Centrales' owners were obliged to settle for the newer district of Bab al Louk.

Fortunately, the proposed site could not have wanted for a better location. For starters, it was adjacent to the Cairo terminus of the Cattaui-owned Bab al Louk to Helwan suburban transit system that served Sayeda Zeinab, Old Cairo, Torah and the budding suburb of Maadi. Interestingly, Halles Centrales' directors were one and the same as those of the Egyptian Delta Land & Investment Company that created Maadi in 1904. Similarly, they were also the proprietors of Helwan's casino, palace hotels and thermal facilities that made this resort town south of Cairo so famous.

Another significant bonus for the Bab al Louk market was the tramway junction fronting its proposed northern entrance. Consumers would be a tram ride from Zamalek, Garden City, downtown Cairo and Giza (the tramway and train terminal were both removed in the 1980s).

Acquiring the property was no problem. Part of the land already belonged to the Delta Land & Investment Co. and the remainder was purchased directly from Khairy Pasha (original owner of the American University in Cairo's main building), who received a company directorship as an added premium.

Lacking was an architect capable of putting all the modern conveniences of wholesale shopping beneath one giant roof. Researcher Pascal Garret, whose recent post-graduate thesis centres on the Bab al Louk market, believes the choice fell on the firm of Edward Matasek & Maurice Cattaui, creators of several Cairo landmarks. Or, could the design have been the work of company chairman, Youssef Cattaui? A graduate of the Paris school of engineering, the pasha-to-be participated in several architectural competitions including one for the design of Alexandria's main railway station.

Even before its official inauguration in May 1912, the press was already comparing the new souq with the famous Paris Halles. Agog with praise for the new market, Cairo's French-language daily recited the building's general aspects, detailing each corner, nook and cranny within its 6,000 square metre, two-storey, U-shaped perimeter.

"Everything can be found at the new Bab al Louk market" exclaimed the *Journal du Caire*. "Besides ample office space on the first floor, the ground floor abounds with grocery stores, restaurants, cafés, beerstubes, pharmacies, pastries and bakeries. Even a telephone office and a bank." The newspaper also mentions the availability of excellent docking and loading facilities, something quite novel at the time.

Meanwhile *Al Ahram* enthusiastically described how, 24 metres below a suspended metal roof, the large fish, meat, poultry and vegetable stands benefit from ample light and ventilation. "Even more amazing," *Al Ahram* continued, "is the gigantic basement and its refrigeration facilities where dairy products, carcasses, fruits and much more, can be stockpiled for months on end. If consumers can now enjoy mangoes in January and strawberries in July, they can also find beer and fine wines carefully stored at Bab al Louk for all-year consumption."

"But more importantly" exclaimed another anonymous reporter, "are the new market's sanitary and hygienic facilities... comparable to the best Europe has to offer."

Everyone was served at Bab al Louk, remembers an old timer, and that included members of all faiths. You would go to the fowl stores and there you would encounter both the Jewish Hakham and the Muslim Sheikh slaughtering the birds according to the kosher or the halal rules of tradition.

The new coat of paint the building received in the late 1990s cannot hide the current sad state of the market brought on by decades of neglect and changing consumption patterns. Now it is from the new chains of Western-style supermarkets where the well-heeled get their food and produce. It is a shame, however, to let a landmark with the history and dignity (not to mention location) of Bab al Louk moulder away.

La maison des artistes

From time to time a certain grimy *hara* at the base of the Citadel wakes up to the resonance of loaders and earth-moving equipment. The alleyway is about to receive an anorexic layer of asphalt. That done, gubernatorial flowerpots are laid out in an effort to camouflage the advanced state of deterioration. By now the local residents know the game: someone of importance is about to visit La Maison des Artistes, the celebrated 400-year-old Ottoman-era house, used occasionally for some major social event. No doubt, Darb al Labana's inhabitants are attuned to these shenanigans. For centuries, ever since Salah al Din built the Citadel in 1171, they have witnessed the making and undoing of history at close quarters.

For several centuries the Citadel remained the single most fortified area in Cairo. First the Mamlukes and later Mohammed Ali used it as a stronghold. Then, when the British Army vacated the towering compound after the Second World War, the Egyptian military made good use of it before turning some of it over to a civilian administration. There are also those who remember imposing funerals, bringing colourful corteges to the nearby Al Rifai Mosque, where Egypt's royals are buried. The last such interment was when the exiled Shah of Iran was laid to rest there in July 1980.

And there are those who remember the heyday of La Maison des Artistes when, in 1900, the impoverished Ali Labib family leased part of their three-storey arabesque house to orientalist Pierre Beppi-Martin. A French counterpart of Gayer Anderson, the British officer who restored a pair of delightful Ottoman houses in the same area, Beppi-Martin was so smitten with Cairo's Islamic quarter that upon marrying, he brought his Lyonnaise bride to the area in 1910 "to impress her," recalls his son Père Martin, a retired priest at the Jesuit School in Cairo's Fagallah neighbourhood. "Here you will live in an ancient Islamic chateau," Beppi-Martin senior promised his wife. On her first day the bride discovered a large snake in her washbowl. And when a snake charmer exorcised several dozen more, the Martins moved out. But Beppi-Martin continued to use an upper floor as a private studio until his death in 1950.

Among the better-known tenants were poet Edmond Jabes and Egypt's architect for the poor, Hassan Fathi. The latter subleased an entire floor while Sanad Basta, a renowned portraitist, took the basement. Several years later, painter Raouf Abdel Meguid, whose trademark was idealised minarets and popsicle-coloured cupolas, rented a corner of the celebrated house. Countless others came for long or short periods, and depending on availability, occupied rooms, nooks or crannies. The lucky ones were those tenants with a view.

Yet there were those who were prepared to forsake the external view for the incomparable arabesque interiors. Such was the case in 1962 when David Hockney sketched La Maison des Artistes during his brief visit.

Musicologist and former lodger, Tarek Sharara, claims Maison des Artistes is in the same league as Bayt al Harawi, Suhaymi and Zeinab Khatoun, medieval houses in the Fatamid city. "Each room is different. If one hall boasts arcades, another is a ceramic-fest and the next one a treasure trove of woodwork. While one room has a gold-rimmed ceiling, the other has the most beautiful arabesque chandelier and the third has no ceiling at all— only stars and blue sky. And thanks to a network of fountains, shafts and cupolas, the house is always cool in summer."

Many observers agree it was *Khawaga* Uri Milovitch a.k.a. Milo, an Eastern European, who put La Maison des Artistes (thereafter nicknamed Milo's House) on Cairo's social map. Tour leaders and cultural centres booked at Chez Milo whenever an important group or performing dance troupe was in town. The cinema crowd were also regulars since Milo had spent some time editing subtitles at Titra Film. In a genuine Mamluke setting they enjoyed the best local fare and entertainment—from kofta and kebab to dervishes, *zar* and Nubian dancers. Lantern in hand, Umm Sayed, the hunchbacked gatekeeper, would welcome the guests and direct them towards the roof. A view of a millennium's worth of urban history awaited them.

The not-so-cultural affairs were essentially parties where Milo's stereophonic record player—a novelty at the time—wowed the wide-eyed novices and titillated the ageing, youth-obsessed set. The host seemed to know everyone from Egypt's *haute Juiverie* to its topmost *Copterie* and *Musulmanie*. At Chez Milo, sons and daughters of pashas rubbed shoulders with the salt of the earth, starting with the obliging nearby slum dwellers, most of whom were Milo's friends.

La Maison des Artistes fell on hard times when Milo left Egypt in the late 1960s. A comparable house across the alley was pulled down the day after its Italian occupant, portraitist Angelo de Riz, moved out.

"If La Maison des Artistes is with us today, it is thanks to the efforts of the Aga Khan Foundation!" exclaims its unofficial curator, Ihab Shafik. "It was mainly because of Hassan Fathi that the historic house was brought to the attention of Prince Sadruddin Khan, who for a time leased part of it."

Today, La Maison des Artistes is classified as a historic monument. Worthy causes are occasionally celebrated in its partially rehabilitated quarters such as the one held there by UNICEF when it launched the Luginbuhl Legacy —a civic project for the benefit of working children. But what of the works of art produced on these historic premises?

For starters, the Beppi-Martin collection is on display courtesy of the Hahn Foundation at the renaissance-style Chateau Lourmain in Vaucluse, France. Milo's artwork disappeared when the old Omar Khayam Hotel (today Marriott) was revamped. Of Angelo de Riz' works, a panel still exists at Cairo's Cinema Rivoli. He also decorated a trendy restaurant in Paris, but no one remembers its name.

Meanwhile, paintings and portraits by Sanad Basta and Raouf Abdel Meguid's popsicle cupolas adorn the homes of Egypt's weathered salons.

The pantheon that never was

Tucked away in the back streets only a few blocks from Midan Tahrir sits a regal mausoleum that would not look out of place in a *Prince of Egypt* movie with ancient Egyptian undertones. Inside the paganistic neo-pharaonic building lies not some vengeful mummy, but Saad Zaghloul Pasha, that great twentieth century Egyptian nationalist who, against all odds, led Egypt down the path of independence.

Saad Zaghloul was unconditionally worshipped. Election results and everything else at the time said as much. Not only was his picture a regular staple in the nationalist press, but almost every headline started with his name. With television yet to appear and radio a novel gimmick, admirers opted for life-size, all-size, any-size portraits of Egypt's fiery premier. These were on display in coffee shops, bars, schools and street corners. And if Zaghloul was regarded as the benevolent Father of the Nation, his wife, Safeya Hanem, was called *Umm al Masreyeen*—Mother of the Egyptians.

When Zaghloul died suddenly and without a successor in the summer of 1927, the nation slipped into a coma of such proportions that only a gigantic public send-off—a funeral worthy of the greatest of all pharaohs: Ramses, Tuhtmose, Cheops, Chefren, take your pick—could bring the country back to the living.

The now fatherless nation could not and did not want to believe it had been so unexpectedly abandoned by its spiritual guide, mentor and confessor. Therefore, it decided to immortalise him. Two larger than life statues were commissioned: one for Cairo and one for Alexandria. In addition, there would be the biggest, most impressive mausoleum ever. Something so sacred it would resemble an ancient Egyptian tabernacle—an unconscious reminder that the pharaoh's cult was alive and well in the ancient valley of the Nile.

In order to have the appropriate space for the mausoleum, the government purchased the three houses situated opposite *Bayt al Umma* (House of the Nation), as Zaghloul's home had come to be called. Work could now begin on this 4,800 square metre lot bordering Falaki Street..

But with the passing of time the bickering began and Zaghloul's anticipated commemoration became a sore issue among Egypt's competing political factions.

While the Zaghloul-created Wafd Party bulldozed ahead with its grandiose schemes, the opposition kept calling for something more modest. Nevertheless, by January 1931, the Wafdist Ministry of Public Works had generously supplemented the collected public funds with an additional LE50,000 so that the mausoleum's construction could begin, using the best red granite Aswan could provide.

By the time architect Mustafa Fahmi Bey (later pasha) had completed the mausoleum 11 months later, the new, ardently anti-Wafd Prime Minister, Ismail Sidki Pasha, decided it would not be Zaghoul's alone. Instead, it would become a national pantheon; a final resting-place for Egypt's greats, himself included when the time came.

Understandably, the resulting Wafdist outcry was heard across the nation. Many still remembered the stirring days of the Great Leader. In a tearful communication to Sidki Pasha, Madame Zaghloul stated that if he insisted on his proposal, she would not release the mortal remains of her husband, temporarily buried in the family graveyard in Imam al Shafei. As far as *Umm al Masreyeen* was concerned, the mausoleum was a small-scale Taj Mahal dedicated to her beloved Saad. If anyone else should lie alongside her deceased husband it would be she and she alone.

Ignoring the Wafd and Madame Zaghloul's protests, the royal remains of Egypt's ancient kings and queens were transferred from the Egyptian Museum to the neo-pharaonic mausoleum. Ironically, just a few years earlier, these same royals including a pharaoh from the 17th Dynasty, nine kings and Queen Nefertari from the 18th Dynasty, had all been withdrawn from public exhibition on the grounds of dignity. Also being transferred to the mausoleum that same day, were five kings from the 19th Dynasty, four Ramses from the 20th, and five queens from the 21st.

Despite outcries that public exposure of past monarchs was deemed unbecoming, they would now be in sight of an entire nation.

Back in power in April 1936, following the enthronement of the 17-year-old King Farouk, the Wafdist-led government proceeded to embellish the mausoleum-turned-pantheon on Falaki Street. For one thing, the walls were entirely lined with granite costing the taxpayer an additional LE30,000.

On the summer of 1936, coinciding with the ninth anniversary of the death of Saad Zaghloul, the Pasha's mortal remains were exhumed from the family vault in Imam al Shafei and placed in a coffin atop a gun carriage. These were then transferred to Falaki Street, led by 15,000 blue-shirted Wafdist youths. As anticipated, the cortege quickly turned into a public demonstration as mourners, religious scholars and university students joined the fray.

What happened meanwhile to Egypt's ancient rulers who had once had massive personality cults of their own? While no one noticed or seemed to care, the 24 royal mummies were bundled out of the heretofore-sacred pantheon and hustled across Cairo to a temporary location. There they would rest in anonymity until such time when the Egyptian Museum could have them back.

This was Saad Zaghloul's day and no one, dead or alive, was allowed to compete, for the time being at least. For the next few years Egypt's neo-pharaonic Taj became a site of veneration whenever the Wafd came to power, and on January 13, 1946, the entire nation turned up at its gates to honour the "Mother of the Egyptians" as she was laid to rest. In a way, the nation was also bidding farewell to its 64-year-old nationalist movement.

2. Kasr el Dubara

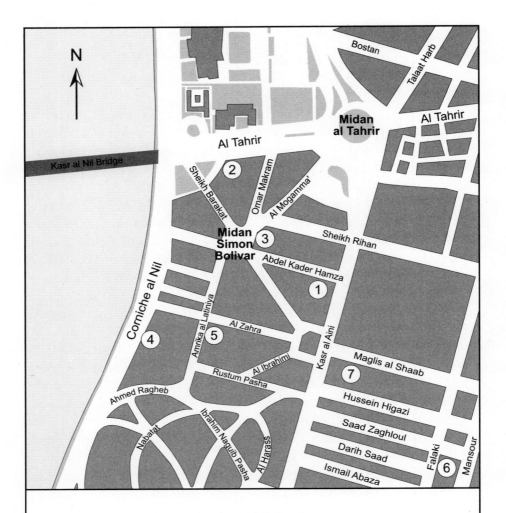

Kasr al Dubara

1 - Villa David Ades / State Printing House
2 - Kemal al Din Palace / Ministry of Foreign Affairs
3 - Villa Casdagli / Abdel Latif School
4 - British Embassy
5 - Fakhry Palace / Banque de Paris
6 - Zaghloul Mausoleum
7 - Shuvikar Palace / Council of Ministers

0   250   500m

Palaces on the Nile

After centuries of living up on the dusty cliffs of the Citadel, Egypt's rulers decided to rediscover the pleasures of a Nile-side residence in the nineteenth century. Together with all the other changes that came during this momentous century, there was the creation of a whole series of palaces along the banks of Egypt's eternal river.

Viceroy Ibrahim Pasha was the first member of the ruling dynasty to move his living quarters to the banks of the Nile: first on the garden island of Manial al Rhoda and later, when he built his palace of Kasr al Aali on what had previously been the marshes and levelled sand bars of Tel al Akareb (Scorpion Hill). The marshes were drained and replaced with orchards and gardens that were further developed by his sons and grandchildren, and soon the area between Masr al Ateeka (Old Cairo) and Boulaq abounded with Kasr This and Kasr That.

One of Ibrahim's sons, Khedive Ismail, built a series of palaces for his wives and concubines called Kasr al Nil, Kasr al Dubara and Kasr al Ismailia. Meanwhile, a daughter-in-law lived in Kasr al Walda Pasha. There was also Kasr al Aini, which would later become Egypt's first School of Medicine.

Somewhat removed from the Nile, as we know it today, were several other palaces of importance. Some of these were turned into ministries or headquarters of important government departments. Kasr Ismail al Moufatish became government HQ and later the Ministry of Finance. Kasr al Amira Iffet Hassan was sold to Princess Shuvikar Ibrahim and, for a short while, rented out to the Council of Ministers. When the princess raised the rent, the Council moved back to Kasr al Moufatish. The Turkish Legation moved in, in its place. Later the princess decided to live there herself. Her lavish New Year parties were attended by Cairo's *crème de la crème*. Following her death on February 17, 1947, and in view of the huge inheritance tax on her estate, a deal was struck so that Princess Shuvikar's palace reverted back to the Council of Ministers.

There is also the nearby Kasr al Mounira that became the French Archaeological Centre (IFAO).

Although some of these palaces are gone, their names live on either as districts or as bridges, streets and squares.

Kasr al Aali, once the scene of many royal weddings, was torn down to make way for the curvy district of Garden City. Meanwhile, Kasr al Nil, which had earned itself the nickname of *The Nursery* because it was there that Ismail sent his pregnant wives, was turned into the barracks of the British Army of Occupation. A clever choice since it was linked to the rest of Egypt by rail. In the late 1950s the *Ingilizi* barracks would be replaced by the Nile Hilton Hotel and the Arab League—the first a symbol of the encompassing American hegemony in the region and the second a potent symbol of Arab disunity, a place where doddering potentates hold ineffectual summits.

Kasr al Walda Pasha, in the Kasr al Dubara district, disappeared when Prince Mohammed Ali Tewfik of Kasr al Manial sold it to developers in 1947 following his mother's (the walda pasha or queen mother) death. Six buildings including the new Shepheard's Hotel came to replace it. Kasr al Ismailia is where the monstrous Mogamaa complex stands today. Part of its garden became Midan Ismailia, renamed in the 1950s Midan al Tahrir.

In between these large royal estates were mini-palaces such as the one still standing opposite the Arab League. From the mid-1930s until quite recently, it was home to the Ministry of Foreign Affairs. This box-shaped 100-year-old structure was built on land that had once been the estate of Viceroy's Ibrahim's eldest son, Prince Ahmed Rifaat. Had it not been for a fatal accident when his Cairo-bound train slipped off a Nile barge at Kafr al Zayat, Ahmed would have ruled Egypt instead of Khedive Ismail.

Upon Ahmed's demise, the Nile-side domain reverted to his heirs. By that time Prince Ahmed's kasr had already acquired a sinister reputation. For starters a young princess died there a few months after her marriage to Prince Ahmed's son.

Prince Ahmed's former estate gave way to new urban developments, including several palaces such as the one designed by Italian architect Antonio Lasciac for Princess Nimet Allah, youngest daughter of Khedive Tewfik.

Abandoned by her first husband Prince Gamil Toussoun, Princess Nimet married her esoteric cousin, Prince Kamal al Din Hussein. He was the only son of the man who would become Egypt's first modern-day sultan. In fact, it was from the princess's Nile-side palace that Sultan Hussein Kamel (nicknamed 'Father of the Peasant' because of his love of agriculture and flora) led his inaugural procession in December 1914. Under normal circumstances that event should have been a happy entry in the palace diaries. Yet quite the contrary; the new sultan had just replaced Princess Nimet's brother, Abbas Hilmi, as Egypt's new ruler. The British occupants had summarily exiled Hilmi, whose sympathies with the Germans were not unknown. He would never set foot in Egypt again.

With time the palace became a sad empty nest. Prince Kamal al Din, who was for a short while Egypt's Heir Presumptive and sometime commander of its army, preferred trekking the desert or travelling around the world than spending time in the nuptial palace. Likewise, collecting oriental artefacts was far more absorbing than attending to affairs of state. A Sufi mystic to boot, the Prince subscribed to the traditions of the Bektashis, that reclusive sect which claimed concealed origins in Albania. Having donated considerable financial support to this saintly order, Kamal al Din was made one of the sect's honorary Brothers.

Either because he shunned public life or because he had no temporal ambitions of his own, Kamal al Din renounced the throne in favour of an uncle a few days before his father's death in 1917. Another happy entry was thus aborted from the palace diaries.

The man who could have been king died in Toulouse, France, in 1932 at age 58, a result of complications from an operation to amputate a leg. Prince Kamal al Din's only wish was to be buried in a specially built vault in the Muqattam Hills above Cairo near where the dervishes dwelled.

A few years later, Prince Kamal al Din's widow leased her palace of sorrows to the Egyptian government so that the Ministry of Foreign Affairs could finally move out of its cramped quarters of Kasr al Bostan (today a multilevel car park) on Bostan Street.

Since that time the Foreign Ministry has gone on to modern headquarters farther down the Nile towards Boulaq, and Nimet Allah's palace is undergoing much needed renovation. Rumour has it that he palace is scheduled to become Egypt's first Museum of Foreign Affairs.

Midan Simon Bolivar (ex-Kasr al Dubara)

A few metres from the palace of sorrows, on any July 5, motorists commuting to work via the district of Kasr al Dubara will notice an assemblage of dapper ladies and gentlemen laying wreaths at the foot of Simon Bolivar's statue, located in the midan of the same name.

Sadly, we no longer call this veteran district by its original name but tend to lump it in with nearby Garden City, in spite of the fact that the latter technically starts three blocks to the south. Indeed, the name Simon Bolivar itself is relatively new. When it was mapped out in the 1880s, the square was known as Midan Kasr al Dubara, in reference to a nearby vice-regal palace that once stood there. It was only when the statue of Simon Bolivar was unveiled on February 11, 1979 that the name change occurred. Today a street sign mistakenly refers to the midan as 'Simone Bovoir,' a misspelled reference to the celebrated French female author.

Attending the inauguration of the revamped Midan were two high-powered Latin American delegations headed by Venezuela's First Lady, Dona Blanca Rodriguez de Perez, who had arrived especially for the occasion. After all, the statue was a gift from her oil-rich homeland to Sadat's Egypt.

Since that eventful day and every July 5 thereafter, representatives from six Latin American countries—Venezuela, Panama, Colombia, Ecuador, Bolivia and Peru—congregate to honour the memory of their shared hero. It was the Caracas-born Bolivar who led these nations to independence from Spain early in the nineteenth century.

While the 500 kilogramme, 2.3 metre high bronze statue is attributed to Venezuelan sculptor Carmelo Tabaco, the accompanying pedestal is the work of fellow countryman, Manuel Silveira Blanco. Another statue commemorating yet another Latin American nationalist—Jose de San Martin—can be found in Mohandiseen next to the Shooting Club. San Martin was responsible for the independence of the southern part of the South American continent.

As South America fought for independence from Spain, Egypt was slowly modernising under Viceroy Mohammed Ali and his descendants. Two of them, Ibrahim and Ismail, were responsible for the creation of Kasr al Dubara and many of the palaces constructed therein.

Understandably, Cairo's political and financial elite followed Egypt's royals to the newly fashionable district. *Fin de siècle* social pages of the time abound with references to their Kasr al Dubara villas and mansions, especially during wedding season. It is there that major events in the lives of Egypt's greats were regularly celebrated. Indeed, the funeral of banker Felix Suares in 1900 did not differ much from that of a pasha-politician in 1950 or an incumbent minister in 1998, for all three corteges invariably led to the clogging of traffic at the prominent midan. Grand funerals still take place in Midan Kasr al Dubara at the adjacent mosque of Sheikh Omar Makram, which replaced that of Sheikh al Abit.

After the power elite came the hotels and embassies. First among the big names within the hospitality industry to grace the midan was the Semiramis in 1908. Built in phases, it occupied most of the block between the midan and the Nile. Mid-century saw the arrival of Shepheard's, a successor to the legendary hotel that was torched to the ground during the burning of Cairo in January 1952.

There is also Villa Casdagli (No. 1 Midan Kasr al Dubara) that is miraculously standing albeit as a government school named after Sudanese nationalist Ali Abdel Latif. It is doubtful any of the students, or their teachers for that matter, have heard of *fin de siècle* architecture or of the Austrian architect who designed this beautiful baroque villa.

Modelled after Central European *hôtels particuliers*, Villa Casdagli was built during the first decade of the last century by Eduard Matasek, reportedly for a wealthy merchant whose name remains a mystery. Yet sometime before 1912 the house became the property of Emanuel Casdagli, the British educated scion of a Levantine family dealing in the lucrative Manchester cotton trade.

According to Christopher Casdagli, now living in London, his father, David Seymour Emanuel Casdagli, born September 24, 1934, lived in Villa Casdagli until the age of four when he returned to the family house in Kersal Hill, Manchester, UK. "It was at Villa Casdagli where my grandparents celebrated their wedding. My grandmother was the daughter of Lord and Lady George Seymour of Wellingore, Lincolnshire and the niece of the Marquis of Hertford so at the time the house appeared in the press in France, Italy, UK, Cairo."

"Wedding in Cairo – Casdagli-Seymour" announces the *Egyptian Gazette* of November 24, 1933, dedicating an entire column to the event. "After the service a reception was held at the Casdagli house in Kasr al Dubara, to which over 400 guests were invited." The guest list reads like a contemporary Who's Who of Cairene society, ranging from the power elite to the moneyed bankers and top military brass.

Almost as soon as the Casdaglis and their lofty British relations moved out of No. 1 Midan Kasr al Dubara, it was the turn of the Americans to move in. During the interwar years the US government leased rather than bought premises. Which is why, for several years before the Second World War, Villa Casdagli doubled as American Legation and official residence of Judge Bert Fish, US envoy to Egypt. Many from that period will remember the Stars and Stripes fluttering above the villa's roof.

In March 1947, things changed. Acting on the instructions of the

American State Department, Ambassador Somerville Pinkney Tuck Jr. purchased part of the present-day embassy compound. This was the first-ever Egyptian real estate owned by the American government. Situated at No. 5 Kasr al Walda Pasha (later Amrika al Latiniya) Street, Tuck's new residence was a short distance from Villa Casdagli. Like the latter, it too had belonged to a wealthy landowner-businessman, this time a Maronite called Alexander Chedid Bey.

As American interests in Egypt expanded, the State Department purchased the contiguous properties, including Villa Rolo, also built by Matasek. Turned into the American Library, it was partly damaged by fire in 1958. In order to accommodate the impregnable American fortress that now occupies ninety percent of the block, Villa Chedid disappeared in the 1980s, followed by a relatively new apartment building that had itself replaced Villa Ades.

Behind Villa Casdagli stood, until very recently, Villa Cozzica, which belonged to a wealthy Greek family of the same name. For a long time they held a monopoly on distilled alcohol in Egypt. During the years leading up to the Second World War, much to the chagrin of the wary British diplomats residing in their large quarters two blocks away, the Cozzicas leased their Cairo residence to the German Legation. The last high-ranking visitor to call was Dr. Joseph Goebbels, the Reich Minister of Propaganda, in whose honour a dinner was held on the night of April 6, 1939.

Also fronting Midan Kasr al Dubara was a ladies-only tennis club. This was transformed in the late 1940s into a U-shaped apartment house designed by another of Cairo's leading architects, Antoine Selim Nahas, for the Al Chams Real Estate Company. Its arrival signalled the latest generation of denizens of Kasr al Dubara and the rise of an Egyptian bourgeois presence in this neighbourhood. Just as the mansions of the Levantine captains of industry replaced the palaces of the royal family, so now it was time for apartment buildings to overshadow the grand houses.

Perhaps friends of Cairo's landmarks within the business community would like to participate in an Adopt-a-Monument programme starting with Villa Casdagli. The positive fallout from such an effort would be enormous. It would strike a rich chord in this highly visible section of Cairo, where it counts most. It would also be perceived as part of the city's effort to repair the moral and physical damage caused by decades of neglectful municipal administration and the onslaught of *infitah* developers.

In the case of Villa Casdagli, an appropriate and highly visible plaque could be appended to its exterior, advertising that this was once the American Embassy. Another plaque would indicate that the restoration of this *hôtel particulier* to its formal splendour was made possible by the generous donations of leaders of the community. In turn, the government, which suffers from a very serious image problem when it comes to saving our architectural cultural heritage, will have its chance to turn over a new leaf and show that it really means business.

The building has so far miraculously survived and is today occupied by a government school whose sole purpose it seems is to add a new dimension to the word 'uglification.'

Bayt al Lurd (The Lord's House)

Just as a coquettish dowager smears lipstick across her old wrinkled face, the British Embassy's century-old wrought iron portico from time to time receives an overdue facelift, with blue, red and gold paint applied to the frame straddling VR (Victoria Regina), the imperial crown and the lone thistle. To those on the diplo-watch, these eleventh hour attempts at rejuvenation usually signify a royal visit. As it turned out this time around it was the Princess Royal who was scheduled for tea and biscuits with a few privileged subjects during a Cairo whistle stop.

Perhaps the princess already knew that it was on the embassy's riverfront lawn, at the very place where Lord Allenby kept a pet marabou stork, that her mother's betrothal to Philip of Greece was brought up in conversation between Lord Mountbatten and the young suitor. India's last empress, Victoria Regina, was related to most of Europe's royal families and so it was that her great-grandson became consort to the future Queen of Great Britain.

The embassy's colonial-style building with its finely painted walls and ceilings was originally an all-in-one residence-chancery designed by R.H. Boyce in 1893. Construction costs reached LE39,894 and building was supervised by a Mr. A. Huntley. The land itself had been purchased in 1890 at a cost to the British Treasury of LE2,580, including LE500 for the construction of an access road. In 1896-7, a further LE144 was spent to raise the floor of the basement above the level of the annual Nile flood in an effort to solve seepage problems.

In those days the British Embassy was referred to as The Agency—*Al Wekala*—just as the old legation on Adly (ex-Magrabi) Street had been. Cramped by a swelling bureaucracy, Lord Cromer had pushed Whitehall to purchase the new, bigger property. The old residence on Adly Street had become for all intents and purposes obsolete. This is amply noted in the correspondence to his superiors in London. On October 26, 1886, Cromer writes:

> The house which I at present occupy, is in no way adapted for an Agency. The reception rooms are far too small for the number of people whom I am obliged to entertain. As regards sleeping apartments there is only just enough room for my family, which only consists of my wife, two children and a governess. If I have to receive any visitors as was the case when the Viceroy returned from India, I am obliged to go to the trouble and expense of sending my children to an hotel.
>
> Nothing can be worse than the arrangements of the Chancery. Two very small rooms, one of which was intended to serve as a pantry and another which is so hot as to be almost uninhabitable in summer are all I can give for my staff, which consists of 6 persons. This accommodation is quite inadequate. The archives have to be stowed away in different parts of the house which cause very great inconvenience. There is not a single room in the house for a European man servant, and the rooms for the native servants are very bad and unhealthy. Yet this is the best house I can obtain in Cairo and I pay LE600 a year rent for it.
>
> I venture to submit to your Lordship that in view of the position occupied, and likely to be occupied for some time by H.M. representative in Egypt it is most desirable that a better house should be provided for the Agency than that which I have described above.

After additional correspondence on the subject, Cromer won the day; the result still in evidence today in Garden City where the largest embassy in Egypt still stands. It was nicknamed *Bayt al Lurd* (The Lord's House), as Cromer's rule over Egypt lasted two decades and it seemed to the local population that the house was his private property rather than that of his government. Few would have known that the man, who at the stroke of a pen could dissolve Egypt's cabinet, appoint a new khedive or annex the Sudan, had, on the other hand, to plead with his government for the purchase of a piece of property.

The British proconsul could not have wanted for a better location for his new residence on the Nile. At the turn of the century the surrounding district of Kasr al Dubara was where Cairo's finest had taken up residence. "For a long time, there were only private houses with marble porches and stained-glass windows in Kasr el Doubara, a secluded district inhabited by a rich aristocracy," writes Fernand Leprette in 1939, in his book *Egypt, Land of the Nile.*

The gardens of the British Embassy expanded considerably when H.M.'s Government purchased an adjoining piece of land belonging to a Mr. Bacos. The road that had previously separated the two districts was also absorbed into the embassy grounds and henceforth Rustom Pasha Street ended where it does today, at Amrika al Latiniya Street and not at the Nile as it originally did. The expanded property now straddled both Kasr al Dubara and Garden City. Would the two precincts eventually merge one day?

In the same book, Leprette inadvertently alludes to this merger.

> Nowadays, the wide streets of these two quarters run into one another. Kasr el Doubara hems with leafy trees the riverbank stretching between the Semiramis Hotel and the gates bearing the monogram of Queen Victoria, behind which Sir Miles Lampson, the British ambassador, still surveys the route to India. The Garden City streets seem to turn in circles on purpose to baffle intruders. In concrete buildings, silent lifts, with metal fittings, rise at one bound to terraces overlooking the Nile. A unique view streaked with light. It is here that the foreign legations reside and also here that the more fortunate Levantine families, their peregrinations through the town having ended, live in grand style.

During the interwar years, press and politicians alike referred to the British Embassy as the Residence. Others within the same milieu regarded the name Kasr al Dubara as an alternate vernacular for British Embassy, a tendency that was quite evident in official dispatches, and later in political memoirs. It was from the embassy veranda and behind its large wooden doors that imperial policy affecting the destinies of Egypt and the Middle East was conducted by empire-builders Allenby, MacMahon and Lloyd.

Up until the fall of the empire, Cromer's successors ran Egypt's affairs in typical imperial fashion. It was from the embassy gates that in February 1942, Sir Miles Lampson (later Lord Killearn) headed with a convincing military cortege towards Abdin Palace to offer King Farouk two choices: appoint a pro-British cabinet or abdicate. The young monarch complied and kept his throne for a few more years.

The embassy ballroom was added at a later date, but that too didn't come easy. When, in 1920, Field Marshal Lord Allenby requested the rebuilding of the embassy and the addition of a separate ballroom, his pleas were summarily rejected by London. Nevertheless, the British High Commissioner persisted, arguing that since, under the Protectorate, the British Residence was also the de-facto British-run Egyptian Ministry of Foreign Affairs, more space was needed to accommodate the swelling administration. London's response was not late in coming. Provisional accommodation should be found outside the Residence perimeter! Once again, bureaucracy overruled autocracy.

As for the crescent-shaped chancery fronting former Al Tambak Street, this came much later, at about the time when the adjacent Walda Pasha Palace made way for several high-rises, including the new Shepheard's Hotel. Up to this point, the British Embassy seemed to be forever expanding, but, in keeping with history, the tide would turn.

The shock of losing superpower status was brought home to the British in October 1954, when Sir Ralph Stevenson saw a large chunk of his embassy grounds disappear. As a result, the embassy, which for half a century had symbolised power in the Middle East, lost its bomb shelter, its swimming pool, its Nile-side dock and 5,000 square metres of freshly mowed English lawn. In their place, a now liberated Cairo would have its corniche.

Contrary to what historians like to say, the land swap was actually conducted with the best diplomatic comportment. In exchange for the land ceded by the British government, Egypt credited Her Majesty's Treasury with the sum of LE300,000 amounting to approximately LE60 per square metre for land originally purchased by the British at LE3 per square metre. It was all very proper.

But the Empire would strike back one last time.

Cairo's corniche was barely two years old when Britain and France, in an unholy alliance with Israel, occupied the Suez Canal area in October 1956. As a result, the Union Jack stopped fluttering above Garden City, replaced instead with the Swiss flag. A framed typewritten declaration stating that this was now the Swiss Embassy hid the 'VR' engraving at the main gate. The office previously occupied by Her Britannic Majesty's imperial envoys was now the realm of Charles Albert Dubois of Bern.

By the time the Union Jack was discreetly re-hoisted in 1959, the mystique of *Bayt al Lurd* was no more. In the national psyche, the British Embassy and its compound had been reduced to the status of 'just another monument'.

Except for faint echoes of earlier grandeur brought on by occasional royal visits, the historic residence is now used mostly to promote trade deals and cultural exchanges. Instead of state dinner parties where guests in white tie and medals troop into the ballroom according to strict protocol, the room has now become a torture chamber for supplicants applying for visas. At least the ghosts of Cromer, Allenby and MacMahon can take comfort in the knowledge that in this area the British still retain total control over the native population.

Monster on the Nile

"Monster Cairo Hotel," wrote *The Egyptian Gazette* in its March 16, 1906, issue, referring to the near completion of the new Semiramis Hotel situated in the genteel district of Kasr al Dubara. Except for the seasonal Gezira Palace Hotel situated on the island of Gezira, the Semiramis was the first Nile-side hotel in Cairo. The Nationale, Grand Continental Savoy, Angleterre and the legendary Shepheard's, all in the same elevated category, were either located off Midan al Opera or on the periphery of the Ezbekiya Gardens.

The 'monster' was situated between the palaces of the Walda Pasha or Khediva Mother, as she was known in these parts, and that of her daughter, Princess Nimet Kamal al Din. The Semiramis was built on part of a 6,000 square metre plot owned by the real estate baron, Moise Cattaui Pasha. He had sold the land in February 1905 to a Swiss hotelier, Franz-Josef Bucher, co-founder of the famous Bucher-Durrer Company that built some of Europe's finest hotels.

Known for his Midas touch, Bucher in turn sold the property the following year for double the amount to the Societé Suisse Egyptienne des Hotels en Egypte, a company that he had helped found. It was his final deal, for Bucher died soon after.

The supervising architect of the six-story hotel was Italian engineer, Tuilo Parvis. His office on Madabegh Street (today Cherif) was among the most prominent in Cairo. The project contractor was the Belgian-run firm of Padova, Leon Rollin & Co., well known for their major undertakings all over Egypt. Padova-Rollin promised to deliver the 200-room hotel to

Bucher-Durrer on January 1, 1907.

True to their word, Padova-Rollin Co. promptly created an Edwardian hotel with a snow-white facade on the promised date in time for a meticulously planned but short-lived dry run. Once ornaments, mirrors, marble columns, Gobelin tapestries, Louis XVI salons, statues and furniture were all in place, an official opening was announced for February 7, 1907.

The widely attended gathering brought together Cairo's leading officials and residents. On hand to greet the inaugural guests were Mr. and Mrs. Theodore Bucher and Max Bucher. Soon enough, manifestations of surprise and admiration were heard on every side as onlookers passed through the handsome apartments. *The Egyptian Gazette* reported the following day:

> To entertain gawking guests and amused aristocracy, an open buffet was laid out for the occasion in the hotel's central halls as the 2nd Battalion Royal Inniskilling Fusiliers band played familiar tunes. Later the same evening, under the glowing cut glass chandeliers and electroliers, an orchestra under the baton of Signor Bracale was succeeded by a sextet providing all night entertainment. The early-to-bed types, could, if they had to, settle in any one of the hotel suites or bedrooms. Except for the large brass bedsteads that were imported from England, the rooms were entirely decorated in Empire style by Messrs. Keller & Co. of Zurich.

What was new and particular to this hotel was its roof garden, a first in flat and arid Egypt. Some said it was inspired by the hanging gardens of Babylon, where the Assyrian Queen Semiramis is said to have found undue pleasure. Little did Bucher-Durrer realise (or perhaps he did!) that his florid undertaking would become an institution within the international café society, written up in countless interwar novels and biographies. From their elevated spot, as they sipped Lapsang Souchong tea in the finest bone china or danced to the sounds of a big band, patrons of the Semiramis roof garden took in the Giza Pyramids and endless palm groves, while large heavily laden *feluccas* sailed down the Nile. A similar vista was also available from any one of the hotel's many west-facing loggias and balconies.

In 1910, Bucher-Durrer sold his controlling shares in the Societé Suisse Egyptienne des Hotels en Egypte to a fellow Swiss, Charles Baehler, who immediately entrusted his manager, Mr. Wirth, with the addition of 50 new rooms and structural renovations. In Egypt since October 1889, Baehler had worked for and then become the owner of the Egyptian Hotels Company that owned and managed both the Gezira Palace Hotel and the famed Shepheard's.

Like The Ritz in Paris, The Plaza in New York, The Savoy in London and a handful of others throughout the world, Cairo's Semiramis occupied the pinnacle of hoteldom. It played host to every single royal in *Burke's Peerage* and later to heads of state, business tycoons and movie stars. When it became the headquarters of the British Troops in Egypt during the Second World War, it was the turn of the generals and field marshals to strut up its landing waving their batons.

One of the last attention-getting events that took place at the Semiramis was in February 1955 when the Aga Khan III was weighed for the last time in precious metal on the occasion of the 71st (platinum plus one) year of his Imamate. He died the following year.

In the 1970s, Cairo's first all-year round Nile-side hotel was pulled down to make way for the new Semiramis Inter-Continental. There is no hall, plaque, or restaurant commemorating the creator of the first Semiramis, or the man who was once regarded as the father of Egypt's hospitality industry.

Our Lady of Kasr al Dubara

To get onto Kasr al Nil Bridge from Kasr al Dubara's Midan Simon Bolivar you have to take the Kamal al Din Salah circular ramp. But the ramp was not always there. Completed in 1966, it replaced Midan Elhamy Pasha that was then flanked by the old Semiramis Hotel and a singular neo-gothic villa built for Minister of Finance Cattaui Pasha. In the 1920s the pasha sold it to *Sitt* Kout al Kouloub al Demerdashia, undoubtedly a remarkable and very wealthy woman.

The daughter of the leader of a religious order, the bejewelled Kout al Kouloub (Victuals of the Hearts), was a so-called feminist who among other things wrote wooing prose in French, including three novellas entitled *Zanouba*, *Ramza*, and *Harem*. Indeed, no visiting French author, poet or writer (Jules Romains, Georges Duhamel) dared visit Cairo without calling on the self-styled queen of the literary salons.

"She had a tiny head, small narrow shoulders and a generally accepted upper body," recalls Malak Khataab, who visited Madame Kout in the late

1950s. "Yet, from the waist down she was simply colossal!" What impressed her most was not Kout's odd physique or the interior of the gothic house trimmed with gold cornices everywhere you looked. Neither was Malak taken by Kout's extravagant display of jewellery, making her "appear like a Christmas tree." Instead she vividly recalls that whenever she entered Kout's house she was immediately drawn to a large gilded glass box positioned at the centre of a large hall. In it was the turban of Madame Kout's late father, evidence of his eminent status within the religious order that he once controlled and was now led by Madame Kout herself.

Moreover, our ample lady of Kasr al Dubara was known to entertain with a difference. If her infrequent dinners were described as extravagant, they were in fact catered by Azouz al Ashi, the most famous food purveyor in Cairo's bourgeois districts. And in case anyone thought he could take early leave of her get-togethers, he had another thought coming. Socialite Kadria Foda remembers how at Kout al Kouloub's son's society wedding, the hostess barricaded the doors so that none of her guests might depart without her say-so.

An eccentric woman, Kout al Kouloub liked to spend time on the Semiramis terrace perhaps only to needle her rival, Aziza Fahmi, said to be even richer than Our Lady of Kasr al Dubara. Both had taken more than one husband and both women decided when it was time to divorce. And like Kout al Kouloub, Aziza Fahmi had her own mansion on the Nile, (today the Akhenaton Museum in Zamalek). Yet she would take to closing up her palatial house and spending several months at a time at the Semiramis, a stone's throw from her competitor.

By the time the ramp replaced the neo-gothic villa by the Nile, *Sitt* Kout al Kouloub had abandoned Nasser's Egypt for Switzerland. There, by the shores of Lake Geneva, she continued to write romantic novels, so that latter-day cultural editors could continue to ignore her existence.

But is our lady of Kasr al Dubara really forgotten? Apparently not if one were to go through some of the responses to a March 2000 article about her. Banker Nevine Shulkami writes from New York:

> I still remember the beautiful villa of Kout al Kouloub and its Tiffany-like stained-glass windows. I wonder if anyone still has menu cards from her dinner invitations? The translation from Arabic into French of certain local dishes was unique. She was by far the richest Egyptian woman of her time. Among her many fixed assets was prime real estate in downtown Cairo overlooking 26th of July Street.

From Canada, computer engineer, Mohammed al Shafei, suggests that one should stop by Ain Shams Hospital where you will find:

> ...an old marble plaque hidden under layers of cheap painting. It tells about the real story of this hospital and who actually built it. It was Kout's father "Al Sayed" Abdel Rehim Mustafa al Demerdash. Al Sayed means "The Honourable". This is one of the titles given to descendants of the Prophet. If you take a walk in the small alley next to it you'll find an old, almost destroyed palace overlooking the Arab al Mohamady Garden. That too belonged to *Sitt* Kout. Most of the land around the palace including the land on which the Coptic Patriarchate was built, was once part of Demerdash's extensive Cairo landholdings.

Amr Talaat writes from Cairo:

> Kout Hanem lived a lavish life in her palace at Kasr al Dubara. In it she held an extravagant wedding party for her only daughter Zeinab Hanem and famous journalist Ali Amin. Kout's close friend the great Umm Kulthum did the matchmaking. After 1952 Kout Hanem fled to Europe. It is rumoured that at an advanced phase of her life she married famous journalist Hussein Abou al Fath.

Someone writes anonymously from the Centre National de Documentation Pedagogique in France that "a chapter on Kout al Kouloub by Julia Madoeuf can be found in the book *Entre Nil et Sable: Ecrivains d'Egypte d'expression Française.* Robert Solé who authored several books on *belle époque* Egypt prefaces it."

The best comment yet came from Omaima Foda: "The name of the Kasr al Nil bridge ramp should be renamed Kout al Kouloub."

3. Garden City

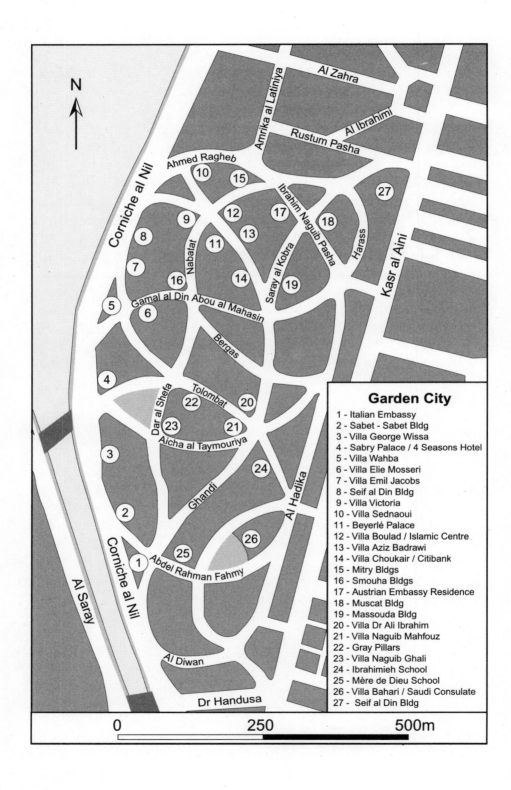

N

Al Zahra
Amrika al Latiniya
Al Ibrahimi
Rustum Pasha
Ahmed Ragheb
Corniche al Nil
⑩ ⑮ ㉗
Ibrahim Naguib Pasha
⑨ ⑫ ⑰ ⑱
⑧ ⑬
Nabatat ⑪ Harass
⑦ Saray al Kobra
⑯ ⑭ ⑲
⑤ Gamal al Din Abou al Mahasin
⑥ Kasr al Aini
Bergas
④ Tolombat
Dar al Shefa ㉒ ⑳
㉓ ㉑
Aicha al Taymouriya
③ ㉔
Ghandi
② Al Hadika
㉖
① ㉕
Abdel Rahman Fahmy
Corniche al Nil
Al Saray
Al Diwan
Dr Handusa

Garden City

1 - Italian Embassy
2 - Sabet - Sabet Bldg
3 - Villa George Wissa
4 - Sabry Palace / 4 Seasons Hotel
5 - Villa Wahba
6 - Villa Elie Mosseri
7 - Villa Emil Jacobs
8 - Seif al Din Bldg
9 - Villa Victoria
10 - Villa Sednaoui
11 - Beyerlé Palace
12 - Villa Boulad / Islamic Centre
13 - Villa Aziz Badrawi
14 - Villa Choukair / Citibank
15 - Mitry Bldgs
16 - Smouha Bldgs
17 - Austrian Embassy Residence
18 - Muscat Bldg
19 - Massouda Bldg
20 - Villa Dr Ali Ibrahim
21 - Villa Naguib Mahfouz
22 - Gray Pillars
23 - Villa Naguib Ghali
24 - Ibrahimieh School
25 - Mère de Dieu School
26 - Villa Bahari / Saudi Consulate
27 - Seif al Din Bldg

0   250   500m

Birth of a neighbourhood

Garden City was born in 1905, at a time when Cairo had a meagre population of 655,500. The three owners of the Nile Land & Agricultural Company, Frantz Sofio, Charles Bacos and George Maksud, asked agricultural engineer José Lamba to create Cairo's newest district. It would rise on what used to be the former royal domains of Kasr al Aali (the High Palace) and two older *sarays* to the north belonging to Viceroy Ibrahim Pasha. Thus was created one of Cairo's most signature neighbourhoods filled with elegant villas and curving streets now packed with banks and foreign legations. To a great extent, much of the city's history in the twentieth century revolved around Garden City and its inhabitants.

Although we don't know the sums paid by the Nile Land & Agricultural Company for Kasr al Aali, which included approximately 50 acres of gardens and buildings, the history of this particular property illustrates the phenomenal rise in the price of land from 1903 to 1905. From the *Egyptian Gazette*'s September 8, 1905, issue, we learn that at the turn of the century, a group of American financiers, acting through the Bank of Egypt, almost succeeded in buying the estate for LE85,000. The deal was about to be concluded when Prince Ahmed Kamal Rifaat exercised, through a proxy, his right of pre-emption and bought the property himself.

Two years later, an offer of LE150,000 put forward by a Belgian consortium, was turned down over a LE10,000 difference. In 1905, with the construction of new bridges across the Nile, the property was once again on the market, this time for LE400,000 or LE2 per square metre.

Cairo's newest khedivial neighbourhood occupied a well-defined hexagon. To the south it was bordered by Lady Cromer Hospital Street (now Dr. Handussa), to the east by Kasr al Aini Avenue and the then-genteel district of Mounira, to the north by the aristocratic neighbourhood of Kasr al Dubara, and to the west by Kasr al Aali Street and that most magnificent of natural barriers, the Nile.

Unlike the contemporary districts of Zamalek, Maadi or Heliopolis, characterised by grids, endless right angles, wide squares and boulevards, Garden City was the work of an art nouveau dabbler who preferred compasses to rulers, hence the absence of straight lines.

José Lamba laid out a series of narrow, winding roads outlining ill-defined triangles and curvy rectangles. Three times out of four, a walk down one street will deposit you back where you started much against your intention. Even as one travels down a single road it erratically changes names at vague intervals. Tolombat becomes Kasr al Aali (Corniche) in the north and Salamlek in the south, while Nabatat turns into Bergas then into Harass and then into Faskia. Moreover, and because of their sinuous delineation, streets like Tolombat and Aicha al Taymouriya intersect each other more than once.

Equally perplexing for anyone without a sense of whimsy, Lamba chose a huge fish as the centrepiece for his Neptunian maze; its head, which stands in as the neighbourhood's only public garden, points towards the Nile.

Designed as a strictly upper class residential community, Garden City had no commercial area to speak of. Communal amenities were therefore at the initiative of the inhabitants.

Garden City's original ordnance survey map shows an area divided up into 273 unequal lots earmarked for villas with small gardens and *immeubles de rapport* (luxury low-rise apartment blocks). These were never to exceed a height limit of 15 metres. Had the lots been exploited as housing units of eight apartments each, Garden City's population would have peaked at 2,184 families, but this was never the case and up until the Second World War apartment houses were outnumbered by villas, many of which occupied several lots.

Street names

Prior to the First World War, Garden City's postal addresses seldom referred to street names. Designations like "Mr. Karl Hasselbach," "Villa Olga," "Monsieur Vincent Mandofia," "Sharia Ritz" and "Legation d'Allemagne" were all the uniformed postman went by for the 40 or so residents of Garden City and Kasr al Dubara combined. Other quaint names included Villa Marica, Larter Cottage, Mog House and Immeuble Badaro.

With a wave of post-war arrivals, the neighbourhood's street names finally caught on. Most names referred to objects or landmarks predating the Garden City project. Vice-regal estates come to mind with names like *Al Saray al Kobra* (grand palace), *Harass* (guards), *Diwan* (ministry), *Salamlek* (reception quarters), *Bergas* (equestrian sport), *Faskia* (fountain), *Nabatat* (plants), and *Hadika* (garden).

Local palace workshops and amenities also left their legacies with *Warshet al Tambak* (gilded pewter factory), *Tolombat* (pumps) and *Ma'mal al Sukar* (sugar mill). Other street names included *Madrab al Nishab* (roller), *Hod al Laban* (milkman's basin), *Salsoul* (source), *Dar al Shefa* (house of recovery).

A few streets were named in honour of lofty personalities. Ismail Pasha, Walda Pasha and Ahmed Pasha Streets were named after members of the ruling family, and Ibrahim Pasha Naguib Street was named after the then-governor of Cairo. As for Khalil Agha, no one remembers who he was. Noticeably absent was a street named after Khedive Abbas Hilmi or Sultan Hussein Kamel. Both had ruled Egypt during Garden City's gestation, so to speak.

Many street names changed once or twice, particularly after 1952, and for almost 50 years Garden City and Kasr al Dubara each had their own Walda Pasha Streets. While Garden City's, named in honour of Khoshiar Kadin (Ismail's mother) became Aicha al Taymouriya, Kasr al Dubara's named in honour of Amina Elhamy (Abbas Hilmi's mother), turned into Fatma al Zahraa and then into Amrika al Latiniya Street. The latter name-change was motivated less by the presence of the Brazilian Legation (today Banque du Caire et de Paris) than by the desire to pique the then-unpopular British and American embassies, which have far greater frontage on the street.

Major proprietors

To this day, Garden City's largest proprietor remains the Vatican, with 12 contiguous lots to its name. Originally intended as a convent, the property was turned over to the Mère de Dieu School for girls in the early 1920s.

The runner up in terms of size is Her Britannic Majesty. The acquisition of Monsieur Bacos' townhouse and its seven attached lots expanded the embassy grounds. The purchase also covered the western portion of Rustom Pasha Street (ex-Ibrahimi). Britain thus has the unique distinction of straddling two precincts; Kasr El Dubara and Garden City.

If foreign institutions owned the largest plots of land in Garden City, three Egyptians and one Syrian were the largest individual property owners.

These were: Prince Seif al Din, Medhat and Adly Yeken, and Syrian financier Aziz Bahari.

Bahari's carp-shaped estate (today the Embassy of Saudi Arabia) comprised ten abutting lots bordered by Salamlek and Gihadia Streets. On the other hand, Prince Seif al Din's property was divided up into disconnected parcels. One property fronted the Nile and housed the much sought after Seif al Din apartments (next to the Mobil Building). The second property is today shared by a Seif al Din Building and Dar al Shaab's printing press and is located between Saray al Kobra and Kasr al Aini Streets.

Medhat Yeken Pasha, the sometime minister of foreign affairs owned a palace that took up seven lots of land. Rumour had it that he won his palace in a card game at the Mohammed Ali Club.

Medhat's cousin, the three-time prime minister, Adly Yeken Pasha, owned five out of six lots in one block of land on which he built a palace. The sixth lot housed the villa of Princess Fatma Fazil. All told, Yeken Palace was Garden City's largest superstructure by far. When the pasha died in Paris on October 22, 1933, the palace took on the name of Kasr Cherif Sabry Pasha in honour of Yeken's only son-in-law, a brother of Queen Nazli. The irony is that all along the palace belonged to neither gentleman but was the property of Adly Yeken's wealthy wife, Zeinab Cherif, a daughter of former minister of finance, Ali Cherif Pasha.

The palace was lost in the real estate boom of the late 1970s when Zeinab Cherif's grandchildren sold it to a Swiss developer who intended to erect a Nova Park Hotel in its place. Financial difficulties sank that project and the property lay desolate until its recent revival as The Four Seasons Hotel.

The botched Nova Park affair is reminiscent of another failed Garden City hotel. During the township's teen years a group of speculators had invited Fritz Hefti, a Swiss architect, to erect for them a mammoth Nile-side palace hotel. It fronted Hod al Laban, Gamal al Din Abou al Mahassen (ex-Ismail Pasha) and Nabatat Streets. They christened it the Grand Hotel Ritz. However the arrival of Kasr al Dubara's Semiramis Hotel and the fallout from the financial crash of 1907 destined the hotel to an early downfall.

The Ritz Hotel went into demise by the end of the First World War, resulting in the fragmentation of this particular block into nine independent properties. Six of these properties were picked up by a group of interrelated Jewish financiers and merchants, namely Isaac Sapriel, Jacques Levi-Garboua, Moise Naggar, Nessim Djedah and Youssef Smouha. The three remaining properties belonged to a disparate grouping—an entrepreneur from Antwerp, the daira of Prince Seif al Din and an Italian architect. All but one of the original buildings are extant. The lavish villa singled out for replacement belonged to financier Nessim Djedah, who sold it in 1947 to Felix Dana. Ten years later it was replaced by the curvy Nile-front Mobil Building designed by Abou Bakr Khairat.

Curiously absent were Nile Land & Agricultural Company's founders, Messrs. Bacos, Maksud and Sofio. Their reluctance at becoming residents of the neighbourhood may have had to do with the fact Garden City had almost ruined them financially. Two years into the project they were hit along with other developers by the 1907 economic crisis.

Also missing in Garden City were the company's senior executives, Hans Mog (a Bacos in-law), Henri Molho and José Lamba who preferred the bustle of Emad al Din Street, Midan Kasr al Nil and Midan Ismailia respectively.

Lofty residents

In spite of its lofty status, Garden City was practically devoid of royal residents. The three exceptions were Princess Fatma Fazil, Princess Iffet Hassan and Prince Abbas Ibrahim Halim. Another exception would have been Prince Seif al Din but his was a sad fate, to say the least. Despite being one of Garden City's largest landowners, the prince never lived there. Having shot and wounded his brother-in-law at an exclusive Cairo social club while defending his sister's honour, he was imprisoned and subsequently placed in an asylum in the United Kingdom. Any hope of his ever returning to Egypt faded when his victim became Egypt's first king as Fouad I in 1922. Prince Seif al Din ended his days in Turkey, where he had taken refuge with his mother, who was also estranged from the Egyptian court.

Among the three royal residents, Princess Fatma Fazil will be remembered as the first royal to expire in Garden City. Shortly after her death in 1933, her mansion became a family *daira* and later a workers' employment union before being replaced by an unsavoury apartment house. Princess Iffet Hassan, on the other hand, was forever changing houses, preferring to lease rather than buy. She would eventually die in exile in Istanbul in 1962 with the satisfaction that among her transitory abodes one is today the Greek Embassy (previously the Iraqi Embassy) on Aicha al Taymouriya Street and the other became an Arab League library (on Tolombat Street).

Although the rambunctious Prince Abbas Halim was a long-term resident of Garden City, he did not own a house, preferring instead to live in the palatial home of his mercantile father-in-law, the very wealthy Medhat Yeken Pasha. The prince's sojourns at No. 3 Tolombat Street did not go unnoticed, especially when workers took to demonstrating outside the palace to show support for their royal advocate, whom they dubbed the "Blue Collar Prince". Needless to say, these public displays of affection did not go down well with his neighbours. In 1948 the prince's now-estranged wife disposed of the palace and relocated to Massachusetts Avenue, Washington, D.C.

But if royalty was practically absent from Garden City, Cairo's fashionable neighbourhood boasted a multi-denominational coterie of pashas, many of whom had a hand in shaping Egypt's artistic, financial, commercial, military and political destiny for almost half a century. By virtue of their collective clout, Garden City became, between the two World Wars, Egypt's main centre of power. A countervailing force, if you will, to Kasr al Dubara, where Britain still had its say in Egypt's affairs.

Garden City's interwar residents had little to complain about. They lived in an exclusive neighbourhood surrounded by like-minded people and their homes were second to none. If the Yekens, Cherif Sabrys, Cattauis and Baharis hired Jansen and Stephane Bodain to decorate their palaces, the Baehlers, Matossians and Levy-Garbouas retained Maison Kriéger of Paris and Cairo. The rest made do with Enrico Nistri, Armando Centofanti, Marius Contessini, Francesco Prinzivalli and Victor Lehman, prompting observers to remark that Garden City's villas were more art museums than family dwellings.

Another plus was that, unlike distant Heliopolis and Maadi, Garden City was a stone's throw from Cairo's commercial and banking hub so that the legion of lawyers, bankers and merchants who moved there during the interwar period commuted to work within minutes. The pasha brigade—senators, ministers and MPs—could walk to work if they so desired. Like the Houses of Parliament, the government ministries and administrative centres were situated east of Kasr al Aini Avenue. Even the Ministry of Foreign Affairs on Sharia Bostan had relocated in 1938 to a nearby palace in the Kasr al Dubara district.

But pashas didn't walk. They were driven. Their groomed chauffeurs and uniformed hired help arrived to work by a tramway that ran along Kasr al Aini Avenue going southeast towards the Pyramids and northwards towards city centre and beyond. No surprise either that Cairo's leading doctors, such as Ali Ibrahim Pasha and Naguib Mahfouz Pasha, chose Garden City as their place of residence, a hop away from hospitals Kasr al Aini and Fouad al Awal.

For distraction, Garden City's best either crossed Kasr al Nil Bridge to the Gezira Club or drove the shorter distance to the posh Mohammed Ali Club on Soliman Pasha Street. Children, accompanied by their European governesses, invariably cycled around Garden City or played in its charming public garden.

If anyone had reason to complain, it was the neighbourhood's devout— a mix of Muslims, Jews and Christians. Eager to exploit every centimetre of available space, Garden City's developers had failed to come up with a house of God, a reflection perhaps of the neighbourhood's secularised character. Yet in any event, the Anglican Bishop of Egypt and Sudan lived in Kasr al Dubara district, just across Rustom Pasha Street where Bishop House abutted St Mary's (today a Malachite church). A few blocks north stood the small mosque of Sheikh al Abit, replaced in the 1940s by a larger one designed by Mario Rossi and named Omar Makram.

For the Jewish residents of Garden City, including Senator Haim Nahum Effendi, Egypt and Sudan's *Hakham-Bashi* (Grand Rabbi), who lived at No. 6 Khalil Agha, this meant a long trek to Adly Street's Chaar Hachamaim Synagogue on High Holidays. Hence perhaps the reason why Midrash Eliahou Curiel Oratory, an informal and intermittent place of prayer, was inaugurated in the 1930s at No. 15 Nabatat Street, on the ground floor of the Elie Curiel Building, designed by Raymond Antonius.

And unless a secret lodge existed in the neighbourhood, Garden City's freemasons would convene at Mason Hall on the corner of Antikhana and Mariette Pasha Street.

Absence of a local temple notwithstanding, when he died in Manchester on September 22, 1924, department store czar Daoud Habib Ades of No. 6 Sheikh Arbein (today Abdel Kader Hamza), Kasr al Dubara, willed LE500 to Garden City's Jewish Hospital. Before becoming a hospital this large villa was the Victoria Nursing Home (now a girls' hostel) situated at the corner of Al Saray al Kobra and Harass Streets.

The presence of the above establishments signaled that what had heretofore been an exclusive residential community was opening up to civic institutions. Other arrivals were Pensionat Mère de Dieu, the Ibrahimieh School for Boys, a secular girl's school that opened on the premises of the former German Legation and the architectural marvel known as *Dar al Hikma*, designed in 1940-1 by Mustafa Fahmi Pasha, straddling Kasr al Aini and Al Hadika Streets.

There were of course those like Regent Cherif Sabry Pasha who did not take too well to these changes, so that when a hospital was suggested next door to his home, the king's uncle lost no time killing the project. Would he have also protested the contiguity of a foreign embassy?

The distinction of first diplomatic legation to lease property in Garden City goes to the Germans. The Hohenzollern emperor's envoy to Egypt at the time was Baron Von Richthofen. While not much is known about this gentleman, his name was famous thanks to other members of his family, such as Manfred Von Richthofen, a.k.a. the Red Baron, the much ballyhooed First World War flying ace. An earlier Von Richthofen (Oswald) was Minister of Foreign Affairs (1900-06) after serving in Egypt as his country's representative to *La Caisse de la Dette*. This was a creditor's club set up to monitor the repayment of sovereign debts accumulated during Khedive Ismail's reign.

Large, gray, foreboding with columns in evidence everywhere, the German Legation at No. 10 Ahmed Pasha Street did not lack in Teutonic trimmings. From the upper floor the baron had an unencumbered view of both the citadel and the pyramids. He could also espy the colonial-style British agency, where Lord Kitchener, that most formidable of imperial foes, ran Egypt's affairs before he became Britain's Minister of War following the hostilities that broke out between Britain and Germany.

It was probably from his home at No. 9 Ahmed Pasha Street, directly across from the German Legation, that the British Commanding Officer, Major-General Julian H. Byng (later Governor-General of Canada), supervised the sequestration of all German and Austro-Hungarian properties in Egypt. Decades later, Byng's mansion would become home to Levantine businessmen Emile and Soheil Boulad, Premier Mustafa al Nahas and now the Higher Council for Islamic Affairs.

After Germany and the Vatican, Italy was the third sovereign entity to purchase prime Garden City real estate, not far from Kasr Cherif Sabry. The neo-classical Italian Embassy on Kasr al Aali Street was designed by Florestano di Fausto and executed in 1929 by Count Paolo Caccia Dominioni.

In addition to the large contingent of Italian attachés were smaller legations. There was Czechoslovakia at Midan Ismail Pasha, Iraq at No. 8 Rustom Pasha Street, Spain at No. 7 Ismail Pasha, Japan at No. 6 Hadika, Yugoslavia at No. 21 Kasr al Aali, Belgium at No. 20 Nabatat and the United States next door at No. 24.

Garden City's never-ending diplomatic minuets eventually came to a complete stop with the outbreak of the Second World War.

What had been a quiet neighbourhood—one could actually hear the roar of the Giza zoo lions across the river—would suddenly turn into a virtual British garrison, its command centre located at Gray Pillars, No. 10 Tolombat Street, right at the centre of José Lamba's ambiguous fish.

The war years

June 11, 1940, shall forever remain a milestone in Garden City's history. The day before, in a bellicose speech from a Venice balcony, Mussolini declared war against the Allies. Within 24 hours, Italy's Ambassador, Count Serafino Mazzolini, took leave of Prime Minister Ali Maher. In accordance with wartime custom the Italian Embassy property on Kasr al Aali Street (the Corniche) was left in the custody of a neutral power. As he stepped out of the compound with 191 diplomats and personnel in tow, the Italian envoy instructed his hired help that, Swiss flag notwithstanding, everything should remain in place. Mazzolini was confident they would all be back on the heels of the victorious fascist legions in a matter of two weeks.

A few blocks away, at No. 24 Ismail Pasha Street, a naturalised Italian banker-industrialist, Elie Nessim Mosseri Bey, was also vacating his Garden City mansion. Having succumbed to a fatal heart attack the day before, he was ferried across town to the splendid family vault in Bassateen.

For the Garden City community, Mosseri's death was a critical loss. To the pasha-politicians, he had been a dependable no-questions-asked source of funds during election time. To the pasha-businessmen, he was the best connection on Egypt's blue-chip boards. To Garden City's wealthy Jews, he was a respected elder of their thriving community. It also didn't go unnoticed by Garden City's residents that the handsome 20-year-old King Farouk took to cheering up Helen Polymires, Mosseri's tantalising Greek widow.

Things were also changing down the road from the Mosseri mansion.

As British military staff swelled to unprecedented wartime proportions, accommodations were found post-haste so that the entire area around the British Residency in Kasr al Dubara district was spoken for within a matter of months. Surplus personnel were therefore moved inside Garden City where entire apartment houses were requisitioned for the khaki-clad arrivals. Garden City's Anglophile elements so welcomed the military brass they willingly loaned villas to senior officers.

Other Garden City residents opened their 'at home' gatherings to anyone above the rank of captain. George Wissa Pasha's villa on Kasr al Aali Street became a favourite Allied rendezvous, particularly the basement that had been converted by his spouse into an informal nightclub.

In July 1941, cables out of London announced that the newly nominated Minister of State for Middle East Affairs would be arriving in Cairo shortly. While the Reuters cable implied Oliver Lyttelton would be the first in the history of British administration to run an overseas ministry, it failed to report that Garden City's No. 10 Tolombat Street had been selected as its headquarters. Where once only the clatter of the king's ceremonial open carriage had interrupted the general silence during its practice runs, Tolombat Street would unexpectedly become the venue for endless outriders and unmarked military vehicles.

With a nod towards the four colonnades that festoon No. 10 Tolombat's stately foyer, the new ministry was referred to in secret dispatches as Gray Pillars. On the other hand, senior officers nicknamed it 'No. 10,' an allusion to the British prime minister's official London residence. The locals, meanwhile, knew the building as the Assicurazioni. A plaque at the entrance evidenced that the building was insured with the Trieste-based insurance company of that name. The only reference to the building's owner, Omar Sirry, was made in the form of his initials incorporated into the beautiful iron grill above the main door.

At any time of the day, visitors to Gray Pillars were likely to run into a forlorn Balkan prime minister, an exiled European royal, a former head of state, an American general or a leader-in-waiting. Iraq's ill-fated future prime minister, Nuri al Said, Britain's Anthony Eden, France's Charles de Gaulle, and World Zionist Organisation leader, Chaim Weizmann, all stopped by during the war. In fact it was at No. 10 that Lyttelton and de Gaulle initialled the August 7, 1941, covenant paving the way for Syria and Lebanon's independence with special post-colonial privileges to France.

Number 10 Tolombat Street would subsequently be headed by Richard Casey and later, Lord Moyne. It was as Lord Moyne was returning home from No. 10 that two zionist terrorists in Zamalek gunned him down. If any building in Garden City deserves to be listed as a national heritage monument, Gray Pillars is surely the one. It meets all the requirements: distinctive style, historical significance, sound condition and architectural merit.

Allied soldiers made routine checks on passers-by and guarded winding roads leading to and from Gray Pillars. This was considered a blatant provocation by some of the British ministry's proud neighbours, particularly for someone like the openly pro-German Prince Abbas Halim.

An intermittent resident at his in-laws at No. 3 Tolombat Street, the British considered Abbas Halim an agent provocateur. Unlike King Farouk, who kept his sentiments in check, his cousin, Prince Halim, was viewed as an overt troublemaker. Apart from his pro-German stance that angered the British, his vocal support of the Worker's Union rendered him unpopular with his own family. It didn't come as a surprise, therefore, when the prince was summarily interned at the 'suggestion' of the British Ambassador Sir Miles Lampson. As a result, No. 3 Tolombat was taken over by Lampson's polished friend, Alexander C. Kirk, America's wartime envoy to Cairo.

With Allied soldiers swaggering in and out of Garden City, empty plots were turned into football and cricket pitches, giving the opportunity to local teenagers to stage quick *sieg heils* before dashing for cover. In their unsophisticated way, Garden City's golden youth were expressing publicly a sentiment that many of their pasha parents voiced privately: war or no war, the imperious Britons had overstayed their welcome.

Neighbourhood architecture

Neither the Great War nor the global crash of 1929-30 held back the architecture of Garden City, where no two structures look the same. Villas and *immeubles de rapport* mushroomed across the district as Cairo's ranking architects battled over who was going to erect the grandest and largest.

The architectural follies of Egypt's rising bourgeoisie were slowly taking shape. As if reflecting Egypt's bias against Britain, Cairo's fashionable community avoided colonial villas, choosing instead a mix of neo-classical, Venetian palladium and Gothic pastiches amidst a festival of art deco.

The most coveted architect at the time was undeniably Antonio Lasciac. Whereas in downtown Cairo he specialised in Islamo-Venetian buildings, in Garden City the Trieste-born creator of the so-called Cherif Sabry Palace indulged in classical palladium with all the playful trimmings.

The neighbourhood's Francophile Syro-Lebanese elite opted for Frenchman Georges Parcq. Having already designed the imposing Sednaoui emporium on Midan al Khazindar, Parcq was commissioned by Elias and Joseph Sednaoui to build their respective Garden City villas. In his unpublished journal, Elias Bey describes his purchase in 1916 of a plot of land on Warshet al Tambak Street from banker Aziz Bahari. He cites the fact that it overlooked the British Legation as a justification for the higher price of LE3.25 per square metre. Six decades later his villa, since famous as the former American Embassy Library, would sell for a sum alleged to equal LE16 million—LE10,000 per square metre!

Another Parcq mansion gone the embassy route is 'Pakistan House.' Built for industrialist Emile Jacobs in 1935, it was subsequently purchased by Aga Khan III, who in turn gifted it to the Pakistan government. Parcq is also credited for the Maratos Building at No. 6 Walda Pasha, built in 1914; the Cassab Building at No. 14 Saray al Kobra, completed in 1925; and the two Sabet apartment houses on Ismail Pasha Street and Midan Ismail Pasha, built in 1925.

During Prince Ahmed Seif al Din's involuntary exile to Turkey, his Cairo *daira* commissioned an Italian architect to design three of the neighbourhood's most celebrated apartment structures, collectively known as the Seif al Din Buildings. While two of these overlook Kasr al Aini Street (Nos. 68 and 88), the third (No. 1095 Corniche al Nil) overlooks the Nile. First-generation tenants fondly remember the monarchy days when *bowwabs* stood guard in their striking, crown-embroidered red kaftans. When the prince died in 1937, his assets passed on to his sister, Princess Shuvikar. The following year she commissioned Giuseppe Mazza to build her four semi-detached buildings on Bergas Street that she promptly christened 'The Elhamy Buildings' in honour of her fifth husband, Elhamy Hussein Pasha.

We meet Mazza again at No. 5 Ibrahim Pasha Naguib Street, a classical concrete building commissioned in 1929 by Air Liquide's agents in Cairo,

Georges and Elie Muscat. Mazza is also credited with designing, together with Limongelli, the villa of Naguib Ghali Pasha (today the Indonesian Embassy) on Aicha Taymouriya Street.

An interesting extant Venetian villa in the south-central section of Garden City was built for Menasce-Sapriel at No. 1 Tolombat Street. Rather than accommodating a visiting doge, as it appears it should, the villa was instead leased to Princess Iffet Hassan during the final days of Farouk's reign. For the past decade, the rundown building has housed an Arab League Library. Its garden, meanwhile, has given way to ramshackle auto repair shops.

Other celebrated Garden City architects include Michel Liberman, creator of the 1926-built Villa Choucair-Sarruf at No. 6 Ahmed Pasha Street (today owned by Citibank), and Raoul Zehery, builder of the broad 1934 art deco apartment building at No. 2 Tolombat Street. The purest art deco structure, however, can be found at No. 18 Dar al Shifa Street, built by Nubar Kevorkian in 1930.

Less attractive from the outside, yet harboring palatial interiors, is an *immeuble de rapport* at No. 9 Hod al Laban, built in 1922 by Limongelli.

Another architect famous for his classical concrete is Antoine Selim Nahas. Shafik and Edouard Mitry, founders of Dar al Maaref publishing house, commissioned his two adjoining works at Nos. 14 and 16 Nabatat. The latter building boasts a unique foyer that uses ochre-coloured glass blocks for its light filtering system; an innovation Nahas repeated in several Garden City postwar buildings that were commissioned by Syrian entrepreneur, Sabet Sabet.

At No. 5 Ahmed Pasha stands the pride of Garden City's interwar collection—the palatial mansion of Abdel Aziz Badrawi Pasha, Egypt's wealthiest pre-1952 landowner. He was the second owner of this masterpiece, allegedly inspired by Leon Azema (co-designer of Palais de Chaillot, Paris) and his colleagues Edrei and Hardy. This excellent illustration of stylised art deco was home to American ambassadors in the 1960s before the Embassy of Japan purchased it.

An architectural walk through Garden City reveals many other handsome interwar buildings, notably the three adjacent Smouha-Ades Buildings at the corner of Ismail Pasha and Nabatat Streets, designed by Giacomo Alessandro Loria.

There are also those Garden City buildings whose architects and designers are regrettably unknown. Topping the list are: the Ades Building (No. 20 Ismail Pasha) which houses the Fulbright Commission, the Naggar Building

(No. 23), which lost part of its classical façade when the Egyptian American Bank sought to introduce a separate street entrance, the Massouda-Barukh Building at No. 3 Saray al Kobra, and the Albert Mizrahi Building at No.12 Ibrahim Pasha Naguib. The latter was subsequently sold to Korashi Pasha and recently restored by its last owner. Today the ground floor is the Austrian ambassador's residence.

A few of Garden City's buildings still bear plaques denoting the architect: Mazza, Zananiri, Parcq, Kevorkian, Liberman, Kfoury and Ayrout. These are difficult to find especially when they've been painted over several times or buried under a maze of commercial billboards, air-conditioners and exposed wires. Some apartment buildings have the year of inception engraved on their exterior, such as the mouldering 1919 Olivier Himaya Building at No. 3 Ahmed Pasha. There again you have to have twenty/twenty vision.

Many of these buildings' contractors were Italian. However, considering its excellent track record in Heliopolis, it comes as no surprise that Les Entreprises Leon Rolin of Belgium were sought after by the best architects. Equally reliable were the firms of Frères Hettena (Simplex), Vidon Frères (Al Chark), Frères Ayrout Cie, de Farro, Habert & Darr, Dentamaro & Cartareggia, and Etablissement Lang. Altogether, they were responsible for most of Egypt's public and private infrastructure between 1890 and 1940.

With the end of the Second World War, however, winds of change were blowing through the luxurious architectural carnival of Garden City that would bring new building styles and new materials spelling an end to the unique architecture of the neighbourhood.

What goes up must come down

Architecturally, Garden City has another claim to fame: it is home to Egypt's first skyscraper. The arrival in 1957-8 of the country's then-tallest building symbolised the simultaneous rise and fall of its new and old power cliques.

Sabet Sabet, a Syro-Lebanese entrepreneur who wanted to leave behind his personal monolith, set in motion the rise of the neighbourhood's harsh skyline. Defying gravity, he commissioned structural engineer Naoum

Shebib to build him a 30-storey reinforced concrete building. Not since Andernach volcanic cement was first imported in 1908 had Garden City seen a comparable construction revolution. Crowned with a red neon cigarette advertisement that could then be seen from as far as the Giza plateau, Cairo's tallest structure was nicknamed *Emarat Belmont*, after the publicised cigarette. The name has stuck, though the sign later on read *Schweppes*. This aesthetics-free edifice heralded a new direction in architecture, a drastic change in housing patterns, and a bold spirit of vertical urbanisation.

New and revised agrarian laws limiting rural ownership prompted several members of Garden City's elite to replace their sumptuous villas with revenue-generating apartment buildings, thus setting a regrettable trend that would eventually come back to haunt them. But as far as architects were concerned it was a bull market. Garden City was spreading vertically.

Garden City's rise would also be its fall. Shortly after his building's inauguration, Sabet and his businessmen peers found themselves suddenly marginalised as a result of the sweeping nationalisation decrees of July 1961. Socialism had no need of enterprising captains and kings. As a result, power was rapidly shifting from Zamalek, Garden City and Maadi to areas with a higher prevalence of military officers—Heliopolis.

The new order hit the fading pasha brigade of Garden City with the force of a tornado; every house, mansion or luxury apartment was affected in one way or another. Businesses were closed, liquid assets frozen, entire industries taken over.

To complicate matters further, a series of housing bills that protected tenancy and forbade progressive rent escalation set in motion the long-term, collective depreciation of Egypt's urban structures. Most affected by these combined developments were the companies that had previously created Heliopolis, Zamalek, Giza, Rhoda, Maadi, and Garden City. Equally let down were those who had just invested in new apartment buildings.

As though that wasn't enough, there were the rulings ordering sequestration of the properties of so-called counter-revolutionaries. Particularly unlucky were those who were out of the country when their names turned up on the People's Enemy List. On their return to Egypt, Youssef Cattaui Pasha's heirs discovered their Gothic villa, designed by Marco Olivetti in 1920, had been taken over by the military. Though a few years earlier his unique library had been auctioned by Feldman, Cattaui Pasha's vintage wine cellar remained intact much to the delight of the uniformed squatters.

Levy-Garboua's Villa Victoria on Seif al Din Street was turned into a club for parliamentarians, while Villa Joseph Sednaoui, at No. 13 Tolombat, became home to Misr Re-Insurance Company. The sad story was replicated across Garden City.

The world seemed to be turning upside down. Privately-owned buildings fell into the hands of insurance companies that had just been nationalised. Apartments involuntarily vacated by long-standing tenants were snatched up by senior officers, the military regime's cronies and a coterie of self-serving praise writers who had thrown in their lot with the new order.

In the ongoing mêlée, foreign governments also acquired prime properties at ten cents to the dollar, cutting triangular deals with the State and former owners. This is presumably how the Swiss and Saudi embassies came to own the Elie Mosseri and Aziz Bahari mansions.

As for those entrepreneurs who stayed behind, they saw their revenues dry up so fast they could no longer maintain large homes.

Inspiration from the past was now most definitely frowned upon; it became open season for architectural terrorism. Streetscape, too, went out the window. For starters, sensible distances between buildings were ignored while sidewalks were summarily hijacked. Green space was annihilated for the benefit of new buildings that lacked the minimum basics of proper finishing. And as demand for new housing and offices grew, classical buildings were often piggybacked with three or more upper floors Nasser-style. The end result was tasteless, colourless and disproportionate.

If gynaecologist Dr. Naguib Mahfouz Pasha's house, designed by Mustafa Fahmi Pasha, at the intersection of Tolombat and Aicha Taymouriya exemplifies the transmogrification of mansions into offices, the Islamic Council's lot on Ahmed Pasha Street set the precedent for the transformation of garden spaces into tall ugly buildings. Barely a hair separates the new structure from the old.

What was once an elitist residential enclave had turned into a jumbled third-rate business district. Meanwhile, aristocratic properties were cut up into cheap housing subdivisions. Sixteen unsavoury buildings replaced Medhat Yeken Pasha's palace, many squatting on the sidewalks.

Buildings that survived the architectural holocaust often faced sad prospects. Upon purchasing Murad Wahba Pasha's mansion overlooking the Nile, Saudi Arabia's Prince Sultan Ibn Abdel Aziz made several horizontal and vertical additions so that an already small garden disappeared completely.

Sir Ali Ibrahim Pasha's (first Egyptian dean of Cairo University's School of Medicine) mansion on Khalil Agha Street, designed by Giuseppe Tavarelli in the 1920s, was acquired first by Syrian magnate Akram Auje and later by Sheikh Mubarak al Sabah of Kuwait. Today, it stands neglected, beckoning lawsuits and wrecking balls, not unlike the fate of Mohammed Abdel Khalek Pasha's mansion across the street, now a glass and aluminum complex housing the Arab African Bank.

As the pendulum swings back and privatisation gathers momentum, the slaughter continues with greater force. The writing is all over Garden City's vulnerable walls: if nothing is done to reverse the tide of demolition, the already questionable 'Garden' in Garden City will become nothing more than a cruel joke.

On death row

Hurrying past every day, it's easy to miss the rusty, faded initials 'CS', 'GW' and 'EM' engraved on the massive iron porticos, some of them adorned with thistles and griffins, as though standing guard between a predatory world and the well-kept secrets of three Garden City mansions. Regrettably, all three are candidates for death row.

The most important of the three architecturally speaking is CS. It is also the last remaining privately owned palace in its class and period still in one piece. Hence the temporary deviation from our Garden City tour to learn the who, when and why of this unique dwelling. And rather than extol its different aspects, let us consult an article entitled 'A Palace At Cairo, Egypt', published on February 9, 1910, in *The American Architect* of New York.

> The recent example of a stately home is located at Garden City, a suburb of Cairo, Egypt, along the bank of the River Nile, and near the new Ritz Hotel. It was designed by Signor Carlo Prampolini, architect, who in addition to the regular practice of his profession is Director of Work in the Department of the Ministry of Public Works in Cairo.
> This building, with its dependencies, garages, generating plant, etc., occupies 3,700 square metres.
> The style of the exterior and interior is of the Italian Renaissance.
> The decorative features of the interior are of particular interest, and the colour scheme produced by the introduction of the marble used, presents

an interior of the most satisfying character.

Through the main entrance, by a flight of six steps of yellow marble from Colle di Elsa, flanked by two well-designed candelabra in solid bronze, the main entrance hall is reached. The hall, which occupies the large, central portion, is decorated in Louis XVI style, and serves to impress the visitor by reason of its beautiful vistas and well-balanced proportions.

The columns in the hall are of Fleur de Peché, the ceilings in Vitraux d'Art, to all of which, with the beautiful decorations introduced, the grand staircase at the upper end of the hall, serves as a dignified background.

The columns shown in the terrace of the first floor are of brocatelle marble. To the left of the entrance is the dining room, while on the right is the salon, music room and library.

The walnut interior doors of the hall are fine examples of the wood carver's art, the decorations being carved in high relief, with flower and leaf motives, surrounded with a laurel leaf scroll. This decorative treatment is also used on the "*ecrans,*" which serve to conceal the American radiators set in the wall.

The grand staircase is the dominant feature of the main floor. There are two runs, consisting of 74 steps, each cut from a single block of "*Pavonaz zo Imperiale*" marble, decorated with "*Brocatello,*" "*Pagaccino,*" and "*Skyros O,*" marbles which, combined with a white marble ("bianco di Siena") form the decorative treatment of the pilasters, pedestals, cornices and mouldings which surround the ornamental relief. This staircase was erected by Signor Leopoldo Maccari, of Siena. The large griffons crouched at the foot of the ramps and panels are the work of members of the Academy of Fine Arts, Siena.

The ornamentation in bronze and the large candelabras in the staircase, of the most artistic modeling and design, form an important part of the decorative treatment of this stately hall.

The bedrooms, many in number, have each its adjoining bathroom and special toilet rooms. The general decorative treatment of these rooms is ivory white. In the gardens surrounding the house is located a two-story building for the servants, and also garages, stables and an isolated electric generating station.

Designed in 1907-8, this was one of the first structures in Garden City to use the then-revolutionary Andernach volcanic cement technique. Thomson-Houston provided the extensive electrical fittings. This colossal Italian Renaissance edifice, sporting outlandish gargoyles and fantastical accoutrements, evokes a Wagnerian opera rather than a habitat for ordinary mortals.

Meant to have been the retirement home of Karl Heinrich Beyerlé, it became instead his transitory mausoleum.

A native of Frankfurt, Germany, Beyerlé immigrated to Egypt where he made his fortune in agricultural and venture capital projects. Eventually he became chairman of the country's largest bank, the Credit Foncier Egyptien, which he co-founded in 1880. He was also deputy chairman and board member of other industrial concerns including the Compagnie Frigorifique d'Egypte.

From the September 1901 *Bulletin de L'Union Syndicale des Agriculteurs d'Egypte*, we learn that Beyerlé was responsible for the creation in the province of Sharkia of two large agricultural concerns known to us today as Kafr Denohia and Mit Rekab. It was there that Beyerlé fashioned his mechanised model crop and dairy farm on 1,500 feddans (acres).

The palace in Garden City was meant to crown Karl Beyerlé's spectacular achievements in Egypt. But this was not to be.

The Beyerlés never lived in their palace. According to Dorothee Von Brentano, both her great-great-grandparents were already dead by then. Marie Rose Pachoud died in 1905, followed by her husband, Karl Beyerlé, on December 12, 1908. He was 71 years old. And since their only son, Charles, died young, we are left with the Beyerlé daughters, Margarete (Mrs. Von Loehr) and Jeane (Mrs. Garcia).

By 1908 both daughters were married and living in Europe, which is why Karl Beyerlé's body had to be embalmed and the funeral postponed until their return, five days later. According to a related announcement in the *Egyptian Gazette,* Beyerlé resided in his new palace all of three days, having moved in on Wednesday, December 9, only to die there the following Saturday.

In order to pay tribute to its founding director, the Credit Foncier Egyptien closed its doors for one day.

Margarete's husband was the former German Consul to Egypt, Joseph Von Loehr, which is perhaps the origin of an unfounded tale often told about Palais Beyerlé—that Germany's kaiser was expected to stay there on his proposed visit to Egypt. But Wilhelm II never came. The Great War intervened and Germany's last sovereign went into irreversible exile in the Netherlands. It must be said, however, that the palace was, between 1912 and 1914, German territory. And if there was ever talk of the Germans coming to a more permanent arrangement with the Beyerlé daughters regarding the purchase of the palace, these were defunct when the German Legation was evicted from Egypt on the eve of the First World War.

In 1924, CS was transformed into the Kasr al Dubara Girls' College, an elite school for upper crust girls. Its Swedish headmistress seems to have struck the right chords in Cairo. "If in Stockholm Madame Dagmar Berg translated the works of Montaigne into her native tongue, in Cairo the graduate of Uppsala University stage-managed western liberal education blending it with local customs and traditions." Positive words from the usually caustic Maurice Fargeon in his book *Silhouettes d'Egypte*.

"She was one of the kindest educators by far," recalls former alumna Bouthaina Younes who, along with several other well-born girls, had transferred from the neighbouring Mère de Dieu. Younes describes Berg as an upright woman with short hair and a long body. As for her gym teacher Ms. Vison, "she was exceedingly supple despite her chunky physique."

Despite the accolades and the personal backing of Minister of Education Ali Maher Pasha (later prime minister), Madame Berg faced tough competition from the nearby Mère de Dieu. With time, the temporal lost out to the divine and the headmistress along with her assistants, Ms. Lictchtenberger and *Abla* Dawlat al Saadi, moved to new premises in Giza in 1932-3. Palais Beyerlé had to find a new occupant.

Rather than lease out their Garden City property, this time around the Beyerlé heirs decided to part with it once and for all. The buyer was Chahine Serageddin Pasha (hence the "CS"), a rich landowner with a large family. From now on, Palais Beyerlé would become a worn out hillbilly *dawwar*.

Seen at eye level from the junction of Garden City's Ahmed Pasha and Nabatat Streets, CS lies hidden behind dusty rotting foliage and massive overgrowth. The final lord of the manor was Egypt's last pasha and the chairman of the opposition Wafd Party. Fouad Serageddin (son of Chahine Serageddin) died at the age of 91, in August 2000. His departure still has people speculating on the fate of his subverted palace. What will happen to the mansion now that the pasha is gone? Will developers transform it into a Disney-esque casino or will some Gulfionaire turn it into a weekend Shangri-La?

There is of course the option that while Cairo's governor and his cronies look the other way, the palace will abruptly disappear and a Four Seasons tower of some kind will go up in its place.

EM is located at No. 24 Gamal al Din Abou al Mahassen Street. Its original owner, an Italian-Egyptian Jew, died the day Mussolini entered the war on the side of Hitler. One of the richest men of his day, Elie Mosseri

Bey's boardroom control extended from Tora Cement Company to the Hotels Company of Egypt that included the Mena House in Giza and the King David Hotel in Jerusalem.

Through his mother, Elie Mosseri was the grandson of Yacoub Cattaui Bey, the founder of a powerful banking, industrial and real estate dynasty. Through his first wife, Laure Suares, he was connected to the founders of Egypt's two most important banks, the Credit Foncier and National Bank of Egypt. Through his second marriage to Georgette Hirsch-Kahn, Mosseri acquired shares in France's mega-department store, Galleries Lafayette. And through his third marriage to Helen Polymires, he was re-connected to the Alexandrian cream of the crop.

In *Too Rich*, a biography of King Farouk, William Stadiem details how, after Nessim Mosseri died, Egypt's monarch installed a red 'hotline' telephone at Villa Elie Mosseri so that whenever he needed special entertainment, Mrs. Mosseri would come up with the best courtesans Cairene society had to offer. Eventually *la belle Helene* committed suicide by jumping from the mansion's roof.

An accommodating arrangement between Denise Dreyfus-Harari (Mosseri's only daughter and heir) and the Helvetian government made it possible for Villa Mosseri to become the property of the Swiss Embassy in Cairo. This strategic move ensured the survival of the villa and saved Garden City's last garden from certain extinction. To this day, Mosseri's resplendent park can be enjoyed by Cairo's best whenever the Swiss host a garden fête. But will it soon end?

In a way it already has. The 40-plus-storey Nile-front Four Seasons Plaza Hotel right across the street from the Swiss Embassy property has all but choked Garden City's last garden. Injunctions for a stay of execution were all for naught.

The third blighted property, GW, stands opposite the former Meridien Hotel. Although it is not proven, the villa's design is attributed to Italian architect Mario Rossi, the same man who designed many private homes, as well as the famed Sidi Morsi Abou al Abbas Mosque of Alexandria.

This recently restored Nile-side villa dates back to the close of the First World War, when court physician Mohammed Chahine Pasha lived there with his family. It was only when his wife died prematurely in the mid 1920s that he moved to Zamalek, selling the house to George Wissa Pasha, an affluent Coptic landowner from Upper Egypt.

Wissa enjoyed several honorifics, including that of America's 'Consular Agent' in Assiut. That is why, in his day, the house was a regular stop for important politicians and visiting statesmen.

It was also at 'GW' that Wissa's daughter-in-law, Marie Fanous, entertained many an officer and a gentleman. As heir presumptive of Gezira Club's teatime crowd, Edward G. Wissa's widow threw parties in the ornate salons or in the basement-turned-cabaret, nicknamed *Chez Marie*.

Indeed, GW was a favourite pre-revolutionary venue for Allied generals and high-hat diplomats. All were inclined towards Marie's well-laden buffets that seemingly took precedence over hobnobbing with Egypt's fawning Anglophiles. Conversation invariably drifted from Monty's routing of Rommel to avocado ranching, a delicacy introduced to these parts by none other than the obliging hostess.

Today, drawn out litigation among GW's heirs will decide the fate of the fallen villa. Flanked between two mountainous skyscrapers, the villa certainly appears to be on the dreaded architectural death row that has claimed so many of Garden City's once grand villas.

The statue of Soliman Pasha and Groppi's

These two long-time Cairo landmarks suffered different but equally sad fates; Soliman
Pasha's statue was exiled to the Citadel while Egypt's foremost teahouse went into steady
decline. The square is now named for Talaat Harb Pasha, the Egyptian industrialist,
whose statue replaced that of Soliman.

Talaat Harb Square

A century ago, mansions overlooking this legendary Cairo square were replaced with handsome high-ceilinged and spacious apartment houses well suited to the uncrowded, leisurely life of the first half of the twentieth century. Most of these have since been converted into offices and commercial space.

The nation's plaza

Sheikh Omar Makram is a recent arrival to the forever-changing Tahrir Square. The statue stands next to the the palace of Princess Nimet Kamil al Din, recently restored for the benefit of the Ministry of Foreign Affairs.

The Davies Bryan building

Commissioned in 1911 by four Welsh brothers, the St. David was a centre of fashionable activity up until the Second World War when its ground floor store "Davies Bryan" finally ceased activities. Purchased by four Syrian brothers the St. David fell into decline after the passing of the sequestration laws in 1961.

Midan Mustafa Kamel/Suares

Midan Suares, so named after a wealthy Jewish banking family, was renamed for Mustafa Kamel when King Farouk unveiled the French-made statue in 1940 in honour of Egypt's first modern-day nationalist.

Palace of Said Halim Pasha

Built in lavish style by court architect Antonio Lasciac around 1900, the palace of Said Halim Pasha, once prime minister of the Ottoman Empire, was turned into a state school for the sons of pashas and beys. With the disappearance of the sons the palace fell on hard times and today desperately awaits salvation.

The Tiring building

Attracted by Tiring's globe-like cupola beaming into the night, people came in great numbers at the beginning the twentieth century to shop on Attaba Square, home to several of Cairo's first European-built emporiums. One hundred years later these are tumbled-down shanties and squatter settlements.

Fouad Avenue and Taalat Harb Street

A bustling intersection in Cairo's Ismailia district conceived in the late nineteenth century by Khedive Ismail. The main thoroughfare with electric trams then running its length was called Fouad al Awal Avenue in honour of the khedive's son.

Monster on the Nile

For lovers of belle époque palace hotels the tearing down of the Semiramis in the 1970s was like a page wrenched from Cairo's rich narrative. The replacement is the giant and uninspiring Intercontinental Semiramis Hotel.

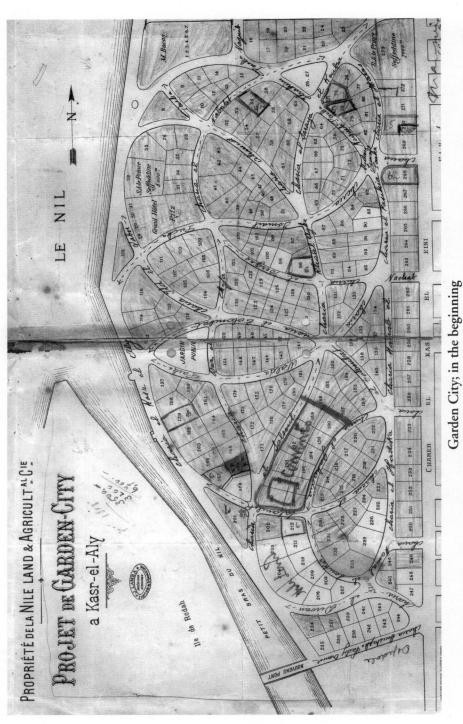

Garden City; in the beginning

An original 1906 plan of Garden City whose component parts suggest that its designer, Jose Lamba, was inspired by water denizens. The new Cairo suburb would replace a group of palaces and parks owned by the ruling dynasty of Mohammed Ali.

4. The island

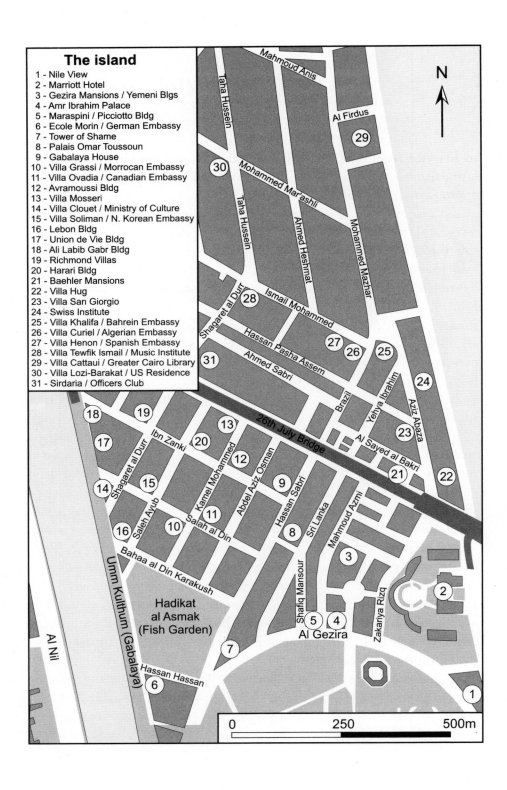

The island

1 - Nile View
2 - Marriott Hotel
3 - Gezira Mansions / Yemeni Blgs
4 - Amr Ibrahim Palace
5 - Maraspini / Picciotto Bldg
6 - Ecole Morin / German Embassy
7 - Tower of Shame
8 - Palais Omar Toussoun
9 - Gabalaya House
10 - Villa Grassi / Morrocan Embassy
11 - Villa Ovadia / Canadian Embassy
12 - Avramoussi Bldg
13 - Villa Mosseri
14 - Villa Clouet / Ministry of Culture
15 - Villa Soliman / N. Korean Embassy
16 - Lebon Bldg
17 - Union de Vie Bldg
18 - Ali Labib Gabr Bldg
19 - Richmond Villas
20 - Harari Bldg
21 - Baehler Mansions
22 - Villa Hug
23 - Villa San Giorgio
24 - Swiss Institute
25 - Villa Khalifa / Bahrein Embassy
26 - Villa Curiel / Algerian Embassy
27 - Villa Henon / Spanish Embassy
28 - Villa Tewfik Ismail / Music Institute
29 - Villa Cattaui / Greater Cairo Library
30 - Villa Lozi-Barakat / US Residence
31 - Sirdaria / Officers Club

Re-christening an island

When he annexed the shifting islands of Boulaq to his vice-regal *ciftlik* of Giza, Khedive Ismail unwittingly laid the foundations of a new Cairo suburb: Al Gezira (the island). The newly appropriated land was first used as a nursery and for the khedive's benefit, a kiosk was erected in the centre of the main island, near its eastern bank. A few years later, a summer *saray* (now the Marriott Hotel) was added nearby thus formally paving the way for the eventual development of the exclusive, leafy residential suburb.

At first, land surveyors and early residents referred to the island as Gezirat Boulaq, an allusion to the thriving eighteenth and nineteenth century port situated on the Nile's eastern bank. The 'Boulaq' was eventually dropped and Gezira became the commonly used vernacular. The landmark that had nevertheless adopted the name of Zamalek very early on was the smaller bridge linking the island's midsection to the then mainly rural expanse of Giza. It was borrowed from a nearby Giza hamlet called Al Zamalek situated south-west of Imbaba village.

Over the years different interpretations for the meaning of Zamalek have come up. One says Zamalek is the plural of *zomlok*, an Albanian or Ottoman expression meaning 'straw hut'. Fishermen or perhaps servants working in palaces belonging to rich merchants living in Boulaq used these huts for shelter. Some say Zamalek comes from a corruption of the Arabic *zou-molk*, meaning asset owner. A definitive interpretation is yet to materialise.

Although the 1873 map sketched by geographer Mahmoud Falaki Pasha reveals no huts, it shows that Boulaq Island, as he calls it, was united to Giza except during the August-October high flood when three islands appeared, the largest one situated in the middle. Hence the designation *Gezira al Wosta*—middle island—used later as the name for a Zamalek street. An earlier, unsigned map gives 1300 AD as the approximate date for the creation of Boulaq Island.

Originally, Gezira's southern edge was closer to Rhoda Island, while its northern was closer to where 26th of July Street now runs. When Khedive Ismail diverted the Nile's course—part of his grand plan to modernise Cairo—the river moved silt and mud to form what is today northern Zamalek. The Nile would fortuitously give birth to a new Cairo district when the bobbing islands were further consolidated into one mass, the result of a channel having been burrowed on their western flank.

For a clue as to the creation of the township of Gezira let us refer to the *Egyptian Gazette* of May 16, 1903, where we find the following item:

> A native contemporary [an Arabic-language newspaper] has fallen into an error in stating that the Egyptian Markets Co. Ltd. have purchased 100 feddans from the Fathers of the African Mission. It is about a month ago now since Mr. Allan Joseph, on behalf of an English syndicate, purchased the land in question for 80000 pounds sterling. It is intended to spend 8000 pounds sterling or 10000 pounds sterling in continuing the river wall which extends from Ghezireh Palace and to divide up the land into building plots.

From the above we gather that the urbanisation of Zamalek had seriously begun. But what of the Fathers of the African Mission, who were they and what were they doing on the island?

The Mission alluded to in the *Gazette* was founded in the late nineteenth century by priests recruited from Verona and Southern Tyrol. They were also known as the Austria-Sudan Catholic Mission, 'les pères de la Nigritie' or the Comboni Fathers after their founder Daniel Comboni. The Mission's ultimate purpose was to 'enlighten' the natives of Sudan.

During the Mahdi's uprising the missionaries and their Sudanese disciples fled to Egypt, establishing in August 1888 temporary headquarters on 120 feddans of secluded Boulaq Island land provided by Khedive Tewfik at preferential terms. There, they discreetly set up a church, a school and an agricultural farm supervised by Reverend Father Angelo Colombarolli. In her study of the Roman Catholic Mission to Central Africa and its protection by the Hapsburg Empire from 1846 to 1914, Dorothea McEwan writes:

> In Gesirah near Cairo, Monsignor Sogaro built the agricultural and anti-slavery colony 'Leo XIII', the church of Saint Joseph and institute for missionaries and for nuns in 1888. In addition he founded a village for the Sudanese who occupied themselves with the cultivation of 50 hectares for fruit plantation.

When it was safe for the Fathers to return to Sudan, then under joint Egyptian-British control, most of the farm was parcelled out in 1913-15 and sold by the Catholic Mission, at a considerable profit, to the newly formed Gezira Land Company and several other private developers, such as Messrs. Legrelle and Geday. The remaining ten feddans at the northern tip of the island was sold in June 1934 to Leon Rolin.

With the help of their replenished coffers, the Comboni Fathers proceeded to invest part of the profit in real estate in Zamalek and in other parts of Cairo, hence their ownership, until the 1960s, of a variety of smart-looking apartment buildings and villas.

One hundred years later, vestiges of the mission are still in evidence on the island. While four of the streets named after priests have been changed, there is still a Morseline (Missionaries) Alley. A successor church and school, both named St Joseph, can be found in the area where the Mission had set up its original headquarters at the island's centre, safe from the annual floods.

To this day, some old homes in Zamalek still receive utility bills in the name of the Mission. Moreover, the Comboni Fathers can rightly claim to have introduced the island's first cinema theatre where, on certain days, Père Zohrab offered his viewers a variety of feature films and documentaries. The ciné club ended with the retirement of Reverend Father Roberto Zanini.

During the first decades of the twentieth century, the island's northern section was almost uninhabited but for some ragtag farms. The island's first British residents referred to this marshy inhospitable area as North End.

With the construction of Boulaq Bridge and the rapid rise in urban development after the First World War, it was a matter of time before the marshy area north of the island's Avenue Zamalek (26th of July Street) was developed. Nonetheless, in 1926 a square metre in this section sold for LE1 whereas the elegant area south of the avenue sold for double that amount.

By the middle of the twentieth century, Avenue Zamalek became the island's *qasaba*, its tramway tracks creating an unofficial north-south boundary. As though to make a geographic and sometimes social distinction, old timers to this day will refer to the area south of 26th July as Gezira. Likewise, during the first quarter of the twentieth century, the mention of Gezira Gardens invariably meant you were referring to that elegant urban area developed on what had been the khedivial palace grounds encompassing the island's midsection.

As the island's population steadily rose, the area north of 26th of July Avenue would be increasingly referred to as Zamalek. By the middle of the century, the entire island would adopt that name. The island's commercial section had won the day.

If lions could speak

If you ask connoisseurs what Sydney Harbour Bridge and Kasr al Nil Bridge have in common, they'll tell you they're both located within range of their city's opera house. Well yes, except that Down Under's celebrated bridge and opera house are potent symbols of Australia with world-landmark recognition status. Their Egyptian counterparts, although worthy of particular credit, cannot profess deserved acknowledgement even from their own home crowd. Yet it wouldn't hurt to give the Kasr al Nil Bridge crossing credit for being the first in its league to span the world's longest river.

Ten time zones and hemispheres apart, the two bridges were inaugurated within 15 months of each other; the 503 metre long Sydney Harbour Bridge on March 19, 1932, and the 382 metre long Kasr al Nil on June 6, 1933. Dorman, Long & Company Limited of York, UK, constructed both bridges.

Internationally renowned for its steelwork constructions, Dorman Long accounted for another famous bridge in Africa: Birchenough Arch Bridge above the Sabi River in what is today Zimbabwe.

Given our propensity to change street names it hardly comes as a surprise to know that this extends to bridges too. Our handsome steel bridge started out in life as Khedive Ismail Bridge. Less known is the fact that it wasn't the first crossing to appear at that particular section of the Nile.

In 1869-72, with the participation of French steel makers Fives Lille, a St Simonian engineer by the name of Linant de Bellefonds had strung what amounted to a narrow causeway across the Nile linking the very same embankments we are so familiar with today. The toll bridge departed just south of Khedive Ismail's palace (later the infamous British-occupied Kasr al Nil Barracks), ending at the southern tip of the uninhabited island of Boulaq that we know today as Gezira-Zamalek. These were the days when the French still had a say in Egypt's economy. The crossing was referred to as Kobri al Gezira or Gezira Bridge.

The construction of Gezira Bridge served first and foremost as a catalyst for the development of Gezira Island and the expanse that lay beyond. It would unwittingly serve as the first nail in the coffin of history's most celebrated panorama. Within a century, the timeless 4,000-year-old Giza pyramids could no longer be gawked at from downtown Cairo as office building after office building, apartment skyscraper after apartment skyscraper, some reasonable, the rest ugly cement boxes topped with garrish neon adverts, made for a harsh new skyline.

The Gezira toll bridge was the bane of traditional ferry operators and *felucca* owners, but a boon to pedestrians, camels, donkey-carts and stagecoaches that could now remain on *terra firma* all year round. Gone were the days when summer floods separated the Nile valley into two alien lands.

With the arrival of the horseless carriage, the Department of Public Works found it necessary in 1913 to commission Cleveland Bridge & Engineering Company to give the ageing crossing a badly needed facelift. In July of the same year floorboards reinforced with concrete blocks were added to the bridge and its narrow sidewalks were widened. Gezira Bridge would thus have a new lease on life linking a city in perpetual effervescence to the still bucolic province of Giza.

By 1930 it became apparent that Bellefonds's bridge had to go. With more than 3,000 all-category vehicles licensed in Egypt, cars were becoming the norm not the exception. Bridge builders from all over the world were invited to submit their tenders.

Of the thirteen received by the Roads and Bridges Department, only two made it to the final selection in January 1931. This time around Cleveland Co. lost out to its arch rival Dorman, Long & Co., represented in Egypt by Colonel Vivian Beaconsfield Gary of the Associated British Manufacturers (ABM) Limited.

With a LE308,000 deal tucked under its belt, Dorman, Long & Co. Ltd., established an Egyptian bridgehead, so to speak, when it opened a temporary office at ABM's headquarters in the prestigious Khedivial Building (Block B) on Emad al Din Street. Dorman, Long & Co.'s new telegraphic address: Dormbridge, Cairo. The local boss was one Mr. T. Biggart.

Once Barclays Bank had issued the appropriate letters of guarantees to the Egyptian government on behalf of Messrs. Dorman and Long, it was simply a matter of hiring competent foreign and local personnel.

Sir John Burnet & Partners and Mr. (later Sir) Ralph Freeman of Sir Douglas Fox & Partners prepared the design of the Kasr al Nil Bridge. Ralph Freeman was similarly involved with the design of Sydney Harbour Bridge.

In January 1931, the four lions guarding Gezira Bridge were relocated to the Zoological Garden in Giza. The larger than life bronze lions that were created by French sculptor, Alfred Jacquemart, were originally intended to stand guard around Mohammed Ali's statue in Alexandria, but Linant de Bellefonds thought better of it and brought them to Cairo instead. They could stand guard on his Nile opus.

It took five months to dismantle the old, narrow bridge. It was agreed that the new, larger replacement would be placed along the identical alignment of the Gezira Bridge. During these five months, suggestions on what to do with the old bridge poured in. One recommendation was that it be reassembled in Luxor for the benefit of tourists wanting to cross the Nile. For an inexplicable reason or perhaps for ecological purposes, the suggestion was mooted so that up until 1996 the Luxor crossing would be by *felucca* or ferry as it had been for the previous seven recorded millennia.

Once the old bridge was no more, the finest bridge builders of the day had exactly 30 months to come up with the product, which included rebuilding the foundations, as the old ones were deemed unsafe. During construction, a daylight steam ferry service operated every half-hour between a pier situated below the Semiramis Hotel and an embankment south of the Pont des Anglais, renamed Evacuation Bridge (Al Galaa) after 1947.

Like Sydney Harbour Bridge, most of the hardware and equipment for both the foundations and the bridge came from Britain. But unlike the fixed Australian bridge, Cairo's new seven-span arch-type steel crossing was designed so that a 67 metre section, powered by Sulzer motors, could swing open electrically within three and a half minutes.

Thirty months later, the bridge builders could pride themselves on both meeting their deadline and delivering an excellent piece of work.

In order to soften the overall aspect of the steel structure, lampposts were introduced at given intervals. For the first time a Cairo bridge shimmered over the Nile like a bride on her wedding night. Except for the two pairs of Aswan granite pylons and the pair of lions at either end of the bridge, there was little else to remind Cairenes that an older bridge had once stood there. Not even a commemorative plaque.

On June 6, 1933, at 10am, King Fouad inaugurated the Nile's newest crossing. Understandably, it was christened Khedive Ismail Bridge, in honour of the king's father. It was during his visionary reign that the original bridge had been built, linking the khedive's then-budding metropolitan Cairo to a little known island he would render world famous during the Suez Canal opening celebrations. The original name is still in evidence on the etched granite slabs located under the lion to the right as you enter the bridge from either direction. The name Khedive Ismail is also marked in English on the Dorman & Long plaque attached to the belly of the bridge.

On hand at the ceremony held at the Gezira-end of the bridge were cabinet ministers, Egyptian and foreign notables as well as the accredited diplomatic corps. To mark the occasion, Major F.W. Stephen representing Messrs. Dorman, & Long, offered King Fouad a golden pen and inkstand in the shape of the new bridge, which can today be seen in the Royal Jewellery Museum in Alexandria.

Also present were members of the large British colony residing in the now fashionable suburb of Zamalek. They were especially pleased since the latest British-built addition to Cairo's skyline considerably reduced the distance between downtown Cairo and the Gezira Sporting Club. The alternative was the cumbersome detour via Boulaq Bridge and the dusty Boulaq Avenue, both of which had been renamed Fouad al Awal the previous year in honour of the reigning monarch.

Court photographer Arakel Artinian documented the ceremony, as Richard Milosh from Australia tell us:

> On the day of the inauguration of the new Kasr al Nil Bridge, Monsieur Venus, as my grandfather was also known, took the official photos showing the motorcade procession of King Fouad advancing from Gezira. The policemen lining the route were wearing their white summer uniforms. My grandfather took the photos from the top of the old Semiramis Hotel. His studio was located at 25 Kasr al Nil Street.

A lesser event that took place behind the scenes that day was the official handing over of Kasr al Nil Bridge. Representing Messrs. Dorman & Long was T. Biggart. Representing the Roads and Bridges Department was Chief Inspector Gawdat. He was standing in for the Minister of Communications, Ibrahim Karim Pasha. Accompanying him were senior civil engineers Selim Amoun Bey and Taher al Sirgani. Both had played a leading role during the construction phase.

After careful examination, some minor adjustments had to be made to bring it in total compliance with the *cahier des charges*. For example, the lampposts absorbed rather than deflected light, which meant the glass had to be changed. Manhole covers and bridge footpaths needed adjustment. A further adjustment was, "the insertion of plates in the clearance between the expansion plates and the abutments to prevent any washing-water from falling on the bridge terraces."

Minor adjustments notwithstanding, the most important issue was that the bridge successfully opened twice a day to let the goods-laden *feluccas* through. With the eventual motorisation of fluvial transport in the 1960s it would henceforth open on rare occasions, mostly to enable Nile cruise ships to pass.

Shortly after the toppling of King Farouk in 1952 and the coming to an end of almost 70 years of British occupation, Khedive Ismail Bridge was officially renamed Kobri Kasr al Nil.

Meanwhile, the Kasr al Nil Palace that had lent its name to the bridge disappeared in 1955. In 1964 the house of writer Kout al Kouloub al Demerdashia, at the downtown entrance to the bridge, was pulled down to make way for the ramp leading onto the bridge. By 1967-8, the Nile flood no longer swelled almost to the level of bridge, thanks to Aswan's High Dam. The *belle époque* Semiramis, witness to the original bridge, was pulled down in the 1970s in order to accommodate a newer glass and concrete hotel.

If the lions were to speak they'd tell about elapsed events that took place on the bridge itself. Maybe they know the secret surrounding the February 19, 1946, car accident that killed royal cabinet advisor and sometime desert explorer, Ahmed Hassanein Pasha. He was also Egypt's first Olympic medallist. The incident triggered endless speculation of foul play, ranging from a monarch seeking to silence the wags linking his mother to the royal advisor, to Britain's MI5 liquidating an anti-British element within the palace entourage.

Another event that made history on Kasr al Nil Bridge was President Gamal Abdel Nasser's September 1970 funeral procession, when thousands of official mourners marched across the bridge. In the ensuing fray, Emperor Haile Selassie of Ethiopia fainted and Archbishop Makarius of Cyprus lost his consecrated baton.

How ironic that while Nasser's funeral was beamed across the world, on any other given day, anyone photographing the bridge risked detention by Sate Security. Never mind that souvenir shops across the city sold exquisitely detailed postcards of the bridge and its surroundings.

It seems that the camera phobia started in the Second World War when military police attempted to secure the area surrounding the Kasr al Nil barracks. The stubborn rule survived long after these were removed. Thankfully the 'No Photo' signs are gone so that today Kasr al Nil's lions top the list of Cairo's favourite photo-ops. Moreover, the view from the bridge is a preferred all-year backdrop for newlyweds.

A bridge misunderstood

We move on to another Nile bridge that ended up in the scrap heap in 1998 despite the extraordinary legends surrounding it.

Cairenes first learned of the second bridge linking downtown Cairo to Gezira Island on December 2, 1905, from the local dailies. The *Egyptian Gazette* reported "A new bridge is to be built across the Nile, the government having decided on the construction of a magnificent structure to unite Boulaq and Ghezireh. The work will be taken in hand shortly." Note the contemporaneous spelling of the island. Over the years the appellation Gezira (which means island in Arabic) would have different spellings: Gezirah, Gezireh, Ghezireh etc.

Besides informing us that the new crossing would be called Boulaq Bridge (no mention of Abou al Ela yet), the article casts a few valuable details on the proposed bridge, plus inklings on the status quo of the island and its famous hotel.

> Boulaq Bridge will be twenty metres in width and will form a most convenient connecting link between the fashionable new suburb of Ghezireh by the Boulaq Avenue. The Ghezireh quarter will thus soon form an integral portion of the capital especially as a double line of tramway is to be laid across the river. The Ghezireh end of the bridge will be about two metres to the north of the Ghezireh Palace Hotel and will divide the estate of the Egyptian Hotels Company in two parts.

The bridge was built as reported but contrary to local legend its opening mechanism worked from the moment it was completed. In fact, the bridge opened for Nile traffic twice a day from 12 noon to 12-45pm and again from 3pm to 3-45pm (closed on Sundays). As for the romantic tale claiming that Alexander-Gustave Eiffel designed this bridge and later took his own life when it failed to open—nothing could be further from the truth.

The bridge's opening mechanism must have been of an unusual kind for it solicited great interest all around. In fact, a special lecture entitled, "The Building of the Boulac Bridge" was given in June 1913 at the YMCA where the focus was on the rolling bascules (drawbridge apparatus) and locking mechanism.

> The latter is comparatively simple, but nevertheless it effectively prevents 'jamming', the secret of the device lying in the fact that one leaf is constructed so that it forces its fellow into position during the process of lowering. The weight of each opening section is roughly 900 tons, yet each is so accurately counter balanced that a ridiculously low power is required to overcome the frictional losses.

Despite the hullabaloo regarding the revolutionary opening mechanism, the ornate span-type metal Boulaq Bridge did, however, stop functioning several years after its inauguration and if anyone was accountable for this deficiency, it should have been American engineer, William Donald Scherzer. Not only did his Chicago firm design the Boulaq Bridge, but it was Scherzer who invented the above-mentioned rolling bascules and locking mechanism necessary for opening it to fluvial traffic. As for the bridge's alleged French connection, this was limited to the manufacturing of steel girders by the well-known company of Fives Lille and to the steel beams produced by the famous French conglomerate, Schneider.

Scherzer was chosen at the suggestion of a commission charged with the examination of the tenders for the construction of the bridge. The commission's recommendations were submitted in 1908 to the adjudication committee headed by Mr. Perry, the Under-secretary of State for Towns and Buildings. In turn, Perry referred the report to another commission made up of Mr. Webb, Under-secretary of State for Irrigation, Macauley Bey who was general manager of the Egyptian State Railways (ESR), and Mr. Holt, sub-director of the Cairo Polytechnic School.

Erecting the 274.5 metre long bridge was no easy feat. Construction took three and a half years with the foundations poured at 18 metres below sea level. In the pre-High Dam days, the portion of the Nile that ran through Egypt was a potent body of moving water, its strong currents and giant swirls, especially during high flood, causing serious challenges to bridge constructors. Several piers, large girders and wide spans were put in place before the bridge could be opened for business.

In sharp contrast to the pomp and ceremony surrounding the inaugurations of Cairo's older bridges or the multiple celebrations at the opening of the Aswan and Qena Reservoirs attended by Khedive Abbas Hilmi and the Duke of Connaught, Boulaq Bridge was quietly opened to the public in July 1912. Summers in Cairo were hot and the entire government had moved to Alexandria the previous April. Khedive Abbas Hilmi was summering in Europe with his new Hungarian wife and Lord Kitchener, Egypt's de facto ruler, was attending an important meeting in Malta. It was left to Ismail Sirry Pasha, the Minister of Public Works, to cut the ribbon on their behalf.

A month later, on August 18, 1912, Cairo's press corps was invited to a magnificent champagne breakfast buffet at the Giza tramway station, courtesy of Fritz de Lancker, the Belgian director of the Cairo Tramways Company, which had partially financed the Boulaq Bridge. Together, they celebrated the launch of the new Ataba al Khadra–Pyramids tram route No. 3, by way of Boulaq and Zamalek bridges. In de Lancker's own words:

> Gentlemen of the Press, we are assembled here to inaugurate this new line of the Tramway Company which already has extended its ramifications in every part of Cairo and its suburbs. We have been careful to choose a route that would be of service to all the villages and suburbs in the district. I need not describe to you the working of the new Boulac Bridge with its wonderful opening mechanism, only the other day observed by you on the occasion of its formal opening by Sirry Pasha; nor indeed the complete change which the Zamalek Bridge has undergone since this new route was projected. We fully believe therefore that our new enterprise will meet with the good will and patronage of all, especially when its utility is pointed out to the travelling public. I drink, then, gentleman, to your health.

Since the Belgian-owned Tramway Company generated its own electrical supply for the running of the trams, it was from its power plant in Boulaq that it extended the 500 volts needed to operate Boulaq Bridge's opening mechanism. Of the lift type, it took two minutes for the bridge's two central movable spans to roll back on their wheels into a vertical position, thus allowing the waiting Nile traffic to sail through a 27 metre wide opening.

Boulaq Bridge was renamed Fouad al Awal on February 4, 1932, in honour of the king. Another renaming would occur after the toppling of King Farouk when the bridge became Kobri Abou al Ela, a reference to Sheikh al Saleh Hussein Ibn Ali (a.k.a. Abou al Ela) whose shrine and mosque stand nearby. The bridge with three names was dismantled in 1998.

Mapping the island

As streets were drawn, designated names had to be found. The north-south street forming the island's horizontal axis was named Gabalaya Street because of a man-made bluff created there in the late nineteenth century, when that entire area was part and parcel of Gezira Palace.

Due to political caprice or simply to honour or discredit someone, names of streets in Zamalek, like the rest of the city for that matter, have undergone a bewildering variety of name changes in the past century. But let's concentrate here on the original names.

In 1924, at the peak of the monarchy, the streets of Gezira west of the former khedivial palace had a decidedly royal tinge. To the west of Gabalaya Street, several Ayyubid Sultans were honoured including the infamous Armenian-born Sultana Shagaret al Durr, the first woman to rule Egypt since Cleopatra. To the east of Gabalaya almost all streets were named after male members of the existing royal family: Amir Fouad, Amir Gamil and Amir Hussein etc. As it turns out, Ayyubid royalty remained acceptable after the monarchy was overthrown but streets named after more recent royals were all changed.

Several of the streets north of Fouad al Awal (renamed 26th of July) were named after Egyptian residents of the island. Bahgat Ali Street was known in the 1920s as Rue Chawarby in reference to Mohammed Chawarby Pasha who owned a large mansion there, and also as Rue Doctor Fathi Bayoumi because the successful practitioner was one of the first true Egyptians to live on the island.

Aside from doctors, civil and hydraulic engineers also managed to pick up a few street names, including British irrigation engineers (Sir William) Garstin, (Sir Scott Colin) Moncrieff and (Sir William) Willcocks. Not forgotten were a few of their Egyptian counterparts, such as Ismail

Mohammed Pasha, Mohammed Sakib Pasha and Mohammed Mar'ashly Pasha.

There were also streets named after several of the island's foreign residents like Privat, Diacono and Doctor Milton. And there were those three streets named after religious personalities: Archbishops Francesco Sogaro and Daniel Comboni, and Kadis Youssef (Saint Joseph).

Some streets were named after adjacent establishments, hence the western section of Mar'ashly Street (the eastern part did not yet exist) was called Mahkama (Tribunal) Street. In 1926 the Indigenous Court of Imbaba was located where Mar'ashly today intersects with Bahgat Ali Street.

Flora too lent its name to parts of the island; there was a Ward (Flower) Street, and the area surrounding the Anglo-American Hospital was, and still is, known as *Zohria* (Floral) in view of the botanical gardens created there.

Demographics

Since there are no separate statistics dealing with the island's early twentieth century population, the best alternative is a French-language 1913 Egyptian commercial directory that lists in its address section 84 long-term residents of Gezira. Given a five percent margin of error and assuming most names mentioned had families plus one or more live-in hired help, one can deduce the island's population that year was somewhere between 400 and 450.

The directory spells out 52 Britons, most of them top executives in the Egyptian administration, major companies and banks. This impressive list includes directors of the Survey Department, the Prison Administration, the Egyptian State Railways, the Customs Administration, the Coastguard Administration, the Irrigation Administration and the Department of Health. Among the joint stock companies we find directors of the Menzaleh Navigation Company, the Egyptian Markets Company, the Egyptian Dredging Company and Thomas Cook. Topping the banking list is the National Bank of Egypt, the Agricultural Bank and the Imperial Ottoman Bank.

The two topmost British residents on the island were Sir Frederick

Rowlatt, Governor of the National Bank of Egypt (Central Bank in those days), and the *Sirdar*, Sir Reginald Wingate, Commander in Chief of the Egyptian Army and Governor of the Sudan.

Next comes Belgium with six residents including the directors of the Sino-Belgian Bank and the Sugar Company. Three of these Belgians lived in lawyer Gaston Privat's (himself a Belgian) *immeuble de rapport*.

Sharing third place were four Swiss and four Jews. (At this time, religious appurtenance often stood in for national identity when the latter was unclear.) Among the Swiss we find the directors of the Egyptian Hotels Company and Banque Hug as well as the Von Heller family who would make a career in civil construction. The more notable of the island's tiny Jewish population was a leading moneylender.

The Germans follow with two illustrious residents, Consul Baron Von Falkenhausen and the celebrated Egyptologist Ludwig Borchardt. With them in the lower single-digit category are two Austrians, a Greek tobacco magnate, a Dutch consul and a Swedish count.

Last on the list are five residents of unknown origin and three Egyptians. By far the most senior of the Egyptians is Sir Ismail Sirry Pasha, Minister of Public Works and War. His address: Ibn Zanki. Yet according to his descendants, Sirry had a permanent address in another part of Cairo during that period, which implies that Zamalek was either his secondary residence or simply a convenient postal address. Of the remaining two Egyptians listed, one was a Coptic landowner pasha and the other a Moslem physician bey. All three Egyptians had strong British connections and were thus reservedly welcome on the British island-colony.

In those days Gezira was a strictly residential community, hence no commercial street, no Sunday market and no shops. On the other hand, the island had several important tourist facilities. The best known by far was the Gezira Palace Hotel that provided the islanders with a park, a post office, a telegraph and a public telephone.

For nature lovers there was *Hadikat al Asmak*, Egypt's only fish aquarium. Introduced and landscaped by Captain Stanley Flower at a cost of LE1,150, it was originally called Grotto Garden; home to a rare collection of African fishes that inhabited the 24 especially constructed water tanks. As of November 1902 the Aquarium was open daily to the public between 8-30am until 5pm. The price of admission was 5 millimes except on Sundays when it was 10 millimes.

The Colombo gardens were another island attraction. They were revitalised and renamed Zohria during Sultan Hussein Kamel's short reign. Situated nearer Kasr al Nil Bridge, Zohria would later spawn an Andalusian garden, *Hadikat al Fardos*. It was inaugurated in the early 1930s and later mutilated into three separate gardens.

As far as pre-First World War addresses are concerned, 'Gezira Palace Gardens' was by far the most common. Most of the island's inhabitants lived near or around the hotel, for a long time the island's hub. In other instances, the directory lists names followed simply by 'Gezira', indicating that the whereabouts of these particular individuals were well known and needed no further elaboration. The only addresses with house numbers were located on what we know today as 26th of July Street, then called Avenue Zamalek.

While some villas sported names like Villa San Giorgio, Villa Beauregard, Villa al Shagartein (two trees) and Red Court, others were named after their owners like Villa Lyons, Villa (Gaston) Privat, Villa (Levy) Garboua, Villa Gordon and Villa Badaro. Also listed is 'Hareem Building', suggesting that Palais Gezira's annexe had been transformed into an apartment building.

The only apartment buildings on the island were Gezira House and Grotto House. All the occupants were British. Likewise, whenever we find two names associated with one address we know this concerns one of Gezira's semi-detached villas, such as the ones still extant on Ahmed Heshmat Street.

Two *dahabiahs* are listed: the *Herodotus*, occupied by the director of Thomas Cook and *Hathor*, occupied by a Mr. G. W. Fraser, who worked for the Ministry of Finance.

Whereas names of the island's non-British are listed in full, we find that the British preferred to give their surname only with one or two initials appended as if it was no one's business to know more.

If the 1913 directory gives us a general picture of the island's demographics prior to the First World War, what then was it like on the eve of the Second World War?

Needless to say, by the late 1930s the island's population had grown significantly, with new schools, different foreign legations and several *pensions* making it across the Nile. As though to illustrate the aggregate affluence of Gezira-Zamalek's burgeoning residents, two service stations—Socony Vaccum and Shell—opened on Avenue Fouad al Awal (26th of July) thus setting the tone that this was Zamalek's High Street.

The population mix is, however, difficult to determine. For sure Egyptians had become a principal component of the island's population but at what ratio? To get a full picture would require a detailed enquiry that exceeds the scope of this book. However, we know from a 1936 *Who's Who* (*Le Mondain Egyptien*) that the makeup of Hassan Sabry Street (Ex-Gabalaya) was as follows:

Gheita, Mohammed, 2 Gabalaya
Deiches, Cavaliere Stasche & Mme. née Kramer, 3 Gabalaya, 'Villa Billy'
Ades, Maurice A., 4-6 Gabalaya [partly replaced by Al Abd building; Four Corners Restaurant]
Mosseri, Maurice Nessim, 10 Gabalaya [replaced by German Embassy chancery building]
Cattaui Pasha, Mme Vve. Moise de, 13 Gabalaya
Cattaui, Edgard de, 13 Gabalaya
Cohen, René M., 13 Gabalaya
Bidair, Mohammed Pasha, 18 Gabalaya
Levy, Isaac, 18 Gabalaya
Naggar, Jacques, 20 Gabalaya [today Amer building]
Zarmati, Moise Lionel, 20 Gabalaya [today Amer building]
Zaidan, Choukri & Emile, 20 Gabalaya [today Amer building]
Zananiri, Fernand; Schemeil, Raymond 22 Gabalaya
Levi, Guido, 24 Gabalaya [today Dutch Embassy]
Gannage, Emile & Mme., 26 Gabalaya, Gabalaya House
Templeton, Dr J., 26 Gabalaya, Gabalaya House
Ceysens, Albert, 26 Gabalaya, Gabalaya House
Barne, H.H., 32 Gabalaya
Coates, E.W., 32 Gabalaya
Kelsey, Easton T., 40 Gabalaya
Mackintosh, Charles, A.G. 41 Gabalaya, Villa Scarabé
Neuville, Paul, 41 Gabalaya, Villa Scarabé'
Curiel, Nessim, 42 Gabalaya
Abdel Latif, Mohammed, 44 Gabalaya
Tousoun, Prince Omar, 51 Gabalaya
Waly, Hussein, 55 Gabalaya
Zaki, Mahmoud, 69 Gabalaya

Khalifa, Mahmoud, 71 Gabalaya
Greenwood, Gabalaya
Mahfouz Bey, Dr. Abdel Halim, Gabalaya
Reynolds, Alexandre, Gabalaya, 'Villa Egizia'

Himself a long-time Hassan Sabry Street resident, Professor Alaa Gheita MD, points out that of the 31 families who lived on the island's longest residential street in 1936, only eight were *bona fide* Egyptians including his two grandfathers, Gheita Bey and Bidair Pasha. The non-Egyptian families are broken down into eight British, 11 Jews, three Syrians and one Belgian.

The first institutions

A religious order was the first to address education on the island. The Fathers of the African Mission opened a tiny school in the nineteenth century that later expanded into the St Joseph Preparatory School for Boys off Brazil Street. The next two pre-1925 schools to open in Zamalek were run by the church—the Mère de Dieu, off Bahgat Ali Street, and the Alvernia Franciscan Sisters at No. 2 Kadis Youssef Street.

It would not be long before non-denominational and secular schools opened on the island as well. Foremost among the island's schools was the Zamalek School for Girls, operated by Valentine and René Morin. First located at No. 25 Mohammed Mazhar Street, in 1933 it moved to a one-acre property overlooking the Fish Aquarium at No. 4 Ibn Mashtub Street.

Years later, when relations with France soured, the Morins were expelled and the small schoolhouse overlooking Bahr al Aama and its adjoining garden were purchased by businessman-tycoon François Tager. But since he too left Egypt in the 1960s, the empty property was re-sold, this time to the Federal Republic of Germany. The deal had hardly been concluded when Egypt and Germany severed diplomatic relations. The property remained an empty wasteland for more than a decade with nothing but a rusty sign indicating this was German Embassy property. The 1980s saw the arrival of the futuristic all-in-one German chancery-residence and its frigid Bauhaus interiors, certainly not a candidate for any architectural award.

Aside from academic establishments, in its early years the island hosted a series of colonial and foreign institutions including German and Swiss archaeological foundations, the Anglo-American Hospital and the all-important British *Sirdaria*—home of the British Commander of the Egyptian Army.

A long gone pre-Second World War landmark was the celebrated Thomas Cook & Son docking facility. Visits to Luxor and Aswan aboard Cook's legendary paddle steamers (from the *SS Setti* to the *PS Karnak* and *Tewfik*) began and ended at Gezira's southern embankment. It was also at Cook's Gezira wharf that several dozen cases containing objects from Tutankhamun's tomb arrived on Monday, May 21, 1923, en route from Luxor to the Egyptian Museum.

An old Nile-side landmark can still be found, all but hidden below the 6th of October Bridge. This is Al Gezira Mosque, the island's first Muslim place of worship. Constructed in 1876 by Khedive Ismail, it was completely restored during the reign of King Farouk, who prayed there on its re-inauguration. Another Zamalek mosque visited by the young king during Friday prayers is the Hassan Nachat Pasha Mosque, designed by Nasr al Din al Beyali, on Bahgat Ali Street. Egypt's wartime ambassador to London commissioned it in 1941-2 in memory of his first wife.

And unless someone proves otherwise, Gezira's first private apartment building is Charles Baehler's Gezira Mansions, designed in 1907 by Ernest Jaspar of Heliopolis fame. Today the building is better known as Emarat al Yemeni (Yemeni Building) despite 'Gezireh House' written across its grand entrance. Observe the following advertising that appeared in the June 5, 1908, *Egyptian Gazette*:

> GHEZIREH HOUSE, GHEZIREH. First class flats to be let in a modern, up to date building, close to Ghezireh Palace Hotel and Khedivial Sporting Club. Latest perfected system of sanitary installation; automatic electric lift; every convenience. Apply to Anglo-Belgian Co. of Egypt, Ltd., Savoy Chambers, Cairo."

Prior to the First World War, Café Gezira was one of the island's only places to relax and later to gamble according to turn of the century travel writer Amédée Baillot de Guerville. This lone convenience on an island mostly devoted to villas and palaces came courtesy of two Italians, Messrs. Dalbagni and Corbetta. In her book *New Egypt*, published in 1905, de Guerville describes Café Gezira as:

A curious roofless building of white stone, made up of a stage and boxes, which is used, I believe, in summer as a café-concert. An enterprising gentleman attempted a year or two ago to establish there a miniature Monte Carlo. He arrived one day with his luggage composed exclusively of roulette boards and pretty women, the latter more charming than virtuous, and was convinced, that, armed with irresistible weapons, he would encounter little difficulty in plucking rich visitors and spoiling the Egyptians.

The only diplomatic agency in Gezira prior to the First World War was the Agence Diplomatique Néerlandaise that moved to Zamalek on November 1, 1912, and had as its address: Mr. P. C. van Lennep, Villa Beauregard-sur-Nil, Gezira. Unlike today, most diplomatic agencies were then situated in downtown Cairo and Kasr al Dubara.

One year after the first Royal Agricultural Society Exhibition took place in makeshift quarters, the Cotton Museum was inaugurated in 1899. Gezira was now host to Egypt's first modern-day exhibition hall. The annual agricultural fairs at Gezira would become world-famous. In 1988, these same fair grounds became home to Egypt's Japanese-built opera house.

And just as Khedive Ismail had commissioned the building of his summer palace of Gezira in 1866, other members of the Egyptian royal family elected to live on his island the following century. Two of their palaces were converted after 1952 into government-owned establishments. The palace of Prince Amr Ibrahim is now the Ceramic Museum and Palais Toussoun is today a branch of the Council of Ministers.

A latter-day museum, designed by Ramses Wissa Wassef, would appear on the island in 1960 housing the works of sculptor Mahmoud Mokhtar. Not too far from the Mokhtar Museum stands the former royal Rest House at the southern tip of the island, which served as the headquarters of the Revolutionary Command Council after July 23, 1952. A 1999 presidential ordinance (No. 204) has set it aside for a '1952 Revolution Museum' at an estimated cost of LE40 million.

Hardly anyone remembers that Gezira was once home to the Museum of Civilization, which opened in 1936 in the then imposing Grand Palais and Petit Palais, together occupying 5,000 square metres. These were designed by Mustafa Fahmi Pasha and executed by Giovanni Bianchi Contractors. The museum buildings and its annexes are located behind the opera house and have been empty for the past few decades awaiting some form of revival.

The only Gezira institution that can rightly claim to have preceded the founding of the township by two decades is the Gezira Sporting Club, which of course features later in this book. But for the time being let us briefly dwell on its poorer cousin, the *Nadi al Ahli* (National Club).

In an interview published in *Al Mussawar* April 9, 1937, the National Club's first secretary, Mohammed Sharif Bey, recounts that it was thanks to a suggestion made by Omar Lotfy Bey in 1907 that the club came into being that year. Lotfy, then a senior member of the Department of Education, was concerned that young Egyptian graduates, especially those who had returned from scholarships in Europe, had nowhere to go for sports and leisure activities.

His like-minded colleagues immediately picked up Lotfy's suggestion. A petition was presented to the government's financial advisor, Mr. Mitchell Aines, who quickly agreed, recommending that a *de novo* club board be formed post-haste. Four feddans were set aside on the island of Gezira at a symbolic rent of one piastre per annum.

In order to raise capital for the start-up expenses and modest infrastructure, bearer shares were issued and divided among the club's founding members. First to subscribe was Aziz Izzet Pasha, Egypt's future ambassador to the UK. Next came a dozen or so members of Egypt's pasha-politicians, many of whom would soon occupy senior cabinet posts: Hussein Roushdy, Abdel Khalek Sarwat, Idris Ragheb, Ali Abou al Fotouh, Amin Sami, Daoud Rateb, Ahmed Fouad Anwar, and Engineer Ismail Sirry. The latter kindly volunteered to design, free of charge, the clubhouse and other such amenities.

The club's first president and treasurer were Mitchell Aines and Mohammed Ali Delawar respectively. The accounts were audited by none other than Talaat Harb, who would later spearhead the creation of Banque Misr and the Misr group of companies.

Despite the monies raised, the club was still short of cash and ultimately had to turn to the Ministry of Education for financial assistance. Enthused with the idea of a club for young Egyptians, the minister disbursed the amount of LE200. In token of its appreciation, the club board offered him the post of first honorary president. Thus, Saad Zaghloul Pasha's name would forever be associated with Egypt's National Club.

When Mitchell Aines resigned as president, he was fittingly replaced by the club's main benefactor Aziz Izzet Pasha.

From empress to emir

Contrary to several Marriott Hotel printouts, the purchase of the Gezira Palace Hotel by the Lotfallah family did not take place in 1908, but was instead concluded in 1919. For nearly two decades prior to that date the palace had been an exclusive hotel.

The building's early history has become a well-worn cliché: this was the palace that Khedive Ismail built to host Empress Eugenie during the 1869 celebrations marking the opening of the Suez Canal. Even so, two minor footnotes are worth adding. Emperor Franz-Josef of Austria-Hungary also stayed there in 1869 with a retinue of 40 courtiers. And as of January 17, 1873, and for 40 days thereafter, the palace became a much-talked about venue for the highly publicised khedivial nuptials, when Khedive Ismail simultaneously married off three of his sons and one of his daughters.

The palace was completed in 1869 in time for the Suez Canal celebrations, but not all of it was hastily built in a matter of months as claimed by a multitude of writers. That description would only apply to the Salamlek area, built to accommodate the khedive's imperial guests.

Chief Court Architect Julius Franz Pasha designed the palace, concentrating his efforts on the main building (today the hotel's central block). Assisting him in some aspects of the project was his colleague Del Rosso. Other parts of the Gezira Palace complex were handed out to different architects. Of the many different sections, only the U-shaped Salamlek remains, acting as the nucleus of the Marriott Hotel.

One of the first sections to go was a large circular gazebo building that gave way to the Boulaq (Abou al Ela) Bridge in 1911. Hardly anyone remembers the Haramlek Buildings since these disappeared in the 1920s. That section of the former palace-turned-Gezira Hotel was for guests who wanted year-around accommodations. These were eventually replaced by the twin Baehler Buildings located on 26th July (ex-Fouad, ex-Boulaq) Street.

Last to go was the *Küçük*, also called the Kiosk, a long narrow wood and plaster building decorated with ornate cast iron trimmings designed by Karl Von Diebitsch. He also designed the iron decorations currently found on the main building. The Kucuk became Casino al Gezira before being transformed into the Lotfallah family *daira*. Ultimately, it was slated to become an exhibition space. On Tuesday, May 31, 1955, on the eve of an

International Tourist Art Exhibition scheduled to take place there, the Kucuk was gutted by fire. The site is now the location of All Saints' Cathedral.

All these buildings were surrounded by the extensive palace gardens, which spread over 60 acres and were reportedly created piece by piece by court landscapers Gustave Delchevalerie and Jean Pierre Barillet-Deschamps. The latter was also responsible for the famous Ezbekiya Gardens in downtown Cairo.

The first royal visitors to stay in the palace were not Empress Eugenie and her retinue, but the Prince and Princess of Wales in March 1869. It wasn't until November that the empress arrived. Her rooms in the palace were supposedly replicas of her rooms at the royal palace in France. The rest of the palace furnishings were also mostly imported from France.

A few days after Eugenie's departure, Emperor Franz-Josef of Austria arrived with his 40-strong entourage. They were divided between the Salamlek, which housed Counts Frederic Ferdinand Beust, Jules Andrassy, Plener and William de Tegetthoff, and the Haramlek where Count Anton de Prokesch-Osten, Austria's Ambassador to Constantinople, reluctantly took up temporary quarters complaining that he had thus been downgraded. To calm him down, he was told his rooms had been occupied by no less than the most beautiful royal princesses and harem *houris*.

Following Ismail's exile in 1879, the palace was appropriated by the State in lieu of his outstanding debts.

By 1897 the now-abandoned palace was taken over by the Egyptian Hotels Company Limited and began operating as the Gezira Palace Hotel. There would be two further hotel incarnations on this site in the ensuing century. In the mid-1960s, there was the Omar Khayam, and two decades later the Marriott came into being.

According to a November 1903 newspaper clipping, the Gezira Palace had just completed major renovations and improvements. These included the refurbishing of 80 bedrooms, the rearrangement of the Grand Restaurant and the re-modelling of the billiard room and bar. One of the participating architects in the transformation of the palace into a hotel was the Italian, Angelo Ercolani.

Moreover, a fence was put up around the entire perimeter of the garden to ensure some privacy. In the same year, improvements were made to the steam ferry service from the hotel to the eastern bank of the Nile where one linked up with the tramway network. The ferry service was discontinued in

July 1912, when the Boulaq Bridge was inaugurated.

As befitting a palace originally built for an empress, the Gezira Palace thrived on an exclusive composite of European aristocracy. To keep up with its clientele, the management periodically rejuvenated the palace adding staterooms and bathrooms, expanding public areas, and refurbishing apartments located in the Haramlek section so that guests wanting to remain after the hotel closed down for the long summer season could do so in opulent comfort. Agatha Christie was one of these guests. In 1910 she and her mother spent a leisurely three months at the Gezira Palace Hotel.

The Great War signalled a slow death for the Gezira Palace Hotel. Aside from losing many of its habitués, whose empires had vanished, the entire Gezira complex was transformed into a British military hospital subsequently to become the headquarters of the Inland Water Transport Authority and other army services.

After the loss of five consecutive tourist seasons, the entire hotel industry was in dire straits. Baehler's decision to unload a costly company asset could not be held against him.

The first hotel phase came to an end with the historic resolution to auction off the Gezira Palace Hotel on October 30, 1919, during the Egyptian Hotel Company's twenty-second annual board meeting in London. The incumbent directors knew better than to go against a recommendation put forward by Monsieur Charles Baehler for he was now regarded as Egypt's undisputed hospitality czar. With an empire that included nearly every luxury hotel in the country, Baehler owned the largest hotel group south of the Mediterranean and was regarded as the ultimate authority when it came to tourism and hotel management.

Enter a white knight bearing LE140,000—allegedly the sum offered by the family of Habib Lotfallah Pasha (no 'prince' talk yet) for the purchase of the Gezira Palace Hotel, lock, stock and khedivial barrel. The patriarch of a rich land-owning family that produced several Syrian nationalist leaders, diplomats and legislators, Habib Lotfallah would receive his munificent hereditary title of *emir* (prince) seven months after the purchase of the hotel. Sharif Hussein of Mecca, whose newly founded kingdom would shortly collapse, conferred the title on him.

Habib Lotfallah was 94 years old when the purchase of the Gezira Palace Hotel was concluded. When he died a few months later, his impressive princely funeral cortege did not depart from the palace gates of Gezira but left from the old family homestead in Fagallah instead. It was left to Lotfallah's descendants to enjoy their new palace along with their new title.

For the next 42 years, the Gezira Palace would be known as Palais Lotfallah. It was there that some of Cairo's most extravagant parties were held. "They would have made Shahrazade's eyes pop out!" exclaimed a regular but seemingly envious guest, who went on to describe her hosts as having given "a new dimension to the word *parvenu*." One of the party-givers was Michel Lotfallah, described by journalist Maurice Fargeon in 1931 as *le leopard*, a reference to his hardy handshake and his tireless roaming of the power chanceries, bidding for no less than the throne of Syria. His brother George controlled the all-important Lotfallah *daira* that looked after vast agricultural properties. George also made sure that he had time to spare for his famous racehorse stables.

In 1961, the government, as part of further socialist restructuring, sequestered the historic property from the Lotfallahs. They were given a year to move out before the palace was handed over to the Egyptian General Organization for Tourism and Hotels. The Lotfallah Palace became the Omar Khayam Hotel. The apparatchiks had arrived, bringing with them an endless reservoir of tastelessness. The former Gezira Palace was a good place to start, hence the wooden cabanas planted all over the legendary garden with a swimming pool replacing the khedivial millpond. Neo-kitsch had come to replace faux-Empire.

The status quo continued for another two decades until the entire property transmogrified into the Marriott Hotel. It would be another ten years, following a complex three-way legal battle that pitted the heirs against the state and the Marriott Company, before the Lotfallah descendants finally received compensation for the loss of their family home.

Socio-cultural imperialism

While no one knows the exact date when Gezira Sporting Club first opened, 1883 is a good guess, for it is during that time that Great Britain consolidated its military hold over Egypt.

The club was already a famous landmark by the close of the nineteenth century as noted by guidebooks and other literature from the time. Back then it was called the Khedivial Sporting Club (KSC) in honour of Khedive Mohammed Tewfik. It was during his reign and due to his largesse that the club was created for the benefit of the British Army and the army of British administrators known then as Anglo-Egyptians. They formed that caste of administrators who acted as guardians of Britain's interests in Egypt during the iron-fisted reign of two powerful proconsuls, Lords Cromer and Kitchener.

Douglas Sladen wrote the following in *Egypt and the English* (London, 1908):

> Cairo has several clubs, but only two are patronised by the best English people, for the luxurious Khedivial is essentially a club for foreigners and Gyppies. I refer to the Turf Club and the Khedivial Sporting Club. With the latter no fault can be found. Its subscription is low and it gives members all kinds of advantages and attractions. It would be charming even if it had no sports, for its wealth of flowers, its broad stretches of turf, its southern trees and beauty.

His use of the term "foreigners" meant anyone *not* British with the exception of the indigenous population for whom he reserved the term "Gyppies".

To get a better idea of the prevailing attitudes, let's refer to some of the contemporary writings regarding the Gezira Club. In *Egypt—Old and New*, Percy F. Martin mentions the Gezira Club in these terms:

> Whilst its hospitable doors have always been opened to visitors non-resident in the capital, the sole requisite for entrance having been a personal introduction from a member, exception has been taken not without some

reason to the policy which tends to bring about the exclusion of the Egyptians from any active participation in the management of the sports; neither have they been encouraged to become members of the Club, except in certain cases. None the less, the institution was primarily established partly with their assistance and certainly with the aid of their monetary contributions.

W. Basil Worsfold, an observant literary barrister who visited Egypt in the winter of 1898-9, remarks in *The Redemption of Egypt* that:

> The English residents have no more to do with the picturesque ruins and mud-heaps of Medieval Cairo than the average West End Londoner has to do with the Mile End Road and Tower Hamlets. Except when they wanted to show a visitor the tombs of the Caliphs or the Pyramids they only left their villas in the European quarter to drive to their offices or the Gezira Club.

Citing the unofficial British headquarters in Cairo, Sir Ronald Storrs writes in *Orientations* how:

> The Turf Club, situated in the Sharia al Magrabi was the fenced city of refuge of the higher British community, many of whom spent anything between one and five hours daily within its walls. The Sporting Club at Gezira, on an admirable site presented in the eighties by the Khedive Tewfik and improved since then almost out of recognition, was the other British headquarters. It was difficult for foreigners to be elected and not easy for Egyptians even to make use of either Club; as I discovered by the glances cast in my direction when I came in with one of the few Egyptian members to play tennis.

The Egyptian tennis player Storrs mentions would become Prime Minister Mohammed Mahmoud Pasha.

Notwithstanding the explicit and implicit racist attitudes nestling in the above accounts, it appears that one of the club's fortes was its flora. Not surprising since the Gezira Sporting Club's 150 acres were carved out of the khedivial botanical gardens, hence the acacias and jacarandas that adorned the area.

Once the land was formally leased to the British military command, club rules were chartered and the land demarcated into several recreational playing grounds. At first, the club was just for the use of the British Army of Occupation. "It is on Gezira polo grounds that officers of the Cavalry Brigade are tested for military efficiency and fitness for command. And on Gezira tennis courts that examinations are held to decide as to the desirability or otherwise of retaining in the service the British officials of the government," remarked a former British administrator in one of his recollections. He was of course referring to peacetime England when inter-regimental wars were played out on polo fields.

What the administrator forgot to add was that over the years, the polo-playing cavalry brigades, whether at the Wellington Club in Bombay, the Calcutta Sporting Club, or the Khedivial Sporting Club in Cairo, were prime attractions for British debutantes, especially those who coveted a husband with a position. These fair maidens who braved the journey to the colonies were nicknamed the *Fishing Fleet*, and they tended to arrive en masse in Egypt or India during polo season. The debs who remained behind in England had to make do with leftovers at the Hurlingham or Rowhampton Clubs. With respect to these elitist clubs, the Khedivial Sporting Club, with its 365 days of sunshine, was the cream of the crop.

As the British rank and file expanded in Egypt, it was thought civilians would enhance the Khedivial Sporting Club's recreational activities. A moving spirit behind the club's creation was a Captain Humphreys of the Mounted Infantry. Not only did he participate in the selection of the club grounds, he was also instrumental in the design of its first racecourse, which had a distance of a little over one mile. It was also on the club's racecourse that he passed away when, one morning, he was thrown off his horse in front of the main stand. The unlucky Humphreys landed right on the brick wall breaking his neck. Unable to move, he lay paralysed at the same spot with a tent pitched over him until his family arrived from England. They were just in time to bid him farewell.

Heywood Walker Setton-Karr of the Gordon Highlanders replaced Humphreys. He was the first in a long line of British secretaries that only ended in the mid-1950s with Captain Eric Charles Pilley. Although Setton-Karr's position carried with it heavy responsibilities, it did not deter him from his other activities and pursuits, which included the discovery of emerald mines in Egypt's deserts.

On February 4, 1903, at the club's Extraordinary General Meeting, chaired by the British Proconsul Lord Cromer, it was agreed that the position of club secretary would no longer be a part-time job. Candidates from outside the British officer class were invited to apply so that after the departure of then-sitting honorary secretary, Captain Alexander Harman, a full-time administrator would be hired. The name of Harry Aspinall of the Turf Club was suggested at an annual salary of 200 pounds sterling.

According to *Twentieth Century Impressions of Egypt* (1909), club membership was restricted to applicants elected by the committee on the recommendation of two members. Army officers excluded, the roll numbered 750 members. It was also stated that an initiation fee of LE2 had to be paid. The various subscriptions were as follows: Life members, LE50; resident members (married) LE5; unmarried LE3.6; country members, LE2. This latter meant those living outside a radius of 23 kilometres from the Cairo Post Office on Midan al Ataba. Guests could visit the club accompanied by members, purchasing day passes for 5 piastres.

It was no wonder that people vied for club membership. In 1914, the Khedivial Sporting Club boasted a tea pavilion, four polo grounds, two racecourses, a 18-hole golf course, six squash courts, 13 tennis courts, and eight croquet lawns. The club's 750 British members were enjoying their finest colonial hours and at the top of this all-powerful community was the British Proconsul, who by tradition was also the club's president.

A day at the races

One of the first recorded horse races at the Khedivial Sporting Club took place in 1885. The starter was the commanding officer of the Egyptian Army, otherwise known as the *Sirdar*, who at the time was General Frances Wallace Grenfell (afterwards First Baron of Kilvey). Grenfell had been present at the battle of Tel al Kebir, which ended with the defeat of Orabi Pasha on September 13, 1882, and the start of the 72-year British military occupation of Egypt.

Another veteran Anglo-Egyptian was the club's first steward, General Charles Coles Pasha. It was Coles who remarked; "Egypt's climate made it possible to follow the races without recourse to binoculars," and that "the colours of the different jockeys were discernible even at a distance." Coles was, however, dissatisfied with the horses. "The European breeds, unlike the smaller Arabians, could not negotiate the course's sharp corners with comparable agility." It appears this problem was the focus of considerable debate during the club's early years.

While jockeys were imported without impediment from England, Arabian horses had to be smuggled from Syria via Al Arish and Kantarah, Sinai, circumventing Turkish restrictions on their import into Egypt. A regular winner in these events was Hadeed, an Arabian belonging to the club's senior trainer, Mr. Langdon Rees. The habitual runner-up was called Sir Hugh. Tired of being shown up again and again by the Arabian favourite, the Anglo-Egyptians clamoured for the English mare, Skittles, a competitor in the same weight and league. But first, Skittles had to be sent for from Malta. When the eventful day arrived, the mare won the day to the jubilation of the Britons whose pride had been bruised for some time now. It was a mournful native crowd that made its way to the Cairo mainland across Kasr al Nil Bridge.

The club's more popular races included the Khedivial Steeplechase, the Newmarket Stakes, the Jubilee Stakes, the Eclipse Stakes and the Koubbeh Handicap. Although Egypt's racecourses were off limits to bookies, this did not stop the stakes and profits reaching stratospheric heights during the First World War, a fact mostly attributed to the arrival of the Australian soldiers who proved to be fanatic gamblers.

The winter race meetings that started in January were interrupted in March by the Gymkhana. Taking part in this annual sport and play event was the upper crust of the British community. They arrived in their boaters and straw hats, armed with their eternal companion, the fly-whisk. Moving effortlessly between the members of Cairo's lofty society of mutual admirers, serving as an astute reminder that this was still Africa, were the turbaned Nubian *sofragis*, balancing silver platters of game pie, roast beef, pork chops and cucumber sandwiches.

The ruddy-faced, thirsty English sire had his choice of sparkling wine, Pimms or Campbells. Also present at these events were the senior army officers, their horses and their wives (in that order); hence the Regimental Races, the Lloyd Lindsay, the Polo Race, the Green Howard Sweepstakes and the Horseback Musical Chairs.

Polo matches, of which ten or 12 were held in the course of the year, were the second most important social events after the races. In 1908-9, a Challenge Cup was added to the polo trophies, courtesy of Seifallah Youssri

Pasha, whose name would be linked to the Gezira Club for the next 40 years. He was one of the club's first Egyptian members and played polo on its fields with the Prince of Wales in June 1922. A club devotee, Youssri Pasha was nominated to be its first Egyptian vice-president. When he died on the golf course on December 26, 1949, the sportsman-pasha was 80 years old.

The ultimate club –
perils of membership

Before he left Egypt for the last time on June 18, 1914, Consul-General Field Marshal Lord Herbert Horatio Kitchener made two recommendations concerning the Khedivial Sporting Club. Firstly, Egyptian members—and there were very few—were to be barred from membership. "No more natives!" The made-in-Liverpool iron picket fence surrounding the club's perimeter had suddenly become an ugly separator.

Secondly, the khedive should be removed from the club's honorary patronage. What Kitchener actually meant by this latter recommendation was that Abbas Hilmi should be removed from Egypt's throne altogether. Kitchener's disdain for his former employer was public knowledge, prompting his recurrent recommendations that someone more agreeable to British interests replace the pro-German khedive.

Attitudes towards 'native' members of exclusive British clubs remained an issue for the length of England's reign as a colonial power all over the world. Percy F. Martin comments on this prickly issue:

> Want of consideration for the wants of the native population particularly of the better classes, permanently inhabiting the countries in which British men and women but temporarily reside, has frequently provided one of the greatest drawbacks to the gaining of popularity and friendship, even where other of our national virtues are generously recognised. It was once said by George Eliot that British selfishness is so robust and many-clutching that, well encouraged, it easily devours all sustenance away from our poor little scruples.

Peter Mansfield in *The British in Egypt* talks of Britain's muddled motives in Egypt. Concerning Kitchener and the Gezira Club he explains how:

> Kitchener was not in favour of British social exclusiveness. In India he had deplored it and blamed it on the club system. In Cairo he did take fairly ruthless action to force the Egyptians members to resign from the famous Gezira Club, but this was not out of any belief in social 'apartheid' but because complaints that members of the khedive's circles were using the club to express anti-British opinions.

Shortly after Kitchener became his country's War Minister in 1914, a volunteer reserve unit was formed from among Gezira Club's able-bodied members, including the 50-year-old *Bimbashi* (officer) Joseph McPherson, subject of that now-famous book *The Man Who Loved Egypt*. It would be thanks to Kitchener's recommendation that the unit, which called itself Pharaoh's Foot, had an all-British character, for by now there were no 'foreigners' or 'Gyppies' left in the club.

Kitchener's other recommendation was realised on December 20, 1914, when the khedive's compliant uncle was placed on the throne of Egypt with the new title of Sultan. With the last of the khedives gone, it was time to find a new name for that great swathe of parkland heretofore known as the Khedivial Sporting Club.

From a semi-autonomous Ottoman *willaya*, Egypt had now become a British protectorate so that the club's Anglo-Egyptian squatters were now officially the country's masters.

The Gezira Sporting Club's apartheid membership crisis was resolved when a small number of Egyptians were allowed back in after the war. They were either related to the reigning royal family or members of the western-educated gentry—that is to say from polite society. To discourage other Egyptian *wannabes*, the trickle was subjected to a convoluted quota and vetting system. Star polo player Victor Mansour Semeika, the son of Wassef Semeika Pasha, Egypt's Coptic former Minister of Communication, had to wait several years before he was invited to join in 1933.

Other Egyptians visited as guests of British members. A classic example is how Kadria Foda, the young daughter of a Cairene notable, made it inside the Gezira Club courtesy of Miss King, her British governess. And whenever Foda and her sisters ran into one or the other Egyptian families on the club grounds, the first furtive query was "How did you make it in, have you become members?" It is, however, doubtful that the young Fodas realised at the time that when it came to membership at the Gezira Club, British governesses represented the base of the colonial administration's totem pole. They were only allowed in so that they could bring comfort to young, single members of the British military.

Interwar expansion

In time for the 1929 Christmas dance, a new LE5,500 dining building, with a veranda facing the cricket pitch, was inaugurated. The firm D.C.M. Brooks was commended for completing the construction in record time thus avoiding a daily LE5 penalty for any delays. The new premises' oak parquet made an excellent dance floor and meals could now be served throughout the year. Above the dinner lounge was an assembly room with a central well looking down on the hall below. It is from there that pretty maidens and wallflowers watched the dances without too much embarrassment. Tea was served and family bridge played on the new building's upper floor. Despite its apparent advantages, there were quite a few members who had been against the project, especially when it meant sacrificing the ladies' rooms, the squash courts and the secretary's office. Moreover, several palm trees, the old cricket pavilion, plus two croquet lawns also had to go.

Black tie celebrations for the new acquisition were hardly over when another part of the club met with unexpected disaster. In May 1930, fire broke out destroying the polo stand. The club's mowing machines, responsible for the excellent year-round maintenance of the greens, were also decimated. While the stands were insured, the machines were not and LE500 had to be raised. The club ladies got together and several successful fundraising bazaars were held. By the time the 1930-31 polo season rolled around, all was back in place and the season's nine tournaments were played out according to schedule. With Japan's Count Nakko on hand to partake in the Visitor's Cup, the season's launcher, that year's polo turned out to be exceptional.

In 1948, it was decided the time had come to renovate the lucrative racing facility that consisted of three separate stands: the King's Stand, the

Grand Stand and the Public Stand. At the club's Extraordinary General Assembly of March 1949, a motion was approved to build a new all-encompassing concrete stand at a cost of LE50,000. In November of the same year, the bleachers were inaugurated, thereby doubling the seating capacity to 1,000 spectators.

Ever since 1907, Gezira Sporting Club was the official home of Egypt's lawn tennis. Open tournaments and championships were held on its clay courts at regular intervals. As of 1925, international celebrities took part in these widely attended events. Despite the launch of the Egyptian Lawn Tennis Association (ELTA) Championship in 1934, Gezira Sporting Club continued to offer its two cups: the Doherty, which was awarded to the winners of the singles, and the Slazenger for the doubles. Until 1929, the former was the preserve of Auguste Zerlendi, an Alexandrian Greek, who rose to the top of international tennis. Another Doherty Cup contender was Sir Cecil Campbell, Marconi's representative in Egypt.

The early 1930s saw the arrival of Joujou and Pierrot Grandguillot. They were consistent finalists, only to be replaced later in the decade by Gezira Sporting Club favourites René Dukich, André Najar and Mahmoud Talaat.

It would take another world war to interrupt the tennis season at the Gezira Sporting Club. Moreover, plans for a new LE40,000 centre court had to be deferred to March 1952 at which time Rolando Del Bello trounced Egypt's Marcel Cohen during that year's International Tennis Championship.

One of the first shows put on at the new centre court was a marvellous performance by the Harlem Globe Trotters in August 1953. That same winter saw Egypt's first ever "Holiday on Ice" extravaganza, and in July 1954, the centre court was transformed into a *corrida* to accommodate Egypt's first and last bullfight. But before giant basketball players and matadors appeared at the club, there were the thousands of Allied military who invaded it during the Second World War.

Throughout the war years, Gezira Sporting Club brimmed with British military personnel, many of whom lived in Zamalek. The more privileged occupied villas and apartments overlooking the club. The polo fields and surrounding flora were welcome sights, especially the firs from Aberdeen, the azaleas from Sussex and the beds of lavender from London.

Except for special occasions, privates and anyone else below the rank of officer were not allowed on Club grounds. There were enough officers as it was to fill the place. With so many eligible uniforms, the maidens from

Cairo's large Anglophile crowd were forever hanging out at the newly-built Lido in search of an M.R.S. Degree in Family Relations. Many succeeded with flying British colours. Every other day the newspapers announced this or that engagement. Not surprising then that Lucette Sapriel, Denise Harari, Mimi Wissa and Yvette Zarb, became Mrs. Makepeace, Mrs. Guysales, Mrs. Spider and Lady Toplofty.

Tweak the lion by the tail

December 9, 1951, witnessed a deadlock between Egypt and Britain over the Sudan Question and Britain's refusal to remove 54,000 unwelcome troops from the Canal Zone, which was bubbling with unrest. Mustafa al Nahas, prime minister of a nominally independent Egypt, decided the time had come to tweak the lion's tail where it would hurt the most.

Indeed, Gezira Club's political symbolism was not lost on Egypt's nationalist politicians. Following a historic cabinet meeting, Minister of Interior Fouad Serageddin Pasha tersely announced that the Gezira Sporting Club would be taken over "for public utility purposes and for the construction of the projected Mohammed Ali stadium." In other words, the last British bastion in the region was to be Egyptianised. Moreover, all remaining British officials serving in universities, government schools, the Ministry of Public Works and the Egyptian State Railways were hereby dismissed.

At that time, the 2,453 strong membership of the club was divided into 743 Britons, 594 foreigners—many of them more British then the British themselves—and 1,116 Egyptians. The latter were those from society's top drawer having made it past the condescending vetting committee. Some of these privileged folks thought that appending the 'GSC' membership next to their name in *Who's Who*, was tantamount to receiving an OBE.

Even though Egyptians—mostly pashas and beys—made up the majority of the club's membership, the picture was very different in the boardroom where Britons were still in control, prompting the French Ambassador to exclaim, "*Les Anglais sont toujours chez eux!*" The future prime minister of France, Monsieur Couve du Murville, couldn't have been more mistaken.

Little did he realise how the looming events were going to bring down the worn-out British Empire.

January 12, 1952. "Gezira Sporting Club Races Cancelled During Weekend," read the morning headlines. As far as anyone could remember, only the First World War and the murder of the *Sirdar* (Commander-in-Chief) of the Egyptian Army had caused the club races to be suspended. Until the previous day it was polo as usual, with a gripping match pitting the home team comprising Saleh Foda, Eric Tyrell-Martin, Mohammed Lamloum and Victor Mansour Semeika against the Crescents. The home team had won 12-7.

The wheels of Egyptianisation, however, were starting to roll. The day's events can be summarised as follows. The club's Egyptian vice-president, Cherif Sabry Pasha (the king's uncle), calls on the governorate to discuss expropriation and compensation measures. The incredulous Britons, from their ambassador to the humblest nanny, are aghast. The British Embassy in Kasr al Dubara where the portraits of so many of the club's former presidents still hang, burns the midnight oil.

January 24. At the club's General Assembly, it is announced that Britain's ambassador, Sir Ralph Stevenson, has resigned from the presidency. Sir Thomas Russell Pasha, former chief of Cairo police for four decades (1917-46) and the club's vice-president, tenders his resignation. With them depart the rest of the General Committee, consisting of Chairman Henry Francis and board members James S. Coxon, Walter Arthur Constant, Joseph P. Sheridan, Colonel P. C. Lord, Colonel Thomas M. Moore, Seifallah Khairy Bey, Abdel Salaam al Shazly Pasha, Mohammed Sultan Pasha and Soliman Naguib Bey. Former cricket champion, R. Etches, also steps down, thus vacating the sinecure post of acting-secretary that he had occupied since 1928.

An Extraordinary General Assembly is scheduled for February 8, at which time a new committee would be elected. According to a press release, these measures were "Taken to ensure the continuation of the club in accordance of the new circumstances aiming at Egyptianising it."

January 26, Black Saturday. Zamalek is a ghost island. Instead of preparing for one of her well-attended après-polo soirées, Cairo hostess Kadria Foda watches in disbelief from her fourth floor apartment on Gezira Street as downtown Cairo burns.

Foreigners perish in the Turf Club fire while other British properties in

Cairo are torched by an unruly mob. Across from Foda's apartment stands an abandoned Gezira Sporting Club. Cairo's great green lung had stopped breathing. Had its Egyptianisation been delayed by a few days perhaps it too would have gone up in smoke.

The self-important *Ingilizis* and their self-serving toffee-nosed committees were gone at last. No more Empire Day celebrations and Coronation Dances. No more parades and searchlight tattoos on the club's polo grounds with poppies raining down from the skies. Also gone were the wartime parties for two or three thousand British soldiers at a time with tea served by Lady Lampson. No more provocative strains of *God Save the King* each time Sir Miles heaved into his box at the races, dressed in his gray frock coat and topper.

The days of the Newmarket Stakes had ended. Even the *hedayas* or black kites seemed intoxicated, for they too remembered how the British ambassador had found perverted pleasure in shooting them down because they mistook his golf balls for eggs! '*Ma'a alf salaam ya Khawaga Lambson,*' they seemed to cry as they circled far above the Egyptianised Gezira Sporting Club.

February 29. On that leap-year day, a new Gezira Sporting Club board of Egyptian pashas and beys is duly elected. A downsized Captain Eric C. Pilley is asked to stay on as club secretary until a suitable replacement can be found. As it turned out, the club secretary remained another four years. Another first in the club's history was the printing of the assembly announcement in both English and Arabic. The latter had never been seen before within the club sanctum.

The Gezira Sporting Club had reached a turning point and it was now open season for the new administration to assert itself and to purge what remained of the British legacy. The new board's first resolution was to change the club's name to NASR. The acronym stood for Nadi Amir al Said al Riadi (Prince of Said Sporting Club), honouring the six-week-old heir to the throne whose official title was Prince of Said (Upper Egypt). Even during the tottering monarchy's last days, fawning courtiers and obliging notables were not lacking. Only this particular bunch seemed unaware their titles and privileges had a few more months to go before it all came tumbling down around them. In this instance, however, no one was going to begrudge the Revolutionary Council for giving back to the club its old name.

1955. The former Egyptian ambassador to Washington, Maitre

Mahmoud Hassan ('maitre' had replaced pasha after 1952), abruptly resigns from the club's honorary presidency. An upright gentleman, he refused to agree to the government's decision to expropriate several feddans of the club grounds, entailing the amputation of nine holes from the world-famous golf course. An officer promptly replaced the diplomat.

As though mirroring what was taking place in the rest of Egypt, the club's civilian administration was replaced by a military version, an action that in many ways brought the club back to where it all began when the British military brass ran the show. Paradoxically, Gezira Club would outlast the imperial power that created it but would continue to perpetuate that twisted spirit of selectiveness, a poignant legacy of its founders. Today, like so many years ago, Gezira Club still stands apart from society at large, imperious and lofty with only one kilometre separating it from another world called Imbaba.

1959. John M. Keshishian was in Egypt on an assignment for National Geographic. He stopped at the Cairo Tower to take photos of the city from above. Lo and behold, military helicopter pilots were landing and taking off from part of the Gezira Club grounds temporarily used as a training pad. Many years later military helicopters would use the club grounds again, once in order to bring Gamal Abdel Nasser's coffin from Koubbeh Palace for his historic funeral procession departing from Kasr al Nil Bridge. And again during the February 26-27, 1986, Central Security Police riots in Giza and Cairo when, for security reasons, the Queen of Denmark headed off by chopper from Gezira Sporting Club to Cairo International Airport.

1999. Kadria Foda, by now the Grande Dame of Cairo's salons, watches from her apartment building across the street as several surviving palms and other decorative trees are bulldozed in the Gezira Sporting Club to make way for new sporting facilities. Cairo's great outdoors is rapidly vanishing in an attempt to accommodate a struggling population that has quadrupled in four decades. The city's exhausted lungs are collapsing. Increasingly, its skyline is silhouetted against a dark, polluted pall evoking the Black Saturday of January 26, 1952, that fateful turning point in Egypt's history that was supposedly going to sweep all the wrongs of the past and remake the country for the better.

Home of the Sirdar

One of the very few times Gezira Sporting Club suspended its activities during Britain's occupation of Egypt was when Sir Lee Stack Pasha, *Sirdar* of the Egyptian Army, was assassinated in Cairo by an Egyptian nationalist. The club refrained from all social and sporting activities for two days. This unprecedented action on the part of its administrators attested to the importance of the victim and the magnitude of the crime.

Aside from the fact that he was vice-chairman of the club, the sirdar was also a Gezira resident, occupying one the largest properties on the island.

The *Sirdaria* fronted King Fouad Avenue (now 26th of July Street). Home to a beautiful lawn and clusters of tall trees, it stretched three blocks from just above what is now Brazil Street all the way to Shagaret al Durr Street. Not only was the thought of entering it next to impossible, passers-by avoided its sidewalk for fear of the choleric looks they would receive from the tall Sudanese sentry on duty.

Everyone knew the Sirdaria was impenetrable, and for good reason. It was the seat of British military intelligence in Egypt, ranking second only in colonial importance to the British Residence at Kasr al Dubara. And as the name indicates, the Sirdaria was the official seat of the sirdar, a borrowed Persian-Indian title denoting the British Commander-in-Chief of the Egyptian Army, who, due to another colonial quirk, was also Governor General of the Anglo-Egyptian Sudan.

Several sirdars made their mark on British imperial history, Horatio Kitchener and Reginald Wingate foremost among them. Kitchener later became Britain's proconsul in Egypt and when the First World War broke out, his country's Minister of War—the sirdar of all sirdars.

Sirdar from 1899 to 1916 and High Commissioner to Egypt from 1917 to 1919, Sir Reginald Wingate was instrumental in quelling Egypt and Sudan's nationalist movements. Small wonder Egyptian commuters cursed the *Ingilizi* commander whenever their tram passed the Sirdaria on its way to the pyramids.

But on November 19, 1924, the harmless curses turned into extreme action. On his way back to the Sirdaria, Wingate's successor, Sir Lee Stack and his Australian driver were shot at. Rather than drive to the Sirdaria, the motorcade drove straight to the British Embassy in Kasr al Dubara where an incensed High Commissioner, Lord Allenby, swore revenge.

A day later, Stack died at Gezira's Anglo-American Hospital. British reprisal came an hour after the state funeral.

To begin with, Egypt's popular Wafdist government was made to resign. The culprits had to be apprehended, brought to trial and hung for their deed. Then came the blood money. A check made out to the British government for half a million pounds was to be hand-delivered post-haste to the Residency. But more importantly, there was the prickly question of the Sudan. Ever since 1882, when Britain occupied Egypt, the Sudan had been under joint Anglo-Egyptian administration. The opportunity to get Egypt out of the deal was here at last. All Egyptian officers and regiments were ordered out of the Sudan.

Sudan was henceforth a British colony with the newly appointed governor general (Sir Geoffrey Archer) residing permanently in Khartoum. The Sirdaria in Cairo lost its duality and half its functions. Likewise, the title of sirdar lost its lustre and was seldom heard of again.

But it would appear that for all that British justice was swift and pitiless, not all of those implicated in the plot to assassinate the sirdar met the hangman's noose. Michel Habib, an Egyptian-Canadian recalls an incident that marked his youth:

Back in the forties, still a student at the Faculty of Engineering at Fouad University, I was waiting at a tram station opposite the Collège des Frères at Daher. I believe the street's name was Sharia al Daher. Suddenly a well-dressed man in a three-piece suit plus tarboush approached me and said "Ana Abdel Fattah Enayat" (I am Abdel Fattah Enayat). I knew whom the name designated from reading books on the 1919 Revolution and from my elders who never failed to mention the murder of the *sirdar* and the catastrophic results it caused.

Before me, stood the man who had been indicted for killing the *sirdar*. I stretched my hand and said 'Abdel Fattah Enayat?' He repeated, 'Ana Abdel Fattah Enayat.' We shook hands firmly. I wanted to tell him I knew who he was, but did not. I thought the firm handshake conveyed my feelings. I was so stunned I do not know what happened next. Maybe the tram I was waiting for came to the station and I hopped into it. Until this day the incident haunts me. Was he just released from jail? He seemed to want to tell the world "I am the man who suffered; the man who dared." Was I among the first people he met then? Or maybe he was wrongly accused, or framed. I still don't know. I am now 75 and have lived in Canada for over 30 years. "Ana Abdel Fattah Enayat" still resounds in my ears. I should have spoken longer; I wanted so much to tell him I knew what he felt. And I still see the man, the strange expression of his face, the suit, the tarboush, coming forward to me.

The last occupant of the Sirdaria was Al Ferik Major General Sir Charlton Watson Spinks Pasha, Inspector-General of the Egyptian Army. Relieved of his functions following the Anglo-Egyptian Treaty of 1936, Spinks and his wife moved into Nile View's fourth floor apartment at No. 18 Saray al Gezira Street. As a result, one of Zamalek's largest properties was looking for new tenants. Enter the Anglo-Egyptian Union on one side of the old Sirdaria, and the Egyptian Officer's Club on the other.

From its name alone, one imagines the Anglo-Egyptian Union to have been a beacon for better relations between Britons and Egyptians. Here at last was a venue that could erase unhappy memories of the Sirdaria and its former occupants. Well, no. As it turned out the Union section of the ex-Sirdaria was out of bounds to locals unless they had proper introductions—British, of course.

It took another world war to make the place more accessible. The Union's bar, library and garden became a favourite with Allied forces stationed in Egypt. Writers like Lawrence Durrell, Freya Stark and Olivia Manning also frequented the bar. Manning captured the mood of the establishment in *The Levantine Trilogy*. It was during this time that a few Egyptians succeeded in becoming members.

In the words of Artemis Cooper (*Cairo in the War*), the Union had become:

> A genteel place, but the influx of writers, refugees, and shade-seekers made it rather scruffy and battered about the edges. This contrasted sharply to the other side of the garden, which belonged to the Egyptian Officers' Club. Here, immaculately uniformed Egyptians, with rows of medals on their chests, play backgammon and baccarat.

Ironically, it was in that same Officer's Club, right under the Union's nose, that a *coup d'état* was already fermenting with one basic aim: toppling the monarchy and ousting what remained of British presence in Egypt.

The Richmond Villas

Clustered north-west of the Gezira Club, that most venerated of British sporting institutions, 19 government villas formed the fenced suburban refuge of the higher Anglo-Saxon community, many of whom started or ended their careers in British-occupied Egypt.

Constructed circa 1906-7, they were among the first villas in Zamalek. In *Orientations*, former British diplomat Sir Ronald Storrs mentions that there was some litigation over their original cost. Not only that, but there appears to have been some secondary litigation over the sum disbursed to the experts brought in to look into the matter—the prickly issue made the pages of the *Egyptian Gazette* in June 2, 1908:

GHEZIRAH ALMSHOUSES: Judgment in the case of S. Cademinos Tromboff and Fitzio v. Konessios and Allam was delivered last week. The Plaintiffs were the experts selected to examine into the condition of the government buildings at Ghezirah erected by the first defendant, and claimed the LE100 each, at which figure their fees were said to have been agreed. Defense was that the amount was excessive in view of the time occupied (viz. three months). Me. Cademinos, for himself and colleagues, pointed out that an accountant employed by Defendants in the same matter had received LE50 from Konessios for one week's work and that the sums now claimed were just and reasonable. The Tribunal decided in the favor of Plaintiffs with cost against Konessios including legal fees of himself and his co-defendant amounting to LE4 each.

Not mentioned in the *Gazette* is Ernest Tatham Richmond, chief architect of the 19 government-owned villas and son of English painter Sir William Blake Richmond. Having worked for an undisclosed period at the Ministry of Awqaf (religious endowments), Richmond had been exposed to a considerable wealth of Islamic monuments. Richmond supervised the restoration of parts of Al Aqsa Mosque in Jerusalem between 1917-19. Above King Solomon's Stables in the Temple area, he discovered the original furnaces and kilns in which the mosque tiles had been fired.

The villas were owned by the Ministry of Public Works and the first tenants were government officials from the ranks of the Anglo-Egyptian civil service. Their role was to restructure the country's governing institutions, transportation sector, educational system and agricultural production. Among them we find the three knighted engineers, Willcocks, Moncrieff and Garstin, who had Zamalek streets named after them, and Sir Ernest Dawson, Egypt's eminent Surveyor-General. Like Richmond, he would spend part of his career in Palestine surveying and mapping a portion of the Levant.

Their work completed, the engineers vacated the premises to be replaced by economic and political advisors. One such advisor was Sir Walter Smart. Those in the know claimed Smart (nicknamed Smartie) was the chief intelligence officer in Egypt, but to outsiders he was the all-important Oriental Secretary, one of the minor (yet key) positions in the Middle East. Invariably this meant he was the ablest hand at the British Embassy when it came to understanding the locals. "He's the Englishman who'll put these fellows in their places, and keep 'em there!" is how a seasoned colonialist described Smartie's position.

By tradition the three villas at the western end of Ibn Zanki Street were reserved for senior officials of the British community in Egypt. While Nos. 19 and 20 are still around today, No. 22, by far the largest of this unique collection of homes, was replaced in the 1950s by an apartment building designed and owned by architect Ali Labib Gabr.

Hardly anyone remembers that up to the end of the Second World War, Nos. 20 and 22 were contiguous and that the street separating the two plots today once ended at their northern sidewalk. Indeed, with the English still in command, no one in his right mind was going to axe part of Sir Thomas W. Russell Pasha's award-winning garden. He was, after all, still Commandant of the Cairo Police.

Even before Mansour Mohammed Street connected with Gabalaya Street, some of the villas had started to change hands. Egyptians had taken over posts previously occupied by the British and as such were the latest beneficiaries of government housing. By December 1941, only five of the Richmond Villas were occupied by Britons; four of them embassy staff with Walter Smart as their doyen.

Walter Smart's intelligence-gathering duties must have been substantially enhanced when he realised the identity of his next-door Egyptian neighbour. Engineer Hussein Sirry Pasha was not only pro-British but he was also the queen's uncle by marriage. It was not unusual for the king to drop by and seek his advice. Had he wanted to, all Smartie needed to do in order to fill in his daily reports was to sit quietly under his mango tree and listen in on King Farouk's wartime conversation floating across the hollyhocks hedge that separated No. 19 from No. 17 Ibn Zanki Street.

Number 17 gets high recognition status today because it stands at the corner of Ibn Zanki and Shagaret al Durr Streets, and more importantly, because the present owner, the government of Tunis, has restored it beautifully. Hardly anyone remembers that this was once the home of Sirry Pasha, confidant to King Farouk and several times head of government.

The substitution of British administrators by their Egyptian understudies heralded a new era in the Richmond Villas annals. The more optimistic among the new arrivals thought that the heretofore anachronistic term 'Anglo-Egyptian' would take up a new connotation: lofty Anglos and Egypt's elite living together as enlightened neighbours. But not for long as it turned out. The dramatic dates of 1952 and 1956 were right around the corner.

Although an individual account of each of the villas would be practically impossible to obtain, any forthcoming titbit is a source of elucidation and enjoyment. Such was the case with a December 14, 2000, communication from Mahmoud Sadek, a retired professor of classical archaeology in Victoria, BC, Canada:

> I was born in December 1930 and lived at No. 4 Shagaret al Durr Street near the Aquarium. It was the house of my maternal grandfather, Ali Gamal al Din Pasha, who was minister of war (1931-1933) in Ismail Sidki Pasha's government. He was humorously known as the Pasha of the Seven Airplanes for having introduced the air force into the army. I remember that the house next to my grandfather's belonged to Mahmoud Shawki Pasha who was the secretary of King Fouad. Next to him lived Attorney-General Taher Pasha Noor, and next to him was the house of Zaki al Ibrashi Pasha, Director of the Royal Estate.

Sadek's account of the Richmond Villa tenants appears to confirm that, by the early 1930s, Egypt's political elite had firmly entrenched itself in Zamalek. This was the first time that a sitting prime minister was actually living in Zamalek. Others would soon follow.

Villas, power and politics

By 1940, almost every one of the neighbourhood's shaded streets boasted a former or incumbent prime minister, former minister, court chamberlain, physician, speaker of the house, under-secretary, or senior magistrate.

Each of course possessed his own stately villa, leaving Zamalek today with quite a collection of elegant buildings dating from the first half of the twentieth century, each with its own special connection to the nation's history.

When Prime Minister Hassan Sabry Pasha unexpectedly died in November 1940 while reading the 'Speech From The Throne', one third of his coalition lived in Zamalek. Just as Sabry lived in a villa overlooking the Zamalek street that would one day bear his name, four out of his 15-member cabinet were also his neighbours.

Foremost among them was Engineer Hussein Sirry Pasha, who headed public works, and the able Abdel Hamid Soliman Pasha, running finance. And since the latter ranked No.1 in the ministerial pecking order, it was to him that the royal condolence—Royal Proclamation no. 65 for 1940—was addressed. But when it came to the choice of a new prime minister it was to Soliman's brother-in-law that the king turned. Hussein Sirry Pasha bore impeccable credentials aside from the fact that he was the son of a famous khedivial minister of public works. Nonetheless he probably owed his accession to the fact that he was also the queen's uncle by marriage. Just as they do today, matrimonial alliances counted for something.

Abdel Hamid Soliman Pasha no doubt comforted himself with the fact that whereas his brothers-in-law, Sirry Pasha and Kamel Nabih Bey, lived in neighbouring government-owned villas, Abdel Hamid had built his villa to his own taste. Villa Soliman is today home to the forbidding, tight-lipped Embassy of North Korea, at No. 6 Saleh Ayyub Street.

According to his daughter, library consultant Chafika A. Soliman, her father designed the family home himself in 1928-9. Handsome yet unpretentious, the neo-classical house boasts a prominent feature visible from the outside: the wrought iron and glass gate is embossed with a large 'S' and fitted with a large stained-glass panel depicting the four seasons.

The varied interior included an inimitable *escalier d'honneur* devoid of any bonding material and made entirely from wood. And since most of the craftsmen came from as far away as Aswan and Italy, temporary living accommodations for these clever artisans was provided in the as yet undefined garden.

The house was spacious enough to accommodate Chafika's parents, her many sisters and a younger brother. "I was born in a makeshift bedroom in the villa's topmost floor for the simple reason that construction was still in progress. And as was customary in those days, society ladies seldom gave birth in hospitals. Instead, it was for the leading gynaecologist to make home deliveries."

When Chafika's father died in 1945, the house was sold to press baron Shukry G. Zaidan of Dar al Hilal. Two decades later the Zaidans would sell the villa to the North Koreans, who promptly replaced the garden's pond, gazebo and gatekeeper's loggia with unsightly office buildings.

One event Chafika remembers vividly is the pre-Second World War wedding of one of her sisters. "It seemed like everyone turned up to what amounted to an all-night affair with Umm Kulthum singing away."

With family, power and politics being what they are in the Middle East, anyone who was anyone turned up at the wedding of the daughter of Egypt's seven-time minister. Several royals were present, including those who held the pasha in high esteem for his successful re-organisation of the Egyptian State Railways.

Seldom had the relationship between palace and government been at such a high. In his family memoir, *In the House of Muhammad Ali*, the late Prince Hassan Aziz Hassan fondly recollects Abdel Hamid Soliman Pasha who, for a time, had represented the *Majlis al Balat* (Privy Council) in affairs that concerned him and his older brother Prince Ismail:

> We had a tutor, Sir Abdel Hamid Soliman Pasha, a charming gentleman with the most suave manners, an inscrutable smile and a bronze-coloured face, and hands that shook slightly when holding his coffee cup or lighting his cigarette. He was living in an extremely handsome home which is now an embassy.

It was in 1938 that Soliman's brother-in-law, Kamel Nabih Bey (later pasha and minister of public works), moved into a Richmond Villa recently vacated by the chief financial advisor to the Egyptian government, Sir Frank P. Watson. Located right across the street from Sirry Pasha, it was easy for the two brothers-in-law to exchange government tittle-tattle and real estate tips. It took several years, however, for an exceptional offer to come Nabih Bey's way. For LE4,000 he could own the villa he occupied.

Fifty years later, his son vividly recalls the missed opportunity:

> My father, who was then the one and only under-secretary of the Ministry of Public Works, refused to buy in view of possible conflict of interest. That is why we moved to the Wahba Building at No.4 on the same street. The Richmond villas were sold to some of the other sitting tenants like Dr. Abdel Wahab Mouro Pasha at No.23 Ibn Zanki Street and my uncle, Hussein Sirry, at No.17 Ibn Zanki—or 12 Shagaret al Durr depending on which door you use. Other villas were pulled down and apartment buildings were erected in their stead, which is what happened in our case when a handsome apartment building designed by Mahmoud Riad replaced No. 15 Ibn Zanki in 1950.

With regard to other childhood memories, engineer Kamal Nabih brings up the castle-like house at No. 14 Ibn Zanki designed by Adolfo Brandani in 1925:

> It originally belonged to landowner Erfan Seifelnasr Pasha. Acquired by the Hellenic government, it was visited by Greek royalty during the Second World War, whereupon sentinels in Evzon costumes stood vigil at the gates. The Greeks are still there today, but no royal visits.

In the aftermath of the Second World War both colonial rule and royalty were gradually swept out of the Near East. Barely recovering from five years of fighting, the much-reduced British embassy in Cairo held on to half a dozen of the Richmond Villas, the rest having been acquired by a variety of Egyptians from the political, cultural and diplomatic worlds. But as urban *laissez-faire* gradually replaced zoning laws and as the price of the square metre started its spiralling ascent in the late 1970s, it was inevitable that these villas would fall into peril. Who in his right mind would sit on a plot of real estate worth millions just for the privilege of saying, "I have a garden!"

With the on-going real estate boom and the exorbitant expenses of maintaining a villa by financially challenged Egyptians or by foreign governments with tight budgets, only nine of the original 19 made it into the twenty-first century. Today only one still belongs to the British government.

The forgotten egyptologist

Is it possible that en route to Berlin disguised as broken pieces of pottery, Queen Nefertiti spent a few days on the island of Gezira-Zamalek? After all, her discoverer and kidnapper was a long-time resident.

We all know how Nefertiti's portrait-bust was found practically intact on December 6, 1912, in the workshop of sculptor Thutmose in Tel al Amarna, that ancient but short-lived capital city of the sun-worshipping pharaoh Akhenaton.

Painted in the most delicate manner, the long-necked queen is adorned for ceremony with a crown and a large necklace. So well made "she is virtually alive", imagined her discoverer, the director of the German Orient Society (Deutsche Orient-Gesellschaft). Alive enough so that he could no longer part with her. "Describing her is useless," he writes the following day, "she must be seen!"

The bust eventually turned up in Berlin and a grateful kaiser decorated its discoverer. Later, in an act of recognition for services rendered to the Fatherland, he was nominated honorary cultural attaché at the German Embassy in Cairo.

The Berlin-born archaeologist-turned-smuggler and sometime diplomat is the legendary Ludwig Borchardt, formerly of No. 13 Amir Said Street, Zamalek. Since that time the street has been renamed Maa'had al Swissry (Swiss Institute) and later, Aziz Abaza.

Recognised as Germany's leading egyptologist, Borchardt's achievements convinced his government to purchase the villa next door. It became the German Orient Society, one of Gezira Island's most respected cultural landmarks. And with more discoveries credited to the society each year, the name Borchardt became a household name in the world of egyptology.

However, by some pharaoh's curse, three decades of Borchardt's achievements suddenly became irrelevant. Astonishing, considering he discovered (and smuggled) the world's most highly recognised bust, and spent the best years of his life on Cairo's blessed island.

Attempts to erase Borchardt's memory started when he went into early retirement. It was about this time that the German Orient Society closed shop only to re-open in 1931 in another part of Zamalek as the German

Archaeological Institute, under the direction of Professor Herman Junker.

The new institute's director was Borchardt's former aide and colleague. Both savants had dedicated their lives to the study of the worlds' most ancient civilization. But there was one key distinction that separated them: Borchardt was a Jew and there was no place for him in Germany's prestigious overseas cultural centre.

As Nazism and fascism gained ground, the former director of the Deutsche Orient-Gesellschaft had fewer opportunities before him. This could well be the reason why he decided to create an eponymous privately-funded foundation. Married to the wealthy Emilie Cohen of Frankfurt, money was not an issue and the savant could thus pursue his academic interests unhindered.

Study, however, is one thing, but what about state and nationality? As Europe rushed towards war, a now stateless Borchardt grew ill at ease. Fearing for his interests and a lifetime's wealth of research and artifacts, it was time to look around for some form of legal and diplomatic protection. Options were limited so that ultimately, and in typical pre-Second World War fashion, a deal was struck with the Swiss Confederation.

Professor Borchardt died in Zurich on August 12, 1938, aged 74. Ten years later the Swiss were declared official beneficiaries of his flower and antiquity-filled estate on the Nile—the Ludwig Borchardt Foundation. The Swiss changed the name to The Swiss Institute. In 1952, while purging the city of royalist associations, the name of the street fronting his foundation was renamed Maa'had al Swissry. Who knows, if the Swiss had refrained from renaming the foundation, the street may have been called 'Borchardt'.

Meanwhile Nefertiti is alive and well in Berlin's Aegyptisches Museum having miraculously survived the bombing and looting of the Third Reich. But the question still remains; did the 3,500-year-old queen ever pass through a certain house in Zamalek on her way to Berlin?

La maison du Canada

When Marie-Andrée Beauchemin became Canada's first woman ambassador to Egypt, she left her mark in more ways than one. Her most conspicuous act, according to one Zamalek resident, was the transformation of the exterior of her residence into "a droll pink wedding cake."

In a bold departure from the traditional white, Beauchemin introduced some of the colours that had captivated her in Tuscany. For some, No. 5 Kamel Mohammed Street looks out of place while for others it is a welcome breath of fresh air.

The best comment yet came from the little girl who lives in a next-door building. "Surely, anyone who lives in such a lovely house must be a princess!"

She is not altogether wrong, for at one point the occupant of the most attention-getting Zamalek residence was royal, a queen no less. Shortly after her divorce from King Farouk in 1948, Queen Farida moved into No. 5 Kamel Mohammed Street where she remained without much ado until her own house was completed on Giza's Pyramid Avenue. This was some ten years before it became Canadian property.

But even before an Egyptian queen and a host of Canadian ambassadors entertained Egypt's finest at No. 5 Kamel Mohammed, the stately mansion had already made local history.

In the 1930s, Kamel Mohammed Street was the address found on the calling cards of a varied crowd, including an Italian businessman art-collector, a minister of interior, a prominent lawyer of Eastern European origins and a leading Austrian archaeologist.

The latter went by the name of Professor Hermann Junker. With several major discoveries to his name the renowned Egyptologist was established in Egypt even before the First World War. Upon moving into No. 5 Kamel Mohammed he used the upper two floors as his official residence. The mansion's lower floor and basement became the German Archeological Institute in Cairo.

Junker's library was second to none. His work and discoveries were recorded and taught all over the world. Which is why, whenever a German-speaking visitor of consequence came to Egypt, it was Professor Junker who escorted them around the Giza pyramids or walked them through the

Egyptian Museum. Visitors' eager to learn more about Egypt's treasures would invariably call at No. 5 for a cup of tea and stimulating conversation.

Ironically, it was his last visitor who brought down the veteran Egyptologist along with the rest of Egypt's German-speaking community. Although it is unclear whether Josef Goebbels dropped in at No. 5 Kamel Mohammed, *Al Ahram* recounts in detail how Professor Junker hosted Germany's Minister of Propaganda at the Giza plateau in April 1939.

War was declared the following June. Considered an enemy alien, Junker was *persona non grata* in Egypt, and since all German assets were sequestered, the German Archaeological Centre was promptly closed.

When it became apparent war was not going to end anytime soon, the library was moved to Cairo University. The new owner of No.5 Kamel Mohammed was Ibrahim Amer Pasha, an Egyptian-Sudanese merchant who died there on December 28, 1942. His heirs sold the house the following May to Ovadia Mercado Salem, a wealthy Jewish businessman.

It was about the time that Salem was interned during the first Arab-Israeli War of 1948 on alleged charges of harbouring zionist sympathies that he leased No. 5 to Egypt's former queen. When, a few years later, she moved out, the Salems found it pointless to move back, especially since their children had all immigrated to Europe. The house was leased to the Hungarian Embassy, which used it as both residence and chancery.

Upon Ovadia's death in Cairo in March 1958, his heirs sold the house to the Canadian government.

In May 2000, Ambassador Beauchemin was advised that the blushingly handsome Canadian Embassy residence on Kamel Mohammed Street had been earmarked as a Zamalek historic house. A commemorative blue plaque was presented to the Canadian government stating that Egypt's former queen had once lived there. An enthusiastic ambassador promised to append the plaque on the mansion's exterior wall, once it was cleared by the relevant government department in Ottawa.

It took six months for a spokesperson from the Canadian Department of Foreign Affairs in Ottawa to announce that a tri-lingual commemorative plaque would soon appear at No. 5 Kamel Mohammed Street, Zamalek. The delay was due to the fact that any plaque involving a public Canadian building would have to involve at least two languages, French and English—not to mention Arabic as well.

Zionist heyday on Kamel Mohammed Street

While the tortured relations between Israel and its Arab neighbours continue to make daily headlines, in the days before the establishment of Israel, both hawks and doves of the zionist *illuminati* were either residents or frequent visitors to Egypt. And this is where a single Zamalek street can relate part of this forgotten story.

Kamel Mohammed Street stretches northwards from Hadikat al Asmak up to 26th of July Street, intersecting Salah al Din and Ibn Zanki along the way.

Early in the twentieth century, the area flanking Kamel Mohammed Street was an empty field. Subsequently, and as the island joined the urban sprawl, this was carved up into 12 plots of half an acre each for the construction of villas with gardens. Alas, few of the first houses—some of the island's finest—survived the urban onslaught of the 1970s. Yet in the days when Cairo's population was below two million, Kamel Mohammed was just another shaded residential roadway with a handful of inhabitants.

Large villas stood at opposite ends of Kamel Mohammed Street. If the three villas (numbers 1, 3 and 4) overlooking Hadikat al Asmak at the south end are gone, the villa at the northern end of the street is still standing albeit somewhat neglected. This is No. 12, a white neo-Islamic villa (today earmarked for annihilation) surrounded by a shrunken garden that fronts 26th of July Street and what was once the Sirdaria.

What had been a villa at No. 1 became an apartment building built during the interwar period. It is there that banker-businessman Hector de Cattaui died. Like his father, Moise Cattaui Pasha, the long-standing president of Cairo's Sephardic community, Hector and his immediate family had little to do with Zionism. For generations they had graced the top echelons of Egyptian society and saw no need to exchange gracious living for life on a socialist kibbutz.

Things were somewhat different at No. 3 Kamel Mohammed where Cattaui's cousins lived.

Villa Goodman was the residence of Maitre Aaron Alexander, an affluent Ashkenazi with origins in Znin, Poland. A successful lawyer at the Mixed and British Consular Courts, Alexander was legal advisor as well as a board member of several British concerns in Egypt, including Shell Oil, the Egyptian Delta Land Company, and the English School. His practice at the Savoy Chambers was considered amongst the best in Cairo so that amongst his clients we find the old khediva mother, Messrs. Rothschild and the Suez Canal Company. Alexander's wife Victoria 'Vicky' Mosseri was a niece of Moise Cattaui Pasha and a sister of banker-magnate Elie Nessim Mosseri.

The Alexanders and their three children, Arthur-Lionel, Anthony-Nessim and Eileen, led a socially active life. As president of the Rotary Club and a dynamic promoter of Eretz Israel, Alexander's villa was the venue for large receptions and visits by important zionists, including British cabinet minister Isaac Hore-Belisha and Chaim Weizmann, both of whom dropped by whenever in Cairo. In fact, Maitre Aaron often accompanied Weizmann during his meetings with Egyptian government officials.

Alexander and his brother Morris, an advocate in Alexandria, had come to Egypt from Cape Town in 1913. Both married into the local cosmopolitan Jewry and, like many Eastern European co-religionists from South Africa, the Alexanders were obsessed with the creation of a homeland in Palestine.

A member of the assimilated elite of Egypt's *haute Juiverie*, the Egyptian-born Vicky Alexander began to see things Aaron's way. Soon enough she became co-chairperson of the annual Women's International Zionist Organization (WIZO) bazaar held at Groppi's or Shepheard's Hotel. These were well-attended fund-raisers attracting Egypt's society ladies of all faiths.

Although wary of zionist intentions, successive Egyptian governments tolerated WIZO's existence along with its auxiliary agencies. Despite the publication of Lord Balfour's November 2, 1917, letter to Lord Rothschild conveying His Majesty's government's view to the establishment in Palestine of a national home for the Jewish people, Zionism was not yet perceived as a threat in Egypt. It was still regarded by Egypt's unsuspecting intelligentsia as little more than the hopeless yearning for an ancestral homeland by groups of scattered Jews. In other words, their cause was commensurate to Red Indians aspiring to take over New Jersey. None suspected that the European Jew knew exactly what he was about and that he was simply marking time towards something wholly Jewish; namely, the Jewish State of Israel.

Local politicians meanwhile found comfort in the fact that Jews in Palestine represented a mere fraction of the indigenous population owning less than ten percent of the entire territory. What, therefore, was all the brouhaha about?

Any serious misgivings by the more sceptical Egyptian statesmen were countered by multiple promises from the British Foreign Office that the borders of British Mandated Palestine and the status quo of its overwhelming Arab Muslim-Christian majority were guaranteed by His Majesty's government and thus in safe hands. Aaron Alexander and his fantasizing crowd were free to aspire and hallucinate as they pleased. But Alexander was hearing contradictory promises from his British friends. The fabled homeland would soon become a reality.

Maitre Alexander died of a fatal heart attack at age 58, on September 12, 1945, while hosting a dinner for visiting colleagues at Cairo's posh Mohammed Ali Club. He would never learn of the creation of Israel and the several bloody conflicts that followed. Neither would he know that after resting for several years in the Mosseri graveyard in Bassateen on the edge of Cairo, his remains would be exhumed and shipped to the United Kingdom. Even though he couldn't claim an iota of Anglo-Saxon ancestry, Aaron had always felt British.

A few years after Maitre Alexander's death, Villa Goodman was sold, demolished and replaced with the twin Wadie Saad Buildings, designed by Albert Zananiri.

As shown by their English School report cards, Alexander's children were exceptionally bright. It was expected therefore for Eileen and her siblings to pursue their studies in the UK, she at Girton College, Cambridge, and the brothers at something equally distinctive.

Not overly concerned about her academic achievements, Eileen's Mosseri aunts waited in eager anticipation for different news from England. They had learned through the international Jewish grapevine that Eileen had met several eligible bachelors. Singled out was Aubrey Eban (born Solomon). He had the perfect credentials. His Anglo-Saxon education was reason enough for him to be sought out by the Anglophile Levantine bourgeoisie of Egypt. And for someone like Vicky ready to marry off her Jewish princess, the fact that Eban's father had been a prominent zionist in the Cape was more than mere coincidence. Perhaps he had known Alexander Senior? Their references were practically identical.

Despite the absence of any romantic attachment between Aubrey and Eileen, Vicky Alexander thought she heard wedding bells. Eban, now an officer in the British Army, arrived in Cairo in February 1942. But a few months later, news from London announced Eileen's engagement to a Cambridge colleague, Gershon Ellenbogen. They were married in London on March 26, 1944, where the Alexanders kept a house on Marley Road, Swiss Cottage.

In April 1943, Eban was again posted to Cairo, this time in the office of the Minister of State for the Middle East, first under Richard Casey, and then under Lord Moyne.

When the latter was murdered by two Jewish terrorists in November 1944, Major Eban may have had mixed emotions. Once again he had to come to terms with that annoying split allegiance syndrome. On the one hand his patrician British superiors represented everything the young officer liked to emulate, on the other, there were these two young men with a mission. Not unlike Eban, they viewed the redemption of Eretz Israel in political rather than religious terms.

Yet it was never a question of Eban's English upbringing being tempered by his sense of zionist responsibilities. The short of it was that an uninterrupted 30-year exposure to the British way of life amounted to naught when it came to race and convictions. "I belong there, but I have to be here" as he put it himself in one of his writings.

For a few weeks, Aubrey Eban and Gershon Ellenbogen, his erstwhile rival in love, who had rejoined British military intelligence in the Middle East, shared a flat belonging to the Alexanders in the Zamalek Building at No. 11 Kamel Mohammed Street. "The Alexanders' old cook, Adele, and their manservant, Said, looked after us," recalls Gershon Ellenbogen. "It wasn't long after his arrival that Eban became madly enamoured with the proverbial girl-next-door—or in this case, across the street."

Opposite Zamalek Building lived the Ambaches, a Yishuv family of East European ancestry. Engineer Simha Ambache and his wife (born Steinberg) had three daughters and a son, Nahman. They had come to Cairo from the Canal Zone where Simha ran a prosperous contracting business. Their home at No. 12 Kamel Mohammed Street belonged to the late Jacques Mosseri, another one of Vicky Alexander's relations.

Ever since his Cambridge days, Jacques Mosseri had been an impassioned supporter of Chaim Weizmann. Upon returning to Cairo in 1913, Jacques headed the zionist organisation in Egypt. Because of his premature death in 1934, he never saw the fulfilment of his dream or the swearing in of his champion as Israel's first president.

On January 1, 1945, Aubrey Eban was engaged to the Ismailia-born Suzy Ambache, who had just graduated from the American University with a Bachelors of Arts in Social Science. Senator Haim Nahum Effendi solemnised their subsequent March wedding. In his grand blue and black robes, Egypt's chief rabbi was described as "something out of a Hollywood movie."

Eban's wedding at No. 12 Kamel Mohammed had assembled the future leadership of Israel. Perhaps it had something to do with the zionist conclave in Cairo at the time. Standing side by side at Eban's wedding reception were Egyptian notables, the pillars of the local Jewry, senior British officers, and Cairo's leading and visiting zionists. Among the guests were Israel's future prime minister, David Ben Gurion, and his wife Paula. Also present was Theodor 'Teddy' Kollek, a Viennese Jew destined to become the mayor of West Jerusalem.

The newlyweds spent their honeymoon touring the ancient sites in Luxor and Aswan. Destiny would soon take them all over the world before settling and retiring in Herzlia outside Tel Aviv. Before he died in November 2002, Eban wrote numerous books as well as his memoirs when he was not touring the American television studios or attending United Jewish Appeal dinners.

Eban had by then fulfilled most of his ambitions. In conformity with his beliefs he had Hebraized his name to Abba. It was as Abba Eban that he raised the Star of David at the United Nations in New York in May 1949, symbolising the creation of the Jewish State, a state he was to serve as foreign minister under several governments. Although Eban was not present at the historic Begin-Sadat meeting, his wife was witness to one of its outcomes. On December 25, 1977, Suzy Ambache returned to her birthplace during Israeli Prime Minister Menachem Begin's visit to Ismailia. He had asked her to come along when he learned she was born there.

Suzy wasn't the only member of her family to marry a prominent zionist. A year after the Ambache-Eban wedding, Suzy's sister married another rising Anglophile Eastern European zionist serving in the British Army. While visiting the Ambache home in Kamel Mohammed, he was smitten by Suzy's younger sister, Aura Ambache. Aura's marriage to Vivian 'Chaim' Herzog took place in Palestine a few months after their initial meeting.

"It was love at first sight," she would fondly recall in an interview many years later, by which time Aura had become her country's First Lady. The son of Isaac Herzog, former Chief Rabbi of Ireland (also the first Ashkenazi Chief Rabbi of Israel), had become the sixth President of the State of Israel in 1983.

The Alexanders, the Ambaches and the Cattauis were not the only wealthy Jewish residents on Kamel Mohammed Street. There was the Salonika-born Ovadia Mercado Salem a Sephardi who, as mentioned earlier, had purchased the splendid villa at No. 5 that would later become the Embassy of Canada.

A self-made man who started out as an errand boy at Beinisch Jewellery in Mousky, Salem worked for Lloyds Bank before forming, with Alfred Cohen and Alfred Perez, the Societé d'Avances Commerciales S.A.E. (*Sherket al Taslifat al Togareya*). Soon Salem became principal shareholder of Chemla Department Store (ex-Chemla Frères) that was later managed by his son-in-law Youssef Peppo Simha.

Those who remember Monsieur Ovadia or *Khawaga* Salem as his employees alternatively called him, describe him as an astute operator who recognised a good deal when he saw one. Others claim he wasn't too popular with insurance companies in view of one or two doubtful claims. But it would be due to his alleged zionist sympathies that Ovadia Salem was in trouble. "During the Palestine War, my father was detained at Huckstep north-east of Cairo until January 1950 during which time his assets were frozen and put under custodian authority, " recalls his son, Maurice Salem who now resides in Geneva. "My mother, a cousin of my father's and in whose name the Zamalek villa was, leased it out to the former wife of King Farouk. Ex-Queen Farida and her parents, the Zulfikars, lived there for a few years."

Salem was not alone in his internment. With him were some 500 Jewish inmates including zionists and communists, and an even larger number of Muslim Brothers. The overflow of prisoners was sent to Al Tor in Sinai and Abou Kir, east of Alexandria. But with the arrival to power of the Wafd Party, things improved dramatically. Consistently treated better than their fellow Muslim Brother inmates, Salem and his colleagues were released in early 1950 with the proviso that those with foreign passports leave Egypt.

A naturalised Egyptian, Ovadia Salem chose to remain in Egypt where he had several business interests including investments in the famous Misr Group. No doubt he was an accepted and respected pillar of the Cairo business community. Salem died in March 1958 while living in the Albert

Harari Building at No.11 Ibn Zanki.

In addition to upright Egyptian Jews and aspiring Eastern European zionists, Kamel Mohammed Street did not want for illustrious residents during the interwar years. For starters there was landowner Abdel Hamid Ghaleb Bey, son of Osman Ghaleb Pasha, a former khedivial governor of Cairo. He owned the plot of land at No. 6 Kamel Mohammed. Rather than commission one of the many foreign architects available at the time, Ghaleb Bey hired local contractor *Al Hag* Morsi and proceeded in 1929 to implement his own drawing of what he perceived to be the ideal home. Four decades later his heirs would lease and then sell the old home to the Embassy of Rumania. The new owner, claiming the house had suffered during the October 1992 earthquake, proceeded to replace it with an unsavoury communist-era-looking chancery.

Contiguous to the Ghalebs was the ornate redbrick house of Mahmoud Fahmi al Keissy Pasha, a former minister of interior. Sometime in the 1980s a grisly vertical building shot up in between the two villas. At about the same time the Libyan government purchased the Keissy Villa annexing it to their adjacent art deco embassy fronting Saleh Ayyub and Ibn Zanki Streets.

Across the street from the Rumanians still stands Villa Nedda (No. 4) built by tobacco baron Signor Carlo Grassi. Carlo and his wife Nedda were great entertainers, always happy to show off their fine art collection. Aside from being a long time president of the Italian Chamber of Commerce, Grassi was head of the Cairo *fascio* before the Second World War. Today his house is the Embassy of Morocco.

Between Villa Nedda and the Fish Gardens stands the 1950s Lakah Building that replaced part of Grotto House, a very popular pre-First World War address.

Two 'bed and breakfasts' were also located on Kamel Mohammed Street: Mrs. A. Steer's Pension Cromer in the elegant Evangel Avramoussi Building (No. 9) designed by Caligopoulo, and Pension Zamalek at No. 11. Also at No. 11 was the Dutch Legation in Egypt with Baron Bentinck presiding before and during the Second World War.

Thus, by the 1950s Kamel Mohammed Street had already played host to an art-collecting Italian fascist, a Nazi sympathiser, several zionists, a Dutch baron, an enterprising Judeo-Levantine financier, an Egyptian notable, a minister of interior, a future first lady and a former queen.

Villa San Giorgio

A glimpse of what Gezira was like *circa* 1900 can be had from the correspondence unearthed by historian-diplomat Dr. Rudolf Agstner from the bowels of the Austrian Foreign Office archives. This particular story begins in 1894 when, recently retired from a career in the imperial Austrian diplomatic service that took him to Bulgaria and the Far East, Baron Rudiger Von Biegeleben, now 50, decided to tie the knot with Bertha Kubeck Von Kubau. Honeymoon destination? Egypt.

For the next six years the Biegelebens wintered in Cairo, residing in the diplomatic sector of the European quarter on the Nile's east bank. By 1901, however, things were changing. Cairo's population of 400,000 was on the rise. An economic boom had attracted banks, commercial enterprises and new apartment buildings "mostly un-oriental in appearance," according to the baron. "What had heretofore been a quiet villa district had become noisy and dusty in view of all the construction." It was time to move out.

Still attached to Egypt, the Biegelebens opted for a new life on the island of Gezira. Using his wife's savings, the baron found a perfect 1,000 square metre parcel of land, "40 paces from the Nile."

Although their house was one row away from the river there was nothing that impeded the horizon. In fact, the baron's view took in the garden of an important English neighbour—the deputy-chief of the interior. "Aside from the ibis birds that seem to live on the Englishman's lawn there was also the advantage of sharing his police guard," wrote the baron to his brother, Paul.

And so it was. On January 20, 1902, the Biegelebens, with their friends the de Velics from Hungary, P. Fournier from France and a Franciscan chaplain, celebrated the groundbreaking of what would soon become the 'St Giorgio on the Nile.' Also present was the young Dutch architect.

"We are fortunate," wrote the baron to his brother on December 1901, "for we are moving to the country with the advantage of the city. Next to our simple house there is the Gezira Palace Hotel which has a post office, a telephone and a telegraph office."

As recounted by the baron in his prolific correspondence with his brother, Gezira Island was not in want of landmarks. For starters architect Julius Franz Pasha had designed the Gezira Palace Hotel, formerly a khedivial

palace, in the 1860s. And just north of the budding Villa St Giorgio was
what remained of the Austria-Sudan Mission. To the west and east of the St
Giorgio were the two branches of the father of all rivers.

On February 9, the baron writes to his brother, "Our favourite outing
consists of watching the villa growing out of the earth. And so far no
problems."

From the baron's letters we learn that Villa St Giorgio was built in less
than 11 months. "Whereas the workers were Mohammedans, the supervisor
and foreman are Europeans. This applies to the neighbouring buildings as
well. All sport an impervious Orientalism about them."

Describing the building process, the baron elaborates on how, "the stones
were carried by camel from the Helwan quarries to the Nile bank south of
Cairo. Once loaded onto large sailboats they were transported down the
Nile to the island of Gezira just opposite the building site. From there they
were carried to the site by black people. No cranes are in use."

When the Biegelebens left for Europe in late April 1902, the villa was
almost complete.

Returning in November of the same year the baron is overcome and
gushes about the completed villa in his letters. "We found the house finished
in the most beautiful manner," he writes to Paul. "There were palms
decorating the outside steps and in the empty rooms there were flowers
everywhere plus a breakfast table prepared by the Velic's cook. As for our
trusted manservant Mohammed, he had guarded the villa as though it were
his own."

Another unexpected surprise was the St Giorgio garden. A construction
site when they had last seen it, it was now bursting with hibiscus, eucalyptus,
bamboo rushes "and roses everywhere."

Later the baron tells his brother about his ongoing good fortune. "We
have electricity, running water and personnel. From our eastern veranda,
where Bertha and I have breakfast, we watch feluccas navigate the Nile, and
when it gets too cool we simply move to the southern room." Describing
another part of the house, the baron details how Bertha had decorated it "as
though it were a medieval Tyrolean castle except for the palms."

The first Christmas at the St Giorgio was a special affair. Writing to his
brother on December 26, 1902, the baron praises his wife's Christmas tree
"in the corner of our dining room. We entertained guests from the nearby
Mission School including many children aged 2 to 18, their colours ranging

from white to pitch black."

Baron Biegeleben died childless in September 1912. His wife Bertha sold the house and retired to the Austrian Tyrol, where Baron Biegeleben had purchased, in 1893, the former hunting lodge of Archduke Sigismund the Rich in Coins (yes, that's his title), built in 1472-1473.

The Villa St Giorgio is today part of the Amoun School. It is located at No. 8 Aziz Abaza (ex-Maa'had al Swissry) Street. Since it bears little resemblance to the original you are kindly invited to use your imagination should you look it up.

Endangered species

It is hard to think of better candidates for the 'Cairo Rare Buildings Collection' then the assortment of pre-1950 mansions situated directly on the Nile. There are only 14 of them left in the entire city. The 11 most important are located on Zamalek's Aziz Abaza and Mohammed Mazhar Streets. These include the Akhenaton Centre of Arts, the Greater Cairo Library and those prime properties currently owned by the governments of India, Saudi Arabia, Hungary, the Vatican, Iraq and Russia. Of the remaining three, two are on the island of Manial al Rhoda and the third is Bayt al Manasterli in the Bahr al Aazam district of Giza (not to be confused with the Manasterli Pavilion on Rhoda Island).

Perhaps an enterprising governor of Cairo would consider putting these villas on the list of endangered species thus placing an ironclad moratorium on their destruction or structural alteration. It would then fall on the Zamalek residents to hold perpetual vigil to ensure the present owners comply with the basic rules of preservation. Meanwhile, the island's elders should chronicle the history of these buildings so that the information could be passed on to the next generations. For sure these landmarks are part and parcel of the island's architectural heritage.

An example of what could be written in the brochure about one member of this endangered species would read as follows:

Villa Hug is located at No. 3 Aziz Abaza (ex-Amir Said, ex-Maa'had al Swissry) Street. Built in 1907-8 it is one of the oldest villas in Zamalek. Its first owners were Jean (born 1862 in Heinfelden, Switzerland) and Marcelle

Hug. Monsieur Hug was the founder of Banque Hug & Cie located at No. 9 Cherif Pasha Street (ex-Madabegh) in downtown Cairo.

The villa is a fine example of the eclectic movement that characterised Cairo's architecture during the first half of the twentieth century. Its French designer, Raoul Brandon, although not as prolific as his Cairo contemporaries, was the designer of Orosdi-Back (later Omar Effendi) department store on Abdel Aziz Street in downtown Cairo.

Villa Hug's contractor was the Italian firm of Giuseppe Garozzo & Figli, builders of the Egyptian Museum.

Because Villa Hug's exterior remained intact up to the close of the last century we need not second-guess its style or motif. Characterised by special masonry, round balconies, buttresses and an abundance of stucco, one can safely surmise it is the only neo-Gothic edifice on the Nile. Note its pointed roof walls, its awesome gargoyles and the superb stained-glass windows imported especially from France. Examine the villa's main entrance and discover the letter 'H' spun into an amazing web of stained-glass motifs.

After Hug died, his widow leased the villa in the 1930s to the Institute of Education for Girls Amira Fawkia al Gedida. This is where daughters of the elite went if they were not already enrolled in the Kasr al Dubara Girls College or the French-language Lycée Français, Mère de Dieu and Sacré Coeur. Unlike the state-run schools of today that have the propensity to turn concrete buildings into a rubble heap, the fragile Villa Hug survived intact.

When the time came, Hug's widow, Marcelle, sold the villa. It thus became the property of Mr. and Mrs. Mohammed Sameh Moussa. In his capacity as secretary of the pre-1952 Saadist Party, Moussa Bey entertained Egypt's top-drawer politicians. His wife, Wadood Faizi, was equally occupied entertaining members of her own family including her siblings who owned three exclusive—and now endangered—Zamalek riverfront mansions (later, the Indian chancery, Russian State News Agency and Iraqi Embassy).

In the 1970s, Villa Hug was leased to the Republic of Venezuela. Among the prominent Latin Americans who have stayed there are Venezuelan President Rafael Calderas and Ambassador Nava Carrillo. The latter was nominated his country's minister of foreign affairs shortly after returning to Caracas.

Six years ago, the descendants of Sameh Moussa sold Villa Hug to leading Egyptian educator Nawal al Degwi, owner of several private educational institutes. Degwi is currently restoring the villa's interior and adding modern amenities here and there. So if you happen to see something protruding from the roof, it is not an old gargoyle gone awry or a statue heaving out of synch, it is simply an elevator shaft as the villa prepares for its second century of existence.

The wedding cake

Moving on to another riverfront mansion, No. 15 Mohammed Mazhar Street is touted as an 'educational library.' Millions were spent to restore, staff and computerize the Greater Cairo Library. Once the hubbub settled after the library's 1995 inauguration by Egypt's first family, the less privileged decided to go and see the results for themselves.

Time and again, the library director appeared in the media explaining how the Greater Cairo Library is the single largest repository of information regarding *Umm al Dunya*. Every conceivable book, map, document, survey plan and statistic regarding Cairo's history, geography and character is available to the public free of charge. And using the latest technology— meaning Internet—you could tap mines of information on the library's website. Or so he said.

Here's a sample of what was found. To begin with, no one at the library could come up with information regarding the magnificent building, beyond that it had been the palace of Princess Samiha, daughter of Sultan Hussein. That scrap of information aside, no one knew when exactly it was built, the name of the architect, or about any important event that had taken place on the premises of this Zamalek landmark.

How about something about Mohammed Mazhar Pasha, after whom the adjacent street is named?

Blank.

Do they know anything about the next-door villa designed by Auguste Perret in the 1930s for Elias Awad Bey that has since been destroyed and replaced by the Swedish Embassy bunker?

Hmmmm. Berret who?

Where could one get such information?

Abyss.

Tapping into the library's website was equally embarrassing. Although the site echoes much of what the director has said on national television, names of certain books that should be on the library shelves failed to appear on the web database. For instance, *Cairo: The City Victorious*, which was reviewed the world over, was not listed; neither for that matter is its author, Max Rodenbeck. Another book this author searched for in vain was a biography of Egyptian-born poet, Edmond Jabes. The 300-page work by Daniel Lançon discusses the poet's early years in school, his agitated youth in Cairo and his formative years working as a broker at the Cairo stock exchange. All this is set against a backdrop of a cosmopolitan city where multilingual intellectual salons were an everyday affair. The book talks of the poet's first encounter with his future wife, Arlette Cohen, and their subsequent marriage, which took place in 1935 at her family home, No. 15 Mohammed Mazhar Street.

Before her death in January 2000, Maadi resident Vera Bajocchi recalled the occasion. "This was one of the few times I visited my rich relatives' house. We nicknamed the house 'the Wedding Cake' because of its external appearance."

The street on which the library stands has gone through three name changes, Rue Doctor Mario Rosi, then Rue Amir Said and now Mohammed Mazhar, but no evidence of this could be found at the library. There is also no mention in the library's brochure of the fascinating array of tenants who once lived in this building. Beyond that it had been the palace of Princess Samiha, daughter of Sultan Hussein (who ruled 1914-17), neither the brochure nor the library employees had any further information.

As it turns out, prior to becoming a royal abode, No. 15 Mohammed Mazhar was the home of the Cattauis. They had moved to Zamalek from downtown Cairo after the family patriarch, Moise Cattaui Pasha, died in 1924. When the widow of Cattaui Pasha passed away in August 1937, the children leased their home to a number of prominent tenants. There was Rashwan Mahfouz Pasha, the Imperial Embassy of Iran and the representative of the Kingdom of Yugoslavia, Mr. Miloje Smiljanic. It also appears that literary doyenne, Madame Kout al Kouloub al Demerdashia, leased No. 15 sometime in 1942 although it is not clear whether or not she moved in. It wasn't until 1942 that the property was finally sold to Princess Samiha Hussein.

From the sale deed notarised on February 7, 1942, we learn that the villa and surrounding garden at No. 15 was sold for the price of LE13,350 partly paid for by a cheque drawn on Bank Misr. In view of the importance of the buyer, the sale document was signed at Abdin Palace with Murad Mohsen Pasha representing Princess Samiha and Edith Moise Cattaui (Mrs. René Cohen) representing herself and her brothers, the late Hector and Edgard Cattaui. Court lawyer Emanuel Mizrahi Pasha, who also acted as a witness to the transaction, represented the Privy Council.

Jabes was not the only poet to grace the villa. According to those who knew her well, Princess Samiha was an accomplished, though unpublished poet. Born in 1889 and married three times, she led a tumultuous life by court standards. Moreover, she outlived most of her generation ending up condemned to absolute anonymity and destitution.

Unable to survive on her meagre post-revolution state allowance, the princess was forced to clandestinely sell some of her furniture. Neighbours, seeing the 'homeless' lady walking down Mohammed Mazhar Street, would attempt to give her a little charity. Little did they know that she was a sultan's daughter, or that shortly after she died at age 100, her house would become the nation's leading centre for the study of its capital city.

The Anglo

When the British Army of Occupation was holed up inside Kasr al Nil barracks, the red-faced Tommies must have found some comfort in the colonial landmarks surrounding them. To the south stood the new British Legation from where Lord Cromer ran Egypt's day-to-day affairs. North of the barracks, plans were in the offing for an All Saints Cathedral (torn down in 1974, the site is now occupied by the 6th of October flyover). Further away, next to the new synagogue on Al Magrabi (now Adly) Street, stood the Turf Club (former British agency/consulate). And across the Nile dividing the palm-decked island of Gezira in two, were the Khedivial Sporting Club polo fields.

Soon, another landmark came to join the collection of post-Victorian icons. The Anglo-American Hospital, known to most simply as 'The Anglo'.

There was talk of a private hospital for the growing number of British civilians even before Sir Horace Pinching took over the Department of

Public Health in 1902. The idea was formally put forward at the Savoy
Hotel on Midan Soliman Pasha during a March 1901 meeting between
Lord Cromer and Judge John Long, the American consul. As a result, it
was announced that subscriptions and donations for a new Anglo-American
Hospital were now welcome. The site for the hospital was south of the
Khedivial Club's racecourse on several feddans especially purchased from
the Egyptian government by Lord Cromer for LE1,600.

By February 1903, the required money was raised except for the hospital's
Maintenance Fund. To make up the difference, a social gathering was held
at the Grand Continental Hotel on Midan Ibrahim Pasha (Al Opera). "The
ball came off with the greatest éclat," wrote the British-owned *Egyptian
Gazette*.

> The arrangements for the ball, which were carried out under the personal
> supervision of Mr. George Nungovich [the hotel's manager], were perfect.
> The whole of the right wing of the ground floor of the hotel had been
> placed at the disposal of the dancers, and the two rooms composing the
> restaurant were thrown into one and formed a most commodious and
> excellent ball-room which, although 150 couples must have been dancing
> in it at times, never became overcrowded. The terrace of the hotel had been
> covered in with an Arab tent, carpeted with soft rugs, and brilliantly lit up
> with innumerable lights, forming a delightful place to sit out in. The
> ballroom itself was tastefully decorated, the intertwining of the British and
> American flags being a special and gratifying feature of the decorations.
> The Rifle Brigade band was brought in for the occasion and certainly no
> fault could be found with either the music or the floor. Under these
> circumstances it is hardly necessary to say that last night's ball was the most
> brilliant function of this or any past season, and we expect the event of its
> becoming a perennial institution, it will be looked upon as the clou of the
> Cairo season. It would be far easier to say who was absent than who was
> there. We were sorry to notice the absence of Lord Cromer, who, we hear,
> was slightly indisposed. He was, however, ably represented by Lady Cromer.
> Dancing was kept up with the greatest zest until 2 o'clock this morning,
> when the company dispersed.

A month later, the LE6,363 Anglo-American Hospital designed by John
Price Bey of the Health Department was completed. At the advice of Natali
Prosperi, the hospital's Italian contractor, the opening was deferred until
autumn when the building would become thoroughly dry. It was just about

the time the Anglo received its first patient in the autumn of 1903, that a malaria epidemic hit the Nile Delta and a rampant cholera outbreak was announced in Palestine and Suez.

A modest venture with 22 beds, the Anglo contained special, private and general wards charging respectively 100, 30 and 15 piastres per day. Owing to the generosity of Sir Hugh Houston Smiley and the poet Leigh Hunt, two beds were available for those without means. The Anglo's largest benefactor was Sir Ernest Cassel, a close confidant of King Edward. When he died, the hospital's reliance on donations and subscriptions from British and American corporations operating in Cairo increased substantially.

During the first 50 years of the Anglo's operation, preference was given to British and American nationals. Management was vested in an executive council elected out of a general committee of 24 members. The envoys of Great Britain and the United States were ex-officio chairman and vice-chairman respectively.

It would be thanks to two of Britain's officials that the Anglo made world headlines. In November 1924, Sir Lee Stack, Commander of the Egyptian Army and Governor-General of the Sudan expired there following an assassination attempt by Egyptian nationalists. Twenty years later the British Minister of State, Baron Edward Walter Guinness (a.k.a. Lord Moyne), was proclaimed dead on arrival, from three fatal bullet wounds courtesy of two zionist terrorists.

Between the two World Wars, the Anglo broke with its unwritten rules and allowed non-British Fellows of the Royal College of Surgeons on the premises. This was how Abdel Wahab Mouro Pasha and Naguib Mahfouz Pasha (not to be confused with Egypt's Nobel Laureate) became the first Egyptians to practice there on a consultancy basis.

During the Second World War the Anglo became a British-run military hospital. Fred Clayton recalls he was admitted to what was then known as the 15th Scottish General Hospital at Gezira, Cairo. The name refers to the military medical people who operated it. "I recall that it was quite close to the cricket ground on Gezira. I enjoyed watching some of the games when I was recovering from illness. It was on the eastern side of the island overlooking the River Nile."

The last British administrator of the Anglo was reportedly a brother-in-law of General Montgomery, the victor in the Battle of Alamein. He lived on a houseboat near to the hospital.

Following the Suez Crisis of 1956, the hospital, like other British interests in Egypt, was sequestered. Dr. Halim Greiss recalls:

> For three days the Anglo-American hospital was in the throes of the Egyptian Air Force which wanted it for its own exclusive use. But through presidential intervention the hospital reverted to a special panel that undertook its temporary administration until a new one was re-constituted in 1961. New by-laws were introduced to reflect the post-1952 changes. Unfortunately, the hospital's balance sheets plunged into the red as traditional sources of income dried up overnight.

Gone were the British and American companies that had provided the necessary funds for general maintenance and upkeep of what was, for all intents and purposes, a benevolent organization. Gone, also, were the charity balls and well-attended fundraisers so crucial to the hospital's welfare. It had been thanks to one of these events that the main building's large elevator was purchased in 1938.

The Anglo-American also suffered when a sizeable part of its fixed assets was amputated by the State. According to Dr. Halim Greiss, the adjacent building had once belonged to the Anglo. In the early 1960s it was used as a state interrogation centre, when chilling human cries cut through the still nights "frightening the Anglos' patients, inducing early labour in the nearby maternity ward, once the exclusive preserve of chief gynaecologist, Doctor Walter Hodes Hamilton."

While Greiss believes the Cairo Tower stands on former hospital property, Henry Pelham-Burn thinks the tower stands on the property that was once part of Sir Frederick Rowlatt's residence, "The house in Zohria, belonged to the Egyptian government. After 1950, when my grandfather died, it was taken over by the military."

Could the Rowlatt residence thus have been the infamous interrogation centre of the 1960s? In any case, the villa-turned-house-of-horrors was the first residential building in Zohria (aside from the hospital's Sisters' House). First occupied in 1914 by Dr. Graham, who headed the Public Health Service Department, it was subsequently handed over to Major General Julian Byng. During the interwar period the villa was thoroughly overhauled and handed over to the governor of the National Bank of Egypt, Frederick Rowlatt.

The ultimately 'de-sequestrated' Anglo-American Hospital included several leading Egyptian physicians. Most prominent among them was veteran Dr. Halim Doss, who was later joined by Doctors Halim Greiss and Samir Massoud. "In 1985, in recognition of my father's long-term contributions to the medical profession, the hospital's [original] intensive care unit was re-named the Doctor Halim Doss Unit," remarks Shahira Doss, whose brother Wahid and sister Laila carry on their father's excellent name at the Anglo.

Having already celebrated its centennial, the 100-bed hospital is desperate for a heavy dose of re-organisation, and a face-lift to boot. The only novel elements in evidence are smart young doctors armed with mobile phones, beepers and hi-tech gadgets, somewhat incongruous with the decaying surroundings. But to the antiquated hospital's credit, the atmosphere remains congenial. The de-humanisation factor one so often encounters in modern sanatoriums and spotless clinics has not yet reared its unsightly head at the Anglo.

Palace of sorrows

Just like the rest of his kin, Prince Amr Ibrahim realised on November 9, 1953, that he was no longer king of his own castle. His villas, palaces and lodge, as of 10pm the previous day, had become state property by order of the Revolutionary Command Council. In exchange for his bounteous assets, 'citizen' Ibrahim was under due consideration by a special sub-committee for a state pension, the equivalent of which would barely meet the cost of his monthly electricity bills.

Among the prince's more visible assets was No. 16 Gezira Street, Zamalek (next to the Marriott, opposite Gezira Club). If the palace's exterior and encircling garden awed all those who drove by, its interior was no less extravagant.

Designed in the 1920s by Garo Balian, this particular structure was conceived as a neo-Islamic monument that would transcend time and space. The palace departed in style and character from the usual assortment of contrived Trianons and Venetian pastiches dotting part of the cityscape.

Built at a time of rising nationalism and economic opulence, No. 16's discreet wooden *mashrabiyas* replaced French bay windows; domes with symmetric designs took precedence over gilded ceilings with pastoral impressions; Cararra marble displaced parquet; and beautiful faïence stood in for a *gallerie de glaces* (mirror gallery). Plunging from high ceilings were exquisite oriental *mishkas* and lanterns, a welcome change from ormolu and *crystal de Bohème*. As for the dining room, well, it has to be seen for no amount of words will do it justice.

It was in his Zamalek jewel that the widowed prince raised his three pretty daughters, Nimet Allah, Amina and Indji. It was quite a daunting task for someone who had wholly missed out on family life. While still a toddler in 1906, Prince Amr Ibrahim lost his father in a motor accident in Epernay, France. Shortly thereafter he was separated from his mother when she became Madame Serge Yorketvitch, having re-married a Russian diplomat from St Petersburg. By so doing, Princess Saliha Hilmi not only forfeited her copious Egyptian assets but more importantly, she lost all rights to her infant son and daughter. The Egyptian court took a very dim view of family members who married outside their kith and kin.

Years later, Prince Amr Ibrahim's first wife died prematurely. "Sure thing, No. 16 was not a merry dwelling," recalls someone who knew the prince.

Things changed when the prince married for the second time. Nejla Hebatullah was a stunning Turkish royal, half his age. In Ottoman times, betrothal to a sultan's daughter or granddaughter earned the bridegroom the lofty title of *damat*. But since imperial Turkey had exited history in the 1920s, it was the bride's family who was on the lookout for a ruling house to ally itself with.

The Turkish sultana was unhappy at No. 16 Gezira Street. "Too noisy", she complained. The looming next-door building didn't help either. The former Villa Hetata had transmogrified into what became the island's largest building at the time.

"Almost as soon as No.14 was completed in 1938, the nickname 'Elephant & Castle' was coined to denote the two adjacent structures," recalls socialite Kadria Foda. She was one of the first tenants to move into the Elephant, even as the Belgian contractors Leon Rolin were removing the scaffold. "One day, after the war was over, the princely couple simply moved out. They committed a great escape, or *buyuk firar*, as they say in Turkish."

Even as the occupants of No. 16 considered moving to the suburb of Maadi, the Elephant next door was already changing owners at record speed.

Dr. Marespini sold it to Joseph de Piciotto who unloaded it onto exiled Nationalist Chinese before it was taken over by an insurance company.

With No. 16 Gezira Street temporarily vacated, it became easy pickings for Nasser's Revolutionary Council once the confiscation-sequestration binge began. Out of the country at the time, the ex-prince missed out on the fabled April 1954 auctions, when his movable assets were either pilfered or sold at cents on the dollar.

After providing an elegant venue for the 1953-1954 Anglo-Egyptian negotiations, Prince Amr Ibrahim's palace sank into obscurity. The new regime could think of nothing better to do with this unique example of neo-Islamic architecture than turn it into a youth club for the needy.

It would be under another president that No. 16 made history again. When Anwar Sadat assumed Egypt's leadership in September 1970, he needed an executive wing next to his Giza riverfront mansion and so ordered the emptying of the house across the street. Soon enough large government vans arrived on Kafour Street and proceeded to empty the Mahmoud Khalil Museum of all its contents. Its paintings and sculptures were redirected to Prince Amr Ibrahim's former Zamalek palace, earning it the new name of the Mr. & Mrs. Mohammed Mahmoud Khalil Museum.

No sooner had the public become used to the new venue than rumours about a missing Van Gogh painting, *Vase and Viscaria*, made the Cairene rounds. To this day, how the Dutch master's work was lost and subsequently found outside Egypt remains a puzzle.

During President Mubarak's rule, the displaced Khalil collection was moved back to Giza amidst much fanfare and celebration. Ambitious plans were in store for the now emptied palatial gallery. Renamed Gezira Art Centre, it has now become Egypt's first ceramics museum.

Maybe its life as a museum will be happier than its time as a home.

What's in a name

When he moved into his apartment, Mark Huband of London's *Financial Times* wondered why Gabalaya House wasn't standing on the street of the name. Over the years, many others have asked the same question. Everyone on the island knows there is a Gabalaya Street in another part of the Zamalek, so why then is this unique neo-Islamic apartment house standing at the corner of Hassan Sabry and Ibn Zanki Streets?

The truth of the matter is that the building is standing exactly where it was meant to be. When Italian architect Mario Rossi decided to inscribe the name Gabalaya House on the building's handsome façade, he was most certainly sound of body and of mind. It wasn't expected of him to know that the name of the street would soon change.

Still, the main residential street of the island has changed names not just once, but twice—with who knows how many more times to look forward to. Gabalaya Street lost its central position on the island when Hassan Sabry Pasha died in the most unpropitious manner.

It was during the first five years of his reign that King Farouk elevated his former ambassador to London to the post of head of government. A widely respected man, Sabry rose above bipartisan conflicts. Equally important, and unlike Wafd leader Mustafa al Nahas, or the pro-German Ali Maher Pasha, Sabry had no bone to pick with either the palace or Miles Lampson, the country's *de facto* British regent. He was therefore an ideal compromise prime minister. But only for 138 days!

On November 14, 1940, in the presence of King Farouk, the entire cabinet and members of the two Houses of Parliament, plus an assembly of ambassadors and their spouses, Sabry Pasha suddenly dropped dead while reading the 'Speech From The Throne'. Cause of death: a fatal heart attack.

Aside from a state funeral, telegrams and drawn-out obituaries plus an endless parade of floral wreaths, particular homage had to be paid to the country's first wartime 'martyr.' What better tribute than to name a street after him! And since the late prime minister was among the first post-First World War Egyptians to have moved to Gezira, occupying a house on Gabalaya Street (where the Degla a.k.a. Benetton, building stands today), why not convert Gabalaya Street into Hassan Sabry Pasha Street.

No one was about to contest the will of the ruler. Likewise, none within Sabry's 15-strong coalition cabinet was going to let the side down. Indeed, four ministers lived within walking distance: Hilmi Issa Pasha (now, French Embassy Economic Section on Aziz Osman Street), Abdel Hamid Soliman Pasha (today, Embassy of North Korea), Mahmoud al Keissy Pasha (today, Embassy of Libya annexe) and Hussein Sirry Pasha (today, Embassy of Tunis).

The Emile Ganage family, owners of Gabalaya House, did not protest the name change. There was little they could do other than wipe the name off the façade of their building. Wisely they did no such thing and left the original name for posterity.

Rather than discard the name Gabalaya (knoll) altogether, especially since the knoll had almost been flattened out over the years, the Cairo governor of the day thought better of it and transferred it two streets to the west. What had up to now been the narrow back road of Bahr al Aama (Blind Sea) Street, was thus re-named Gabalaya. With only seven villas and a few *dahabiahs* nearby, the confusion would be minimal.

Years later, the northern half of Hassan Sabry Street was renamed Brazil Street—though it's not exactly clear what the politics were behind *that* name change.

Terrorism on Hassan Sabry Street

One of the most dramatic events to take place on Hassan Sabry Street was the murder of Lord Moyne.

The scene of the crime was right by the gates of No 4-6 Hassan Sabry Street, a luxury rococo two-storey villa belonging to Maurice Ades and leased by the British government for Lord Moyne, The Right Honorable Walter Edward Guinness.

A Member of Parliament for Bury St Edmunds from 1907-1931, Guinness was raised to the peerage in 1932. The first Baron Moyne occupied the posts of Minister of Agriculture, Colonial Secretary, Leader of the House of Lords and finally Minister of State and British government representative in Cairo. He was also a scion of the wealthy Guinness family, owners of a beer empire and whose name would become linked to a certain Book of Records.

On November 6, 1944, Lord Moyne and his driver were returning from Gray Pillars in Garden City where Moyne was co-ordinating the British and Allied war efforts in the Middle East.

Hidden in the bushes just inside No. 4-6 Hassan Sabry were two young zionist zealots. Having stalked the place for the previous few days, they were familiar with both the surroundings and their victim's routine. The quiet neighbourhood consisted of a handful of villas and a tiny police station where Hassan Sabry intersects Gezira Street. At the worst of times, this was manned by a lone constable on a bicycle.

The victims never stood a chance. It was over in a matter of seconds. The Right Honourable British Minister and his driver, Lance-Corporal Fuller, were shot at point blank range as they got out of the car. No doubt Lord Moyne could have been regarded as a target for political assassination, but the deliberate shooting of the chauffeur was pure murder. Two lives brutally terminated, not at the front but on a sleepy Zamalek Street, a few metres from Africa's foremost polo and cricket fields.

By the time anyone realised what had happened, the killers would already be en-route to Palestine via a prearranged safe house on the other side of town. That, at least, was the plan.

To their misfortune, an out-of-district police constable was passing by on a motorcycle when he overheard gunshots. Sensing something was wrong, he instinctively gave chase to two men rushing off on bicycles. The fleeing murderers were overtaken on Abou al Ela Bridge.

Confronted with irrefutable evidence, neither assassin could deny his guilt. Nevertheless, they argued their case with a logic known only to die-hard fanatics: they were carrying out the orders of a zionist terror network operating inside British Mandated Palestine. By finishing off Moyne they were sending a message directly to the highest echelons of the British Foreign Office: "Stop interfering with Jewish immigration to Palestine, or else..."

The two assassins, Eliahou Bet-Zouri and Eliahou al Hakim, both in their early twenties, were members of the Stern Gang then controlled by Yitzhak Shamir. Shamir would later became prime minister of the State of Israel. They were tried, convicted and subsequently hanged at the insistence of the British government. The Eliahous were buried in an empty corner of the Jewish Cemetery in Bassateen, south-east of Cairo.

In the days immediately following Lord Moyne's killing, the murderers were publicly condemned and in the most categorical terms by mainstream Jewish communities. *Ha'aretz*, the leading pre-Israel daily newspaper, described the double murder as "One of the worse abominations since Zionism began," while the leader of World Zionism, Chaim Weizmann, (afterwards Israel's first president) described the killings as, "A far more severe shock and more numbing than that of the death of my own son." In his letter to Churchill, Weizmann wrote, "I can hardly find words adequate to express the deep moral indignation and horror which I feel. I know that these feelings are shared by Jewry throughout the world."

David Ben Gurion, who would become Israel's first prime minister, went even further than his most hard-line zionist colleagues when he described the killers as traitors to the Jewish people. "The bullet that struck down Lord Moyne was aimed not only at him but at our hearts," wrote another zionist leader. The *Zionist Review* meanwhile declared, "The dastardly acts of the Stern Gang are morally indefensible and politically crazy. Murder is alien to the high teachings of Judaism. Thou shall not kill is one of the Ten Commandments."

As the mood changed and the Western psyche was increasingly imbued with a feeling of collective guilt regarding the atrocities of the Second World War, the two terrorists were eventually exonerated. They became the subjects of folk tales, books and poems. Lord Moyne's assassination, rather than stem the tide against the fate of the Palestinians, had instead hastened Britain's exit from Mandated Palestine. But the story does not end there.

During a 1975 Egypt-Israel prisoner exchange, President Anwar al Sadat released the bodies of Eliahou al Hakim and Eliahou Bet-Zouri to the Israeli government at the latter's request. No sooner had they arrived in Jerusalem than the then acting-prime minister, ex-general Yitzhak Rabin, personally gave Moyne's assassins a military funeral of the type usually reserved for men of distinguished valour. Moreover, the two men were buried at Mount Herzl in an area reserved for the nation's eminent citizens.

The Hassan Sabry Street terrorists had become champions in the eyes of the Israeli public.

On November 6, 1995, a date that coincides with the 51st anniversary of Lord Moyne's assassination, the world watched another funeral, this time covered live from Mount Herzl. The much-decorated Israeli Prime Minister

Yitzhak Rabin was being laid to rest with full military honours. Two days earlier a Jewish zealot had shot him at point blank range, just as he was about to get into his official car.

The slain Rabin joined Lord Moyne and Lance-Corporal Fuller's killers-turned-heroes.

Maybe a lesson was learned that day with regards to terrorism: What goes around comes around.

Palace of communication

Further north from where the Hassan Sabry Street murders took place are large iron gates behind which stands a grand old arabesque palace. Inside is an inaccessible fiefdom belonging to a government ministry—a sumptuous palace where platoons of civil servants converge daily. Welcome to Palais Toussoun, No. 11-A Hassan Sabry Street, opposite the newly restored Dutch Embassy.

When Gabalaya Street was renamed Hassan Sabry Pasha Street, certain members of the Egyptian royal family were devastated. If anyone deserved to have his name on that particular street sign, it was the highborn occupant of the neighbourhood's grandest mansion, Prince Omar Toussoun.

A direct descendant of Viceroy Said Pasha, initiator of the Suez Canal scheme, Prince Toussoun was the principal benefactor of Alexandria's academic, archaeological and cultural institutions. His generosity towards civic organisations concerned with Egypt's summer capital earned him the informal title of *Amir al Iskandariya*—Prince of Alexandria.

How then did a commoner, who was head of the government for less than a year, bypass Toussoun? And if the villas and mansions fronting the newly renamed street were criteria to go by, the ordinary Villa Sabry Pasha paled next to the magnificent Palais Toussoun.

Perhaps the answer lies in an explanation put forward by a younger member of the Toussoun clan. The naming snub originated with King Farouk's rancour towards his more scholarly cousin. Toussoun's popularity among the peasant class did little to endear him to Egypt's young monarch. The name Amir Toussoun Street was therefore relegated to a little-used Zamalek side street (now Sheikh al Masrafy Street).

The designation 'Palais Toussoun' itself is contestable. A title and deed search shows that the palace did not belong to Prince Omar Toussoun but was instead the property of his wife, Princess Bahiga Hassan, a granddaughter of Khedive Ismail. True, the Toussouns ordinarily lived in Alexandria— their palace is now the broadcasting headquarters in Bacos— but as court life grew busier, their trips to Cairo became more frequent. Shubra no longer being what it used to be, a more suitable residential area in Cairo had become a necessity.

Independently wealthy, Princess Bahiga purchased 6,300 square metres of prime Zamalek land for the construction in 1922-3 of her Cairo townhouse. The choice of location was no coincidence. The epic receptions given by her grandfather at the Gezira Palace during the Suez Canal's 1869 opening celebrations had propelled into urban history what had until then been regarded as some quaint hamlet perched on shifting mud-reefs. It was also at the Gezira Palace that Princess Bahiga's parents celebrated their nuptials, and she may herself have been conceived in Zamalek.

Palais Toussoun consists of two independent units. The main building or Haramlek is at the southern end of the garden. The Salamlek—official quarters—and *daira* are on the northern perimeter. Whereas the princess, the three Toussoun children, Said, Hassan and Amina, and their large retinue lived in the Haramlek, the prince resided in the Salamlek. The family met daily at lunchtime in the Haramlek.

Princess Bahiga survived her husband by three years, dying in 1947. Before her death she deeded the palace specifically to her two grandsons, Hussein and Hassan. By so doing she excluded all other Toussoun grandchildren who might subsequently be born. Would estate problems arise in the future? Not really; as if to pre-empt any upcoming inheritance squabbles, in 1953 the State confiscated all properties belonging to the royal family. Henceforth, Palais Toussoun belonged to the people.

The palace's last pre-1953 occupants were Prince Said Toussoun and his second wife, the beautiful Nawal Zaki, and their infant son Aziz. The fall of the monarchy would ultimately condemn them to a life of luxurious exile between Paris and their country estate outside Deauville, France.

The first post-1953 occupant of Palais Toussoun was Anwar al Sadat. As chairman of the newly established Islamic Interchange Conference, he moved into the palace-turned-offices in the summer of 1954. His awe at the opulent surroundings notwithstanding, Egypt's future president was especially interested in Prince Said Toussoun's vintage collection of radio transmitters. In deference to his new duties and as purposefully underscored in *Al Ahram*'s August 25 front page, Sadat's first directive regarding Palais Toussoun was the conversion of Prince Said's well-stocked bar into a prayer hall.

Since then, a succession of government ministries have moved in and out of Palais Toussoun, last of which was the Regional Information Technology Software Engineering Centre (RITSEC)—the government's information technology arm. It's an appropriate enough tenant considering Prince Toussoun's fascination with radios, though satellite dish technology and high-speed computers have replaced the now antique transmitters.

The red villa

Of the 18 villas that stood on Zamalek's Hassan Sabry Street during the Second World War, only six have survived into the twenty-first century. Number 14 Brazil Street, today the Algerian Embassy, is one of the survivors. Unique for other reasons, it is also the only embassy villa in Cairo that was reportedly donated to a foreign state-in-the-making.

For that story we must go back in time to when that part of the street was still known as Gabalaya and the villa was listed as No. 42. Its owner was Daniel Nessim Curiel, the blind son of a moneylender who made his fortune bankrolling peasants and small landowners during the latter part of the nineteenth century.

Second generation usurers such as Daniel were ennobled with the title of bankers even though their occupation still consisted of *cambio* and money lending. They were needed to bridge-finance their clients' next crop since small farmers and petty landowners knew they would never be allowed through the doors of the National Bank of Egypt, or any other respectable bank for that matter.

Having lived a substantial part of his adult life in the upmarket island of Gezira, Daniel Curiel planned his new house meticulously. He would build it on that large empty tract of land across from where he actually lived. It would be spacious so as to satisfy the needs of his wife, Zefira, and their two sons, Raoul and Henri. It would be high enough so that anyone wanting to admire the Nile could do so from the second floor. There was no question about who would do the decoration—Jansen was all the rage in those days. And if the villa's 17 rooms did not include specific servants' quarters—ten of them in the service of the Curiels—they would have to make do with the basement.

Daniel Curiel also made plans for two exceptional rooms set aside for his personal relaxation. One was for his significant numismatic and medal collection estimated to be worth thousands of pounds, and the second for respite at the piano.

Cairo at the time did not want for first-rate architects so it was only a matter of price. And cost is precisely what delayed the project. This was 1929 and debt collectors across Egypt were in a fix. The New York financial crash had gone global and the Curiels would remain a few more years in their apartment at No. 69 Gabalaya Street. Meanwhile, the haggard employees in Curiel's grubby money-lending agency at No. 6 Chawarby Street in downtown Cairo would have to work overtime to recoup the losses.

It was only when the country's finances picked up in the mid-1930s that Villa Curiel went from blueprint to implementation. And if one believed the gossip, Jansen's premium services were discarded altogether for reasons of expense. Yet judging from its exterior, it is evident that another stately residence had been added to Zamalek's burgeoning repertoire. And even if the music room had to be shared with Zefira, who was herself a first-rate pianist, everything else was roughly as Daniel Curiel had planned. Well, almost.

As was the case with Zamalek's other stately homes, the children of the rich and famous were not as predictable as one imagined. There were those ready to rebel against their sagacious and sometimes bigoted parents.

Even amid the good living in Gezira, Cairo's best schools, the meals with three servants in attendance and the habitual summers in Europe, some youngsters, like the French-educated Raoul and Henri Curiel, found time to flirt with Marxism. But in Henri's case things were very serious for he went as far as declaring himself an Egyptian communist. But in this case the word 'Egyptian' is a little problematic since the Sephardic Curiels held Italian citizenship, a fact that did not prevent Daniel from opening his garden each Sunday to British officers and officials throughout the Second World War.

Singing *La Marseillaise* at school may have had something to do with the young Curiels' decision to end up in France rather than Italy. Raoul was the first to go, much to the distress of his father. A chagrin that paled, however, to that brought on by Henri, when the family homestead was searched for concealed manifestos printed by Henri's bookshop, Le Rondpoint. Moreover, the unrepentant millionaire-scion-turned-communist was preaching *l'Internationale* in Cairo's outlawed communist cells.

Prime Minister Ismail Sidki, whose villa was diagonally opposite Villa Curiel, had just about had it with the young founder of the Egyptian National Liberation Movement (MELN)—whoever his father might be. As far as the entrepreneur-minded Prime Minister was concerned, Henri's preaching was dangerous and infectious, so much so that some of Sidki's own nephews were quoting Trotsky! The Marxist epidemic had to stop.

The resulting fallout was also hurting Daniel Curiel's money-lending business. He died a broken man in November 1948, just as Henri was beginning a two-year tour of Egypt's prisons: Abbassia, Huckstep, Foreigners' Penitentiary and Oyoun Moussa in Sinai. Zefira, finding No. 42 Hassan Sabry overbearingly empty, moved into a *pension* and leased out Villa Curiel, first to Omar Chirine Bey and later to the Afghan Embassy.

Henri Curiel was released in 1950 and very soon after was expelled from Egypt, never to return to the family house on Hassan Sabry Street.

Here the contradicting stories about Villa Curiel's fate clash. One version says Henri Curiel donated his Zamalek mansion to Ahmed Ben Bella, the leader of the Algerian independence movement, to be converted into his country's first diplomatic mission in Cairo once an independent Algeria was established. The two men had become revolutionary comrades, with Henri providing the FLN (National Liberation Front) with tactical support and logistics. Yet according to Algerian statesman Lakhdar al Ibrahimi, it was President Gamal Abdel Nasser, not Curiel, who offered the house to the fledgling Algerian government.

The fact that unknown assailants gunned down Henri Curiel in 1978 at the entrance to his Paris home, and that Nasser had died eight years earlier, leaves Villa Curiel's bequest open to speculation.

On the other hand, since he is still alive, perhaps Ben Bella can set the record straight.

Death of a garden

Opposite the Algerian Embassy is a smart Mediterranean villa designed in the mid-1920s by Michel Liberman for landowner Mahmoud Khalifa. In the days when this villa dominated the northern end of the island's main residential street, it straddled a 6,200 square metre garden. But as is typical of any Cairo suburb, the present and the past have little in common.

For starters the street on which the villa stands has changed name three times. In the 1940s Gabalaya became Hassan Sabry Pasha Street and then three decades later the section north of 26th of July Street would become Brazil Street. Talk about geographic schizophrenia! The villa itself changed owners, colours and sizes so many times; writing its history would require an open-ended sabbatical at the Title and Deeds Bureau.

To make things simpler, let's start with the here and now, going backwards through the decades.

Devoid of its surrounding garden, the stand-alone villa is today the Embassy of Bahrain at No. 15 Brazil Street. Compressed between two large grubby buildings, it overlooks the length of Ismail Mohammed Street. If today the only way to visit its interior would be to apply for a visa, a few years ago it was much more accessible when it served as Bank of America's Cairo headquarters.

Between 1977 and 1981, Cairo's start-ups and upstarts would come to No. 15 hat in hand looking for soft loans during the heyday of Sadat's frenzied *infitah*. Besides easy money, they found eager tellers standing at large wooden counters and the inevitable gray-suited clerks tapping on calculators and adding machines behind glass doors. Everywhere you looked, dull green carpets and matching curtains looked back. The upstairs section boasted three impersonal executive offices and two restrooms also drenched in a similar shade of putrid green. Except for two elegant chandeliers, there was little else to remind you that this had been a home for the posh and lofty.

During its banking-a-go-go days, the villa turned from yellow to white. It took a month to paint its exterior. It took another three weeks for the paint to start peeling. And with the permission of its owner, Madame Tarabishi, a prefab floor was added to the villa's roof as the bank expanded its portfolio and chased after its bad debts.

Several tenants earlier, during the 1960s, No. 15 had been home to the Embassy of Afghanistan when Taliban and Mujahideen were still in the never-never. Kabul's next-to-last envoy to Cairo during the Afghan monarchy was Moussa Shafik. It was an unlucky day when the debonair diplomat was nominated his country's chief minister. He would be liquidated along with his country's political elite soon after.

Jumping a few interim tenants, we come to No. 15's original proprietor. Ibrahim Khalifa, a retired corporate consultant in Washington DC, believes his parents chose to live in Gezira because they were both familiar with its surroundings. Between them, the Khalifa and the Chawarby families owned some of the island's grandest homes.

Whereas Villa Khalifa is still standing, it is missing its lush garden, "which consisted of approximately 6,500 square metres of rich soil including what became a midan at the end of the street." Khalifa is referring to Midan Sidki at the convergence of Brazil, Mohammed Mazhar, and Aziz Abaza Streets. "This was an extension of the original garden." Then, like now, politicians were closet town-planners, a sideline that resulted in the demise of the first chunk of No. 15's garden.

As it turns out, fronting the Nile across the narrow Aziz Abaza Street stood the imposing villa of Ismail Sidki Pasha designed by Giuseppe Tavarelli. When Sidki assumed his first premiership in 1930, a decree unexpectedly appeared whereby a midan was created opposite his residence at the expense of the existing garden. The new square was appropriately baptised.

A decade and a half later, Sidki Pasha commissioned Albert Zananiri to replace his own garden with the rounded Sidki apartment building at No. 17 Aziz Abaza Street. Could it be the capitalist pasha didn't like green, or red, for that matter? His new ten-storey building would interrupt the vista that separated his home from the newly installed Embassy of the Soviet Union. Before the communists moved in *circa* 1944, the stately red palazzo designed by Luigi Manham had been the home of Ali Mahmoud Bey MP, brother of former Prime Minister Mohammed Mahmoud Pasha, Sidki's formidable opponent.

Another part of No. 15's garden was ceded for an unforeseen liquidity crunch. The buyer this time was Salvatore Cicurel Bey. "Thankfully," relates Khalifa, "he kept it intact for his weekend visits. This latest development meant we were surrounded by Egypt's department store czars, for somewhere to the south, off Hassan Sabry Street, was the villa and large garden of Levi de Benzion." That too would later disappear, as did Cicurel's weekend hideaway that transmuted into an outsized apartment building designed by Henri Fresco for account of sometime Sorbonne lecturer, Philippe Drakides. While the latter would henceforth enjoy a panoramic view of Cairo from his now fashionable tenth floor penthouse, Villa Khalifa would never see the Nile again.

"When I bicycled to the National Club (Nadi al Ahli), the only tall buildings I saw south of 26th of July Street were the Ades, Harari, Rodrigues, Naguib Youssef and Gabalaya House buildings. Wherever else you looked you saw front doors with gardens," reminisces Ibrahim Khalifa. His childhood memories will soon appear in book form as he puts pencil to paper somewhere in Washington DC in an attempt to explain to his American-born descendants where he comes from. But will they believe him when he tells them that Gezira Island was once a dormitory, its streets an open-air playground?

Les soeurs Henon

"We reluctantly parted with two properties in Zamalek," declared Marie-Louise and Christiane Henon in tandem. They were referring to two family-owned villas on Ismail Mohammed Street.

The delightful daughters of lawyer Marcel Henon grew up in Zamalek in the 1940s. They witnessed the many changes played out around them like a horror movie. Handsome villas giving way to ugly disproportionate buildings, garages transformed into boutiques, and irregular sidewalks hijacked by flower kiosks and mechanics. Later in the same movie, public alleyways become impromptu mosques with blaring microphones. And through a second floor window, a fly-over looks you straight in the face welcoming you to a concerto of car horns and carbon emissions. As for Zamalek's rooftops, well they had already developed a life of their own, becoming simulated hamlets for migrating labour and their farm animals. A fusion of urban and rural.

"Imagine waking up one day and discovering that the garden next door is a car service station!" exclaimed Marie-Louise.

"The castle-like Villa Assem lies abandoned. The grand Abdel Latif Bey house across the street leased to the Chinese Embassy became a noisy government school... and the few remaining trees are screaming for attention," chimes in Christiane.

After three generations of Henons in Egypt, the sisters opted for Paris where surroundings don't decline overnight.

The sisters agreed to sell their family home on Ismail Mohammed Strret to the Spanish Embassy in the 1980s, but only after receiving assurances that it would not be pulled down. Their grandfather had purchased it in 1929 from businessman Paul Lifschitz. "Before selling it to my family, Lifschitz, who may have run into financial difficulties during the crash, rented it out for one year to the Chawarby family," says Christiane Henon. Her grandfather, Achilles Henon Pasha, a French national, worked for the *Caisse de la Dette*, a debtors club set up in the late nineteenth century to control Egypt's expenditures.

According to the Henon sisters, their father purchased their second villa in 1939 from a bankrupt senator with the intention that they move therein leaving the original house to the now widowed Grandma Elise Henon.

> Our paternal grandmother was a daughter of Comte Selim de Chedid. She had quite a strong personality and I guess our parents wanted to live independently of her. In any case, they never moved into the new house since the British Army commandeered it for the benefit of WAAS, a women's auxiliary army service. It was during the Brits unwelcome tenancy that the mansion's priceless cedar-wood roof went up in flames, probably the result of one of the servicewomen smoking in the bathroom.

At the end of the hostilities, rather than return it to its owner, the British Army sub-leased the mansion to the Egyptian government, which occupies it to this day in the guise of Helwan University's School of Music. Located at the corner of Ismail Mohammed and Shagaret al Durr Streets, the Gothic mansion in question was designed by Adolfo Brandani and Domenico Limongelli (a relation of the Henon's by marriage) for the account of Senator Tewfik Ismail Bey from Upper Egypt. The bankrupt senator's name and emblem are still visible on the mansion's Shagaret al Durr façade surrounded by a sea of nauseating pink paint. Unable to evict Helwan University from the premises, the Henon sisters sold the mansion in 1985 to the State for a below market sum to be paid over five years. "To think that for over 50 years we were the rightful owners of this villa yet never spent a single night under its roof!" exclaimed Marie-Louise while Christiane nodded in support.

What the Henon sisters have not parted with, so far, is a wonderful example of art deco architecture on Mohammed Sakib Street (No. 5). Designed by Michel Liberman for landowner-businessman Hamed al Lozi Bey, the three-storey apartment house is as close to its original condition and context as is possible under the circumstances.

Liberman's opus

Standing back to back with the ex-Lozi Building is a white Mediterranean villa. Its address: No. 10 Taha Hussein Street.

Even before successive American occupants rendered No. 10 Taha Hussein famous for Fourth of July celebrations and coveted dinner parties, the villa was well known to polite society due to the variety of individuals who had lived there. And just as No. 10 was not always US government property, the name of the bordering street was not always Taha Hussein. Teddy Hasbani, the doyen of Willcocks Street, will gladly walk you through its history if asked.

"This was actually Willcocks Street, so named after the knighted engineer who built the Aswan Reservoir, which, incidentally, celebrated its centennial in November 2002." In the same vein, Hasbani, who although leaner bears an uncanny resemblance to Alfred Hitchcock, explains that Sir William Willcocks actually lived on the street bearing his name, in a villa that was the subject of Penelope Lively's novel *Oleander Jacaranda*. "Right next to the Cesar Levi house!" enunciates Hasbani in his Hitchcock-like pitch. "As for eminent writer and sometime Minister of Education Taha Hussein Pasha, he lived a few blocks from here, at No. 3 Baroudi Street."

It was only when the ambassadorial residence transferred to the US embassy compound in Kasr al Dubara, that No. 10 reverted in 1994 to what it had been prior to June 1967: the official residence of senior American diplomats. By tradition, it is the designated dwelling of Deputy Chiefs of Mission or DCMs, as they are better known. The first DCM to move into the house was Gordon H. Mattison in 1950.

A dozen or so DCMs later, just before they departed for Kosovo in May

2002, Reno Harnish and his vivacious wife Leslie shared happy moments with their friends and neighbours at No. 10. The showstopper of their last reception was the villa's magnificent stairway and its stained-glass screen authored by Italian artist Albano Macario of Torino. Missing tiny parts here and there, the screen was restored thanks to Leslie who also took time to dig up the history of the house and its architect.

Prior to becoming US territory in 1949-50, the villa had been occupied by senior party politicians. According to Professor Amina al Lozi, it was her mother's relation who commissioned Michel Liberman in 1924 to build No. 10. "Abdel Halim al Alaili Bey was secretary of the *Hizb al Ahrar al Doustouriyin* (Liberal Constitutional Party). He married Fatma al Lozi, who besides being a lady of many talents was an excellent pianist."

Alaili Bey died unexpectedly, the result of an abscess of the throat. When his childless widow fell sick and passed away shortly thereafter, the villa passed on to Fatma's father and heir, Abdel Fattah al Lozi Bey, who sold the villa *circa* 1938 to the Barakat family.

Thus, No. 10 changed political camps given that its new owners featured prominently among the Wafd leadership. The family patriarch, Fathallah Barakat Pasha, was one of the party's original members.

Eventually it was one of Fathallah Pasha's sons who took over No. 10. And as was customary then, if you couldn't find a bride within your own stock you married within the larger Wafdist circle. Which is why the elderly scion took for a wife the daughter of Wafdist Minister of Defense, Hamdi Seifelnasr Pasha.

The young bride had little in common with her overweight, tarboushed husband, 25 years her senior. Hastily widowed, the childless Siham lived on for a few more months at No. 10 before the Barakat heirs sold the villa for LE 40,000 (US$ 120,000 in those days) to the American State Department around 1949.

Thereafter, a string of American diplomats moved in and out of No. 10, some remembered more than others, each adding part of his persona so that from time to time the villa changed colours and makeup. It was only after the resumption of relations with the US, following Nixon's visit to Egypt in 1974 that No. 10 became home to US Ambassadors. They were successively Hermann Frederick Eilts, Alfred Leroy Atherton, Nicholas Alexander Veliotes, Frank G. Wisner II and Robert H. Pelletreau.

Neighbours like to point out how, when Donald Clayton Bergus lived at No. 10 as head of the American Interest Section at the Spanish Embassy, only one policeman guarded the place. This was when relations between the United States and Egypt were at their lowest following the June 1967 War. Paradoxically, with Egypt-US relations at their peak, it now takes a platoon of uniformed guards and security personnel with machine guns and walkie-talkies to protect Uncle Sam's Deputy-Envoy.

Could Liberman have ever foreseen that defensive walls, crowd barriers and hefty concrete blocks would one day incorporate themselves into the villa's exterior?

Whereas No. 10 Taha Hussein is constantly renovated, another Liberman villa, very much in the same style, is down on its luck. Ironically, the partly disfigured house is the preserve of Egypt's Mr. Art & Culture, the long-time minister of culture, Farouk Hosni. Located at the southern tip of Shagaret al Durr Street, the villa originally belonged to a Mr. Clouet, a Frenchman who worked for the Suez Canal Company prior to its nationalisation. When Villa Clouet became Villa Farid, it had more to do with worship than ownership. Clouet had converted to Islam and taken on a Muslim name in order to marry a beautiful Hejazi.

But what of architect Michel Liberman, who was he and where did he come from?

Like his name that is barely noticeable on a marble plaque above the doorway of No. 10 Taha Hussein Street, Liberman himself seems almost invisible. Not much can be found about him even though he catered to a top-drawer clientele. Unlike his Syrian, Italian and French colleagues, whose CVs and achievements were incessantly depicted in newspapers and magazines, Liberman is nowhere to be found, not even in the colourful *Mondain Egyptien*. No trace of him ever being decorated or receiving awards. No club memberships or group affiliations either. More importantly, no posthumous write-ups in specialised publications such as *Al-Emara*.

A less detailed commercial directory affirms in the 'Architect' section the existence of a Michel Literman prior to the First World War. After the war the name changes to Michel Liberman with a post box address. The same directory lists Liberman in the 1930s with an office in the Marconi Building at No. 18 Madabegh (later Cherif Pasha) Street. In 1955 the directory lists Liberman as sharing office space with architect Joseph Levy at No. 48 Kasr al Nil Street. There is no mention of Liberman after 1957.

The only person who remembers Liberman is George Khoury-Hadad.

Freshly graduated from the school of architecture in Alexandria, he apprenticed with Liberman in the early 1950s. He describes him as "short, bald and suffering from a nervous tick, constantly shaking his neck."

As for family life, Liberman didn't have any. He never married. His last known address was in a small building on Taha Hussein Street that he designed for his brother-in-law Silvio Matattia, an advertising agent. "Liberman had another sister married to a Benaroyo, a well-known Jewish family," says Khoury-Haddad. "I never met her neither was I ever invited to my employer's home." As for Liberman's nationality, Khoury-Haddad believes he held an Italian passport. "Despite his name I never heard him speak German. He conversed either in French, Italian or broken Arabic. He was a very private man."

Zamalek's three grand ladies

"Lebon along with Union-Vie and Ali Labib Gabr are the Three Grand Ladies of Zamalek," was how the late Mona Foda described the three 1950s buildings overlooking the Nile's small branch. A pioneer real estate agent specialising in luxury apartments, she dealt extensively with the Grand Ladies, showing off their respective apartments to foreign envoys, corporate managers and bank directors. One of Foda's favourite lines was "If from the outside they look plain and pockmarked with balconies, the interiors have a lot of presence. They are bright and spacious with an excellent ratio of bedrooms to baths."

No doubt about it, grand in scale these buildings have always been. Built in the heyday of Egypt's boardroom capitalism, two were commissioned for the French capital ventures—Compagnie Centrale d'Eclairage et de Chauffage par le Gaz (LEBON) and the La Compagnie de l'Union-Vie. The third was owned and designed by Ali Labib Gabr, Egypt's foremost Egyptian architect at the time.

Understandably, the arrival of the Three Grand Ladies upset more than just a few old timers. Not only did the utilitarian tower blocks usher in a new era in architecture, but it also meant that villas and gardens were now officially on Zamalek's endangered species list. In fact, one of Zamalek's prized gardens had been sacrificed for Gabr's concrete edifice.

What's more, the Three Grand Ladies trespassed the accepted norm of three to four-storey interwar art deco *immeubles de rapport* scattered throughout the island and sporting names like Dorchester House, Grenville, Gordon House, Air House, Embassy Court, Darenth, Victoria Building, North End. Conversely, Soliman House, Pyramids House, Dar al Hanna and Dar al Salaam were there to remind the islanders they were in Egypt and not somewhere in Highgate, North London. Irrespective of their names, all had respected the island's unsanctioned zoning laws.

Stylised concrete forms and lacklustre streamlined shapes had come to replace pastiches, neo and retro revivals of preceding styles. The age of 'international' or 'rational' style was more for function and return per square metre than into the benefits of high ceilings and whimsical refinements. Le Corbusier had won the day with his plain, ornament-free flat surfaces and straight lines. "*Quelle horreur, mais c'est la fin de Zamalek!*" must have been the catchphrase in some of the island's Francophone salons. Trapped between two worlds, the old timers were persuaded that the island was on a downward slope. It was as though the sleepy suburb had abruptly graduated into a vulgar inner-city borough. Even worse, one of Cairo's vital lungs was about to choke on cement.

Out of the three architects involved, only Ali Labib Gabr was a *bona fide* native. He represented the first generation of modern Egyptian architects and deservedly became Dean of the School of Architecture at Cairo University. Besides his white triangular building on Zamalek's Ibn Zanki Street, Gabr's legacy can be found across Cairo, from international style apartment houses to California genre villas. One of his better-known Zamalek compositions is the Nile-front Yehya Building, mistakenly called *Emarat* (Mohammed) Abdel Wahab after the famous singer-composer who lived there. Another one of his preferred creations belonged to Dr. Mohammed Reda before the latter sold it in 1949 to the newly independent government of India. Henceforth, the villa on Zamalek's Mohammed Mazhar Street became the high-profile residence of India's ambassadors to Egypt.

The principal architect of the Union-Vie Building was Max Edrei, an Egyptian-born Jew from Simbelawein. He had worked in France with the Chief Architect of Paris, Leon Azema, who participated in the design of

Palais de Chaillot on the banks of the Seine.

By far the most prolific architect of that generation is Antoine Selim Nahas, designer of the Lebon. He is also responsible for two of Kasr al Dubara's principal buildings, François Tager and Al Chams, as well as the two monoliths on Midan al Tahrir, the Bahari Buildings.

The son of a Syrian textile industrialist, Nahas was educated at Cairo's Collège des Frères. Much later in his career he would build the extant college in Daher. "He was one of the rare men in the world who cumulated two major prestigious degrees, namely Beaux Arts of Paris and Ecole Centrale. It took him 13 years of university studies." recalls Selim Nahas in New York. "I also remember at King's Farouk's request, my father designed the Shooting Club in Dokki and refused to be paid. He was given the title of Bey in return, which he turned down."

Although Nahas's first major project was the design of Beirut's National Museum around 1930, most of his working career was spent in Cairo where he started as Chief Architect for the Ministry of Education. And if in Beirut Nahas chose an evident neo-pharaonic theme for the museum's majestic façade, in Cairo he steered away from anything Egyptian or Islamic preferring instead to run with the more aesthetic-free international style.

All of the above architects studied architecture in the West at a time when Frank Lloyd Wright made headlines in America and Le Corbusier was still evoked in Paris.

But not everyone is appreciative of postwar international style. Global denizen-cum-self-styled interior designer, Magda Sidki, leases an apartment in Lebon while owning another in a Giza high-rise also designed by Nahas. She complains that their layouts are impractical. "There are too many corridors and ill-placed concrete beams. The space has been badly exploited so that you need to rework the layout. And who needs balconies in our day and age?"

True, the Three Grand Ladies do not lack balconies. This only goes to show that at the time of their conception in the late 1940s and early 1950s, sunny Cairo was noise-free and carbon emissions were still unknown. Gradually, most of the dust-gathering balconies were incorporated into their respective apartments so that they could better showcase the dramatic view outside.

But as attention turned more and more towards interiors, some of them lavish beyond reproach, the exterior suffered in direct proportion.

Individualism had taken over to a point that seen from outside, any one floor looks different from the one above or below it. If one balcony is glassed in with aluminium frames, the one above looks like a wooden cabana and the one below is walled in with red bricks. From time to time there is the perennial *manshar* (washing line) advertising entire wardrobes from ladies' lingerie to children's designer undies. And when you add to these accretions and impositions the adjacent buildings, you are left with a truly unique streetscape. Goodbye concord and harmony, hello egoism!

Until very recently, the Three Grand Ladies suffered from downright neglect. Two of them saw their original owners replaced in the 1960s by thrifty state-owned insurance companies that knew next to nothing regarding real estate management. Currency devaluation coupled with archaic housing laws meant the owners of the Ali Labib Gabr building and their counterparts across the city were raking in a monthly pittance in terms of rent. The protected tenants meanwhile had become used to what amounted to free lodging, abstaining from any collective participation in the maintenance of their buildings.

Another anomaly that has hit the Three Grand Ladies is how uncaring individuals blatantly transformed their apartments into offices, thus abusing and wearing down the common utilities. This phenomenon has been replicated across the city so that, in many instances, entire apartment buildings have been changed into office space with all the negative consequences such a travesty entails.

Understandably, the prematurely aged Grand Ladies have turned into crumpled dowagers in desperate need of facelifts. When businessman Wafik Shamaa asked his wealthy Lebon neighbours to chip in for the upgrading and restoration of the building's utilities and public areas, less than 50 percent responded. "I'm nevertheless pleased with the result," he says. "Had I made that same request 15 years ago the response would have been less than ten percent."

Disappointing outcomes, especially when one learns the Three Grand Ladies are home to the country's leading politicians, legislators, senior diplomats as well as screen goddesses and teen idols.

Shamaa accepts that we are beginning to realise that socialism is dead and that a businesslike approach to maintenance and restoration could extend as well as enrich the city's remarkable architectural legacy. "More importantly we all stand to gain financially from this turnaround."

Figures speak for themselves—a large apartment in Lebon now sells for in excess of LE2 million.

The humble renovation of Lebon's palatial entrance is a welcome sign that, after years of abandon, Cairo's privileged inhabitants are appreciating and restoring to public view some of the city's landmark buildings. And in a departure that some critics will deride as overly capitalistic, these efforts are mostly a result of privatisation and, yes, a belated re-awakening of basic civic responsibilities. As the new millennium dawns, people are beginning to appreciate for the first time the design revolution that occurred in the early decades of the twentieth century, much of it manifested in Zamalek, Garden City and downtown Cairo.

The Three Grand Ladies of Zamalek may have a new lease on life yet.

Roosevelt's waqf

Piercing the Cairo skyline, the lotus shaped *Al Borg* (Cairo Tower) was meant to impress the world as a great Nasserite achievement. It would also become the logo of the nation's capital. Yet no one can blame the Egyptian administration if the tower's April 11, 1961, inaugural ceremony was a low-key affair with only a Nasser crony, Kamal al Din Hussein, unveiling the tower's commemorative marble plaque. There was so much else going on that month plus *Al Rais* had other worldly concerns to attend to.

On April 12 the Cold War climaxed again when the Soviet Union upstaged the United States by putting the first man into space aboard a Vostok-1 rocket. From that day onwards, 27-year-old cosmonaut Yuri A. Gagarin became world famous.

Four days later, Fidel Castro infuriated John F. Kennedy's Camelot, following the botched Bay of Pigs landing. Meanwhile, in Europe, de Gaulle suffered his worst ever humiliation as Algeria gathered momentum towards independence. The indisposition of the West meant that Nasser and Tito, two self-congratulating pillars of the burgeoning Non-Aligned Movement, had a lot to discuss during their whistle-stop tour of the Cairo Tower on April 21.

On the Giza plateau meanwhile, the Great Sphinx was about to speak for the first time in 4,400 years, courtesy of the first Sound and Light show inaugurated on April 13 by President Nasser and Crown Prince (later King) Constantine of Greece. And at the old Opera House, world-famous conductor-composer Aram Khachaturian put the final touches to his *Rhapsody Concerto for Violins* to be premiered on April 20 with the presidents of Egypt and Yugoslavia in attendance.

No wonder the Cairo Tower played second fiddle.

But whatever Al Borg lacked in feisty inaugurals and architectural pizzazz, this was more than compensated in print thanks to its controversial origins. The 187-metre high structure has been written up in countless volumes dealing with Nasser's Egypt. The first to do so was the CIA's Miles Copeland in *A Game of Nations* where he reveals how the LE450,000 tower was built with American hush money intended as a bribe to Egypt's strongman. The main player in this Cold War episode was Kermit Roosevelt, a relative of the two American presidents of the same surname.

Roosevelt, then a roving CIA operative, allegedly gave Nasser's confidant Hassan al Tohami a suitcase stacked with small bills amounting to one million US dollars, reportedly to be used for purchasing presidential "security accessories".

Furious at the suggestion that he could be bought, Nasser resolved to translate the CIA's hush money into the most transparent and un-diplomatic rebuttal. He would build the highest structure in Cairo, 43 metres taller than the largest pyramid at Giza. It would rise from the ground like a giant middle finger so that even the Americans would see it.

Henceforth, the tower was known in Egyptian officialdom as *waqf* Roosevelt or Roosevelt's foundation. Either out of ignorance or a devilish desire to sour relations even more, Arabists in Washington's State Department put a negative spin on the whole affair when they interpreted the word *waqf* to mean *waqef* (erection) underscoring the malicious pun.

Furious at the assumed Egyptian slight, the American administration retaliated by referring to the Cairo Tower as "Nasser's Prick". The *double-entendre* notwithstanding, it has made for entertaining and anecdotal reading. Since then, journalists and authors alike cannot resist mentioning the incident in their political memoirs.

Unaware that the Cairo Tower was a pawn in the East-West struggle, Katherine Hepburn was the first Hollywood great to visit it.

Despite the LE10,000 per year concession given to Shaher Catering Co.

the tower's amenities quickly acquired a characteristic public sector look. Tour d'Argent it most certainly wasn't despite the 30-minute panorama provided by the revolving restaurant. "It rotated with fits and starts so that Stella beer kept spilling from your glass," recalls former airline attorney Tamim Foda, who frequented the tower in his adolescent days. On the other hand, his mother never visited the tower. "It's not due to high anxiety or anything of the sort... it's because Zamalek lost part of a unique garden to make way for someone's big ego."

With the entry ticket priced at 10 piastres, couples took to meeting illicitly high in the sky. The shudder and thrill of an elevator travelling towards the observation deck at the speed of three metres per second was the best thing since the invention of the roller coaster. Like the revolving restaurant, Al Borg was built in fits and starts. According to the tower's chief architect, Naoum Shebib, work on the earthquake-proof lotus-shaped structure was interrupted for almost three years due to the Suez War of 1956. In all, it took five full years and 500 workers to build it.

"Yet for someone who built Egypt's then-tallest structure, his honorarium was surprisingly short," comments one of Shebib's relations in Canada 40 years later.

Honouring the patriot

Mahmoud Mokhtar, the author of *Egypt's Awakening*, that magnificent granite statue in front of Cairo University, died a frustrated man. His court case against the Egyptian government for non-payment of LE8,000, a very large sum in those days, remained unresolved.

The monies in question had to do with an order Mokhtar received from Mustafa al Nahas's Wafd-led government in March 1930, commissioning Egypt's *primo* sculptor to produce two larger than life statues of Egypt's nationalist leader Saad Zaghloul Pasha.

In Paris at the time, Mokhtar travelled to Egypt to understand what was required of him. Upon reaching a preliminary agreement with the Ministry of Public Works on March 19, Mokhtar set off to produce two model statues. Upon their acceptance he could begin work on the real thing.

The stone models were acclaimed and a contract was signed. It was agreed that the two 6.5 metre statues and their respective bases would be produced in France where Mokhtar had the benefit of a studio and a team of experienced helpers. However, somewhere along the way, a new non-Wafd government changed its mind concerning the bases. To Mokhtar, who had already commenced work, this was a flagrant breach of contract.

Mokhtar died before there was an outcome to the litigation. More importantly, Mokhtar never knew his two Zaghloul statues made history standing atop landmark sites in both Cairo and Alexandria. In Cairo, Zaghloul Pasha soars above the Father of Rivers at the main entrance to Gezira via Kasr al Nil Bridge. In Alexandria he faces the city's historic Eastern Harbour. What greater gratification for any Egyptian sculptor than to have his works at the epicentre of the nation's first and second capitals?

The simultaneous unveiling ceremonies took place on August 27, 1938. As was customary under the monarchy, court and government spent the summer months in Alexandria. It was therefore the coastal city's statue that received full honours with the presence of the king and the members of his household along with the acting prime minister and his entire cabinet. All turned out to pay homage to the man who had led the way to Egypt's independence.

Naturally, every Wafdist of consequence was present to honour the founder of Egypt's leading party. From among the 2,000 attendees in the official marquee, the only conspicuous absentee was Saad Zaghloul's wife. The Mother of the Egyptians or *Umm al Masreyeen*, as Safeya Hanem was called, did not attend due to a seating arrangement blunder. Whereas she was meant to sit next to King Farouk during the unveiling ceremony, grumbling from the conservative Muslim clergy resulted in last-minute changes unbecoming for a lady of her stature and position. Madame Zaghloul, who by then was a potent national symbol for Egyptian women, stayed at home and listened to the live broadcast of the event instead. Informed of the blunder after the fact, the 18-year-old king later called on Safeya Hanem to apologise.

In Cairo, the statue was also unveiled at 5pm, this time by Minister of Justice Ahmed Khashaba Pasha. Keeping him company was a much more rambunctious crowd. Despite the passing of 11 years since Zaghloul's death and the time-honoured propensity to confine hero-worship to living incumbents, many citizens had not forgotten the man who had so valiantly fought against the British. It was, after all, Zaghloul who had called for the unprecedented general strike in 1919 that brought the entire nation to a grinding halt, setting off Egypt's long struggle for independence.

There was another reason for attending the Cairo unveiling. The statue stood on an island still considered a virtual British enclave. More importantly, it faced the notorious Kasr al Nil barracks across the Nile where a large British garrison was headquartered. Despite Zaghloul's efforts and those of his successors, the British still maintained military bases in Egypt. Here again was a chance for a poke at that oldest of colonial powers.

Many onlookers at the Cairo unveiling were seized by the statue itself. Was that Zaghloul depicted in one of his legendary fiery speechmaking postures, or was he perched up there giving the finger to his sworn enemies?

But what of the bases, subject of Mokhtar's litigation? Who then was responsible for the two statues' mighty granite substructures?

A local newspaper indicated at the time that the Ministry of Public Works awarded the contract for the Cairo statue pedestal to Andrea Vescia, an Italian contractor. Regarded as the "king of granite", he had undertaken various important contracts across the country. Luciano Zaccour, Vescia's now elderly grandson, writes from Canada, "He supplied granite to several landmark monuments, including the Esna Barrage and Kasr al Nil Bridge. As a matter of fact, he was one of the original sub-contractors who worked on the old Aswan Dam between 1898 and1902. He also owned the unique villa that stood on a granite hill next to Aswan's Grand Hotel."

Working closely with Vescia on the statue's titanic stand was engineer Mustafa Fahmi Pasha. According to Ali Fahmi, now a retired architect living in Paris, "The design of the neo-pharaonic base is the work of my father, court architect Mustafa Fahmi Pasha, whose wife's aunt was Madame Zaghloul Pasha, Umm al Masreyeen." With time, Fahmi and Mokhtar would themselves become related when Ali married Mokhtar's niece.

The Alexandrian base is reportedly the work of one Yanni Nikolaides.

If Mokhtar died a frustrated man, thanks to his efforts Egypt's great patriot received his due and presides over the centres of Egypt's two largest cities. Eventually, Mokhtar would also be posthumously honoured when a delightful Zamalek museum, designed by Ramses Wissa Wassef, was dedicated to his works in July 1963. The Mokhtar Museum, a facsimile pharaonic temple, stands a few hundred metres behind Saad Zaghloul's statue, just a stone's throw from yet another important statue which, this time, was not designed by Egypt's leading sculptor.

Albeit smaller than that of his mentor, Ahmed Maher's statue faces the Nile's smaller branch opposite Evacuation Bridge.

A diehard nationalist, Ahmed Maher Pasha is best remembered as one of three Egyptian premiers assassinated in the twentieth century. The dastardly deed occurred on February 24, 1945, a few minutes after he had declared war on the Axis during a fiery speech in the Lower Chamber. The portly premier was gunned down at short range as he walked out of parliament.

Since Mokhtar was already dead, the author of Maher Pasha's statue was a little-known artist, Mohammed Hilmi Youssef, and this time there was no fanfare and celebration around the pedestal. In fact, the statue remained veiled for quite some time until Mother Nature unceremoniously interceded. "*Il n'ya pas eu d'inauguration officielle de cette statue. Les vents de l'hiver l'ont dévoilée en une nuit de Fevrier, sans temoin et sans etoile.*" reported *Le Progrés* a week later in 1950.

The tower of shame

What if Cairo's governor decided to make a gift to the nation's capital? One suggestion is that he rid the city of one of its worst-ever eyesores and sends a clear message to urban culprits, past and present, that the days when anyone could do as they pleased with the skyline are over.

The Tower of Shame, perhaps inspired by the cardboard tube nestling at the heart of a roll of toilet paper, is the still uninhabited 45-storey building standing at the intersection of Zamalek's Gezira and Hassan Sabry Streets, across from that assortment of ramshackle huts which calls itself a police station.

The Tower of Shame is the brainchild of Khaled Foda, a former under-secretary who in his civil service days worked for Hassaballah Kafrawi, the minister responsible for billions of pounds worth of reconstruction and new settlements projects. Disregarding the 'how' and 'when,' let's just say Foda's fortunes took a timely turn for the better and the Tower of Shame is one of his 1980s watershed trophies.

Likewise, let's not ask whether Foda has heard of Isaac Newton. For the time being his building successfully defies the law of gravity. One hopes it will do the same if exposed to seismic tremors or some other form of natural catastrophe. The Tower of Shame could become the curse from which Zamalek may never recover.

For the time being the building stands empty and desolate earning the ire of those who drive beneath it. But how much longer will it remain inactive? For sure its owner is pushing all available buttons to breathe life into it. According to a source close to the governor, not a day goes by without someone of consequence calling on Foda's behalf for this or that permit or license.

Besides safety hazards and other anomalies, the building has no garage to speak of, which means that if it should ever be used as an apartment building where each tenant owns two cars or more, the resultant traffic jam will make Ramadan rush-hour look like a midnight picnic.

The other option is that the Tower of Shame be turned into a five-star hotel, a project that is likely. But does Zamalek really need a hotel which stands 45 storeys high, hugging two narrow streets each barely six metres wide? We only have to look at what happens whenever a tourist bus heaves out of the Marriott Hotel and how things get ten times worse when mothers rush their loved ones to and from nearby schools and nurseries. Observe the total chaos that ensues at the entrance of the nearby Gezira Club during teen rush-hour. Multiply all that by ten and then add 30 additional tourist buses, 40 eager taxis, a dozen rentals and 150 private cars each time there is a Tower of Shame wedding. Get the picture?

Supposedly, the Tower of Shame's owner is ready to negotiate a lucrative deal with any interested party in order to create an underground garage, be it under the Gezira Sporting Club, the Fish Garden or the ratty police precinct across the street. The question remains, however, why didn't Foda negotiate the parking problem *before* he took it upon himself to reach for the sky? Who gave him the go-ahead for so obvious a problem-maker?

In any case the building is there, sneering at Zamalek's heavyweights and so-called politicos, those who saw it coming yet did nothing about it. The Tower of Shame is there so that our kids can realise how it was open season for architectural terrorism in the 1980s and 1990s when, in the absence of civil society and a democratic system, gluttonous businessmen seconded by corrupt politicians destroyed our cities. It is there so that one fateful day, when fire breaks out on the 38th floor and 30 Swiss and 15 Japanese tourists are trapped and charred, we will be painfully reminded that accountability where it counts most was non-existent. Can we therefore blame the next generations if someday they condemn us for all of this?

In the next few years, encounters with this concrete reality will not be happy ones. Lamentably, Zamalek's inhabitants have but themselves to blame. Their collective silence and lack of involvement made it possible for the likes of Foda and his accomplices to have it their own way.

As things stand, the Fodas reign supreme. The real test is whether our officials and legislators will come out and condemn architectural terrorism, not just when it is against them but when it is against the laws of nature.

Godless architecture or Cairo betrayed?

Built in the dreary 1960s, an era when architects forgot there is a God, Al Borg Hotel should earn its place in urban history as the vanguard of Cairo's disfigurement. The uncomfortable truth is this infamous hotel, with its thicket of concrete walls and garish stucco, was a precursor to a trend that spread unabated across the capital and beyond

Contrary to the Ministry of Tourism's caprice and despite frantic searches for any redemptive virtue justifying this project, any self-respecting architect will tell you Al Borg Hotel should never have been built, let alone dubbed a five-star hotel. A home for mad cows or a refugee camp is more like it. And as things continue to go downhill, one may think it is currently used as target practice for a Third World War.

But then there's the other capital sin. Notice how this Nile-front hotel faces Kasr al Nil Bridge, the Nile Hilton, the Ramses Hilton and the Semiramis Inter-Continental. Where can you go from there?

Hotel al Borg occupies Cairo's most precious real estate. Who then is the lucky one who owns this priceless chunk of property, in addition to the two or so acres that surround it?

How about the Teacher's Syndicate?

The land was given almost free of charge to the budding Teachers' Union back in the 1930s with the intent that developers and builders of the day conceive something of urban coherence. They created a park and a clubhouse surrounded by trees so that teachers from all over Cairo would have a place where they could retire, get inspired and enjoy themselves.

Although it didn't exist officially, in those days there was some form of neighbourhood development ordinance. Its job was to ensure that no single person or group of individuals could introduce at random anything that pleased them thus subverting the rest of the community.

With little more than their straightforward *cahier des charges* and sensible zoning regulations, builders and town planners of the 1910s had devised practical ways to wield an explicit and positive influence on more than just the projects they planned and designed each year. Why can't we do the same a century later?

Ironically, these were the days when government played a minimal role in urban development. That is precisely why new towns such as Garden City, Maadi, Heliopolis, and Koubbeh Gardens were developed with such high standards. For that reason alone it was a very sad day when the developers of these towns and districts were removed in the 1960s. Sadder still when the government took over most aspects of every day life.

And what did Big Brother come up with in the meantime? Nasr City and Mohandiseen! Ah, yes, and Al Borg Hotel. And that's not all. What should have been old but still functional prototypes for creating other new suburbs, we began wantonly to destroy.

The time has come to reverse the bias. Already more people agree that preserving historic buildings and districts is a good thing; that old-fashioned buildings and commercial downtown Cairo could become great pleasures; that if this new trend is destined to continue and grow, then maybe the prevailing architectural madness can turn into hope.

Yet if we really mean business, and in order to make the point clear that there is no returning to architectural mayhem, the first thing to be done is the instant removal of the ignoble Al Borg Hotel.

Basna Shaarawi house
Setting an unbidden precedent in Garden City, Basna Hanem Shaarawi replaced her unique arabesque residence with an apartment building in the early 1950s. Her landmark villa on Tahrir Square belonging to her famous mother suffered the same fate a decade later.

Kasr Adly Yeken Pasha

Designed by Antonio Lasciac for statesman Adly Yeken Pasha and his wealthy wife, this Garden City palace was commonly referred to as Kasr Sherif Pasha Sabry before it was pulled down in the late 1970s. The plot of land will eventually hold a Four Seasons Hotel, scheduled to open in 2004.

Kasr al Nil Bridge and Gezira

Opened in 1933 and originally named after Khedive Ismail, Kasr al Nil Bridge ultimately helped to increase the speed of settlement on the once virgin island of Gezira. This image, from the 1950s, still shows a remarkably empty skyline.

Red Court

The buzzing Zamalek of today was made at the sacrifice of villas like Red Court and its surrounding park. Built for hotelier Charles Baehler in the 1920s, Red Court became the property of Hassan Shaarawi Pasha before developers replaced it with eight tall buildings.

The pressures of space

The division of family properties can result in daunting encroachments as evidenced by Shafik Pasha's villa now copulating with a contiguous construction overlooking the Nile in Giza.

The murder villa

Giza's Villa Solomon Cicurel was the scene of Egypt's most talked about 1920s society murder. Apparently the ghosts of this homicide have not yet gone to sleep.

Tower of Shame
Defying the laws of gravity and municipal common sense, the Tower of Shame reaches for the sky while Egyptian's town planners look on indifferently. The building is still uninhabited!

The Indian Embassy

A reminder of the not too distant past, this Zamalek residence designed by Ali Labib Gabr for a wealthy bourgeois family was purchased by the Indian embassy and is today one of 14 remaining Cairo villas with direct access to the Nile.

Music School, Zamalek

This Gothic mansion, built in the 1920s, has played various roles. It was first home to a bankrupt senator from Upper Egypt, then headquarters of a Second World War women's auxiliary in the British forces, and later became Helwan University's Music School.

The Sakakini Palace

With its centennial-old wooden turrets and metal spires hidden by overgrowth, the backless Habib Sakakini folly, located near Daher, conjures up thoughts of Disneyland and Grimm fairy tales. Its only use today is for contractors to line their pockets when, every now and then, the government half-heartedly decides to restore it.

5. The west bank

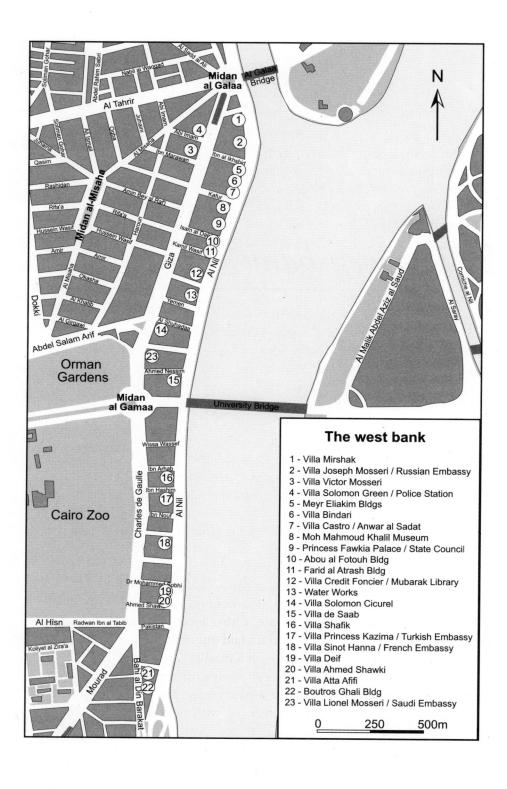

N

The west bank

1 - Villa Mirshak
2 - Villa Joseph Mosseri / Russian Embassy
3 - Villa Victor Mosseri
4 - Villa Solomon Green / Police Station
5 - Meyr Eliakim Bldgs
6 - Villa Bindari
7 - Villa Castro / Anwar al Sadat
8 - Moh Mahmoud Khalil Museum
9 - Princess Fawkia Palace / State Council
10 - Abou al Fotouh Bldg
11 - Farid al Atrash Bldg
12 - Villa Credit Foncier / Mubarak Library
13 - Water Works
14 - Villa Solomon Cicurel
15 - Villa de Saab
16 - Villa Shafik
17 - Villa Princess Kazima / Turkish Embassy
18 - Villa Sinot Hanna / French Embassy
19 - Villa Deif
20 - Villa Ahmed Shawki
21 - Villa Atta Afifi
22 - Boutros Ghali Bldg
23 - Villa Lionel Mosseri / Saudi Embassy

0   250   500m

Gardens of delight

For a long time, Cairo's other half, Giza, was best known for its pyramids, its university and its zoo. The three could be found not far from each other in a predominantly green setting. Generations of Cairenes loved to brag that theirs was the fourth best zoo in the world. In the last few decades, however, since the recession of the 1960s and the *infitah* of the 1970s, Giza has undergone a horrific transformation. The intermittent green patches of the zoo, which celebrated its centennial in 1997, are all that is left of what was once Cairo's fertile hinterland.

Cairo's zoo is a legacy of Khedive Ismail. Originally, it occupied 50.4 feddans, once part of the Harem Gardens or 'Gardens of Delight' as its sequestered inhabitants then called it. Whether it was in his quest to green Cairo or to awe his beautiful Circassian concubines, Ismail imported what resulted in one of the finest collections of flowers, exotic plants and trees that India, Central Africa and South America had to offer. A survivor is the zoo's giant banyan, planted around 1871. As for the collection of animals that came to form the backbone of the zoo, it all began with Ismail's private menagerie.

In the late 1870s, the palace and gardens—the first executed by the Italian contractor Giuseppe Garozzo and the second conceived by Barillet Deschamps, the famous nineteenth-century landscaper whose gardens and parks still adorn Paris today—were passed on to the State in partial settlement of the khedive's accumulated debts. The Harem Building was used as a museum for Egyptian treasures and antiquities until the current museum on Midan al Tahrir was opened in 1902. And while the southern portion of the Salamlek Garden fronting the Nile was sold to the public—resulting in many stately Nile villas—the gardens of the harem remained intact.

Some wonders of the former Harem Gardens included roads paved with black flagstones imported from Trieste. Other footpaths were worked in pebbles resembling sugar-coated almonds laid out in arabesque and Roman mosaics. There was the idyllic pond with a marble island in its centre that later became the zoo's Tea Island where so many notables and their consorts spent their stolen moments. Giant ferns grew under the shade of large trees.

The khedivial park was also ornamented with several grottoes and on every knoll stood a lookout kiosk. Canals sprinkled with a fine collection of water plants and inhabited by the khedive's hybrid salmon trout wound through the gardens. The canals were spanned by rustic bridges of various workmanship, their handrails covered with velvet so as not to hurt the delicate fingers of the khedive's harem.

One crossing that stood out from the rest, joining two artificial hills, was a light suspension viaduct built by Alexandre-Gustave Eiffel. It was brought to Cairo after Ismail visited the Paris Exhibition of 1867. It was, and remains to this day, the only bridge in Egypt associated with the celebrated designer, and if you look close enough you may still find the metal plaque bearing the engineer's name buried under several layers of green paint.

According to contemporary eyewitnesses, the flora that adorned the Harem Gardens was more than sufficient as an attraction. The suggestion of adding fauna for the creation of a zoo was considered by some to be redundant and unnecessary. Apart from aesthetic concerns that cages would disfigure the gardens, Cairo's sub-tropical climate, while ideal for plants and trees, was viewed by some as unsuitable for furred four-legged inmates.

Nonetheless, the project of the zoo went forward at a cost to the State of LE7,400. The responsibility for laying it out between 1891 and 1901 was given to A.R. Birdwood. The zoo officially opened in 1897 and by 1900 the annual cost of running it had reached LE1,600 of which LE1,000 was a grant from the government and the remainder derived from private donations. Captain Stanley S. Flower, who was responsible for the animals, became the zoo's first director, a post that he occupied until 1924. Each year, in concurrence with the zoo's prestigious board of trustees, Flower submitted to the government his celebrated State of the Zoo Report. The report was reproduced in the local papers to be scrutinised by nature lovers and wildlife supporters forever eager to learn what new plant or animal had been imported.

By the end of the Second World War, the zoo boasted 4,700 exhibits including 3,500 birds, 700 mammals and 500 reptiles, a far cry from Khedive Ismail's original menagerie of 78 mammals and 180 feathered creatures.

Gradually, the zoo's inmates increased with a tiny percentage entering this world through the efforts of the inhabitants themselves, such as the two Kudu antelopes born in 1907, making them the first ever to be bred in captivity. As new animals arrived—some to stay, others in transit on their way to other zoos—old inmates died of natural causes, epidemics or heat apoplexy. The bulk of the animals however, continued to be imported from different parts of Africa and Asia.

The number of human visitors to the zoo was climbing as well. In 1899, there were 43,567, yet by 1906 these had increased fivefold to 223,525. Zoo attendance climbed in proportion to Cairo's burgeoning population. Feast days and certain public holidays would result in record highs, sometimes to the annoyance of the animals and their keepers. To this day, and despite its neglected state, Khedive Ismail's former Harem Gardens continue to draw record attendance on any given public holiday.

The way things are going it will be a great sorrow indeed if the maimed Giza zoo becomes the last refuge in Egypt where one can glimpse a bit of fauna and some exotic flora.

The Giza and Rhoda Land Company

By the heyday of Egypt's liberalism in the 1930s, the riverfront stretch, south of the land now occupied by the Cairo Sheraton Hotel, had matured into an exclusive suburb west of Cairo. The row of stately mansions and gardens overlooking the Nile occupied what had been part of Khedive Ismail's Giza estate.

Following Ismail's exile and the subsequent privatisation of his landholdings, his Giza property was carved up into the Giza Zoo, the Orman Gardens, and the precursor of what became Fouad al Awal (now Cairo) University. The rest of the land was sold to the private sector as described in the *Egyptian Gazette* of April 13, 1903:

> Mr. Zervudachi has purchased an extent of 190 feddans of Government land situated at Ghizeh, and consisting of the foreshore of the Nile from the waterworks garden to Ghizeh prison and of a portion of the old Museum garden. The purchase price is the extremely advantageous one of P.T. 40 per sq. metre, which will therefore bring in to the Government the magnificent sum of LE120000. Mr. Zervudachi has also, we understand, obtained an option to purchase a further 30 feddans at the same price within a fixed period. Prince Hussein Pasha Kamel has purchased the remainder of the foreshore extending from the Pont des Anglais to the Waterworks garden at the rate of P.T. 37 per sq. metre.

The following year, the Giza and Rhoda Land Company, belonging to the Zervudachi-Rodocanachi brothers-in-law, launched Giza's suburban section. Its aim was to divide up the Giza property and build upmarket villas for either sale or lease. All that was needed was the promised bridge that would link Giza to the island of Rhoda and the rest of the city. Alas, the coming of the much-awaited bridge would be postponed another four years. Failing to live up to its ambitious blueprint, the company ended in disaster with one of the partners committing suicide in order to avoid financial embarrassment.

The belated inauguration of Abbas Bridge in February 1908 led to the first significant changes to Giza's skyline. The second wave of changes came after the August 1912 inauguration of the Ataba-Pyramids tramway route by way of Zamalek and the Zoological Gardens. Just as the maligned Zervudachi had predicted, both events led to the rapid development of Giza's riverfront when the first set of luxurious villas appeared on the banks of the Nile.

These handsome new structures were the envy of Cairene society, for the proud mansion owners represented the social strata that made up Egypt's wealthy urban class. Not only did they comprise landed gentry, pasha-politicians, Syrian entrepreneurs, Jewish bankers and department store owners, but there was the eccentric royal, the court doctor, a poet laureate, several art collectors, a cabaret entertainer and an international movie director. Most of the above were interconnected either through boardrooms where they held key positions or through party politics or marriage. It was almost tribal. Conspicuously absent, however, were the British civil servants and administrators.

While an integral part of the social landscape during the first half of the twentieth century, for the most part the post-Victorian Anglos kept their distance from Giza, following the dictum that familiarity breeds contempt. They continued to run the country from above, even after Britain had formally ended its protectorate over Egypt in 1922. They lived in semi-isolated communities, preferring the island of Zamalek and the *floradora* of Maadi. Both sites boasted that most famous of English institutions—the Club, with its cricket pitches, tennis courts and golf courses, around which members could enjoy afternoon tea, cucumber sandwiches and buttered crumpets.

Not so the French

The first official detail of starched French diplomats arrived in Giza as late as 1936. In the meantime, *la belle France* was invariably represented in Cairo's top drawer salons by a contingent of *midinettes*, who under normal circumstances could never have afforded an attic overlooking the Seine in Paris, let alone play society hostesses in beautiful Giza mansions overlooking the Nile. Their dreams became a reality when the French Suzettes married the scions of influential Egyptian pashas and rich beys while these young men were still studying on state-sponsored or private scholarships at universities in France.

At first, there was no corniche on this stretch of prime riverfront so that mansions and villas had immediate access to both the Nile and the colourful *dahabiahs* moored on its bank. This privileged situation ended when town planners, armed with slide rules and drawing boards, traced a new Nile-side road. A Giza riverside drive was laid down so that lesser Cairenes could enjoy a wonderful promenade that allowed them a glimpse of how the bold and the beautiful lived.

As though to mirror the developments that overtook Egypt during the twentieth century, the name of the new drive changed several times. From Al Bahr al Aazam (Great Sea), a reference to the Nile's titanic summer floods, the name was changed in 1936 to Sharia al Malek Farouk (King Farouk Street), commemorating Egypt's new monarch. But like all monuments and edifices named after royalty, these were changed in the wake of the 1952 military coup that toppled the king. New names were drawn from an unoriginal list: Gamal Abdel Nasser, Tahrir, Gomhouriya and Nasr. In this particular case, King Farouk Street became Gamal Abdel Nasser Street. But, for some unknown reason, the new name never caught on and reverted to the original with a slight variation. By now the 'Great Sea' had been irrevocably tamed by Aswan's High Dam. The adjective had become redundant. Sharia al Nil or Nile Street would have to do for now.

Had a confused citizen mailed a letter to Anwar al Sadat in the 1970s, he would have addressed it: "President Anwar al Sadat, No. 82 Sharia Gamal Abdel Nasser, ex-King Farouk Street, Giza." Five decades of history on an envelope!

Closest to Pont des Anglais, which understandably changed its name to Galaa (Evacuation) Bridge after 1947, stood the imposing homes of prominent Jews including two Mosseris, a Smouha, real estate mogul Solomon Green, palace jeweller Meyer Eliakim and businessman Charles V. Castro. The tip of the stretch, however, was reserved for a disparate coterie of Syrians, most of whom hailed from Damascus, Aleppo and Beirut. Hence the nickname of 'Tabouleh Heights' in reference to the popular *Shami* dish

Tabouleh Heights expired in the 1950s to make way for an apartment building followed later by the five-star Cairo Sheraton Hotel complex. As one by one the great mansions beyond Tabouleh Heights also started to disappear, an important piece of Cairo's history was irrevocably forsaken. Solomon Green's villa is the only one to have survived in that area thanks to the State, which converted it into the Dokki Police Station opposite the Sheraton Hotel. Not so lucky was the grand villa belonging to Solomon's son, Ralph Green. Occupying the property abutting the police station it is today part of a Russian Embassy recreational centre.

Kobri Badia

It was in 1926 that Damascenes Naguib and Latif Sobhani commissioned Italian architect Domenico Limongelli to build them a three-storey apartment house. The electrical fitting was the task of Aimé Amato. While half the Sobhani Building was occupied by Sobhanis, the remainder was leased to a Syrian architect, a Coptic magistrate, Maitre White Ibrahim, the director of La Genevoise Insurance, Dr. Georges Vaucher, and later to Sobhani Bey's son-in-law, a member of the Totounji clan from Aleppo.

There were also several English tenants in the Sobhani Building. One of them, Major Long of the Royal Air Force, was in a way, responsible for the make-up of the surrounding area. Commuters, upon crossing Pont des Anglais into Giza, would inadvertently come across a large ditch. Following the floods of 1926-27 this was filled with water, forcing motorists to detour through Al Dokhoulia Alley. Displeased with the situation, Major Long, who enjoyed considerable influence within the British-dominated administration, contacted the ministry of public works. The latter promptly proceeded to fill the ditch with gravel and the situation was quickly rectified.

Just north of the Sobhani Building, across Al Dokhoulia Alley, was where another Syrian set up shop on land belonging to Selim de Saab, a Syrian ennobled by the Pope, hence the honorific 'de'. But this was not to be your typical family homestead, for the new arrival was none other than the celebrated Madame Badia Masabni or 'Badaada', as Egypt's unchallenged cabaret queen was often called. But even the queen needed the necessary permits before she could open her nightclub for this was a strictly residential area. Which is why the diva contacted Naguib Sobhani Bey and solicited his support. His condition: all music and accompanying commotion had to end by 11pm. According to Fernand Sobhani, who grew up in the family home:

> Il est à noter que Badia Massabni ne pouvait pas obtenir son permis pour un cabaret (zone résidentielle), et elle avait demandé à mon père Naguib Sobhani de la recevoir pour le convaincre de lui donner son accord pour le permis—autant que je m'en souvienne cela a été fait avec une seule restriction: musique et bruits devaient cesser à 11 heure du soir!

Giza's celebrated Music Hall—Casino Badia—went on to make international history during the Second World War when officer, swindler and spy intermingled under the comforting 'torpedoes' of *Sitt* Badia's famed dancers. It was common knowledge that Churchill's son and the Duke of Gloucester had frolicked in her casino. Failing to win her over, Hitler's propaganda machine found it necessary to slander Madame Badia, accusing her in turn of being a traitor, a dangerous spy and a British secret agent.

Apart from her ten minutes of fame in Second World War accounts, Madame Badia made such an impression on her surroundings that for a long time one of Giza's landmarks was called after her. *Kobri Badia* was how people referred to the Kobri al Ingiliz (English Bridge, later Al Galaa/Evacuation) linking Gezira to Giza. "Meet me at Kobri Badia," was an everyday expression that survived long after the diva exited the scene. Understandably, it sounded better than "Meet me at Kobri al Ingilizi."

Born near Zahlé in Lebanon's Beka'a Valley, Badia spent part of her unhappy childhood in Argentina where many under-privileged Lebanese immigrated to at the turn of the century. Returning to her birthplace, the young girl sang and danced in impromptu theatres. Having successfully performed in the Levant, Badia was determined to try her luck where it counted most, Cairo's celebrated music halls. "It was in Cairo that she met my uncle through a mutual friend, Hussein Riad," recalls Badie al Rihani, now a retired gentleman in Maadi. Badia Masabni had married his father's brother.

Naguib al Rihani was the celebrated creator and star of the famous comedy *Kesh-Kesh Bey*. To the newly-arrived Badia, he was full of encouragement, suggestions and ideas. It was not long before his protégée became almost as famous as he was. Never mind that they came from different worlds. She loved to dance, he preferred to act. She was a Greek Catholic, he was a descendant of King Sargon the Assyrian, with ancestry in Mosul and Upper Egypt. Naguib's father Elias had come to Egypt from Iraq while his Coptic mother, Latifa, was from the village of Akhmin. As Badie al Rihani puts it:

> My uncle and aunt had egos that could easily fill an entire music hall, but love and mutual interest won the day and they tied the knot on September 11, 1924. Unable to agree on a church, the wedding took place in Doctor Khalil Gouda's downtown clinic. He was my uncle's friend from their Hawamdia days when they both worked for the sugar factory. The witnesses were Badie Khairy, [Rihani's partner and scriptwriter] and Emil Assa'isso, a Syrian restaurant owner on Adly Street.

Like everyone else, Rihani knew of Badia's prior involvement with the scion of a wealthy Egyptian landowning family. Badie al Rihani explains:

> This is why, shortly after their marriage, my uncle used all his powers of persuasion to convince his bride to travel with him on a stage tour in Argentina. After much argument she gave in. And since the SS Garbibaldi also stopped in Brazil, the couple agreed to perform Rihani's new play "Al Princessa" in both Rio and Sao Paulo. The play was a veiled portrayal of Badia's life, character and ambitions. The public adored it, especially the "Zahlaweya", who were an integral part of the large Syrian community in Brazil.
>
> Repeat performances took place in Buenos Aires. The tour lasted a year. The return trip to Alexandria was by way of Marseilles. Whatever money they had made in South America, the Rihanis' spent it all during a dizzying Paris stopover where Badia went wild on theatre and shopping. Among my uncle's purchases at the famous Au Bon Marché department store were several caricatures by Semp.

The Rihanis eventually separated and multiple efforts to bring them back together failed, including those of a trusted mutual friend and sometime moneylender, Claire Mossali. For a long time, Mossali befriended and bankrolled both parties while filling in as a French teacher to Badia's adopted daughter, the blonde Juliette. The Rihanis had no children of their own.

Badia's famous dance halls—successively on Emad al Din Street, Midan al Opera and then Tabouleh Heights—were considered Cairo cultural landmarks. Both the Druze-born crooner Farid al Atrash and ex-husband-comedian Naguib al Rihani had their turn on Badia's stage. Badia's was also a launching pad for many a dancer, singer and performer. It was from Badia's stables that famous belly dancers like Samia Gamal, Tahia Carioca, Hekmat Fahmi and Safeya Hilmi began their careers.

Preoccupied with shows and performances, Badia relied heavily on her relations for the day-to-day running of her business. Albert Masabni was the technician who looked after the wiring, lighting and sound system. His wife Rose handled Badia's wardrobes. Years later the couple would open an electric appliance shop on Maadi's Road 9. Managing Badia's personal and financial affairs was her favourite nephew, Antoine Issa. After first falling in love with Juliette, Antoine married one of Badia's chorus girls, Beba Ezzedin. The young couple would become the chief cause of Badia's financial undoing, drowning her in debts. Moreover the conniving Beba turned against her benefactress, becoming her chief rival.

Debt-ridden and hounded by tax collectors, the downcast Badia escaped to Lebanon just before the fall of the monarchy. The prematurely aged diva eventually settled down in Chtaura in the Beka'a Valley, not far from the Syro-Lebanese border. With the help of her young driver she set up a chicken farm. The legendary cabaret queen had come home to roost.

Friends would occasionally visit from Egypt including Naguib al-Rihani's nephew, Badie, with whom Badia always maintained a good rapport. Conversely, the blonde Juliette never saw her adopted mother after the latter's escape. Antoine Issa, meanwhile, died in a car crash on the road to Maadi and his former paramour Beba Ezzedin died in a separate car crash in February 1951 near Kalyoub.

It was Safeya Hilmi who carried on Badia's legacy into the 1960s from her own dance hall on Midan al Opera. Like its predecessor on the Nile, Safeya Hilmi's casino was a sunny spot for shady personalities and, from time to time, influential thinkers.

Long after the departure of Cairo's favourite shisha-smoking entertainer Pont des Anglais continued to be called Kobri Badia. And since the next bridge down the Nile was called Kobri Abbas in honour of the khedive, who inaugurated it in 1908, the two Nile crossings together represented Egypt's far off version of 'The Prince and the Showgirl.'

Neither Villa Sobhani nor Casino Badia exist today. Villa Sobhani was demolished in the 1950s to make way for the Mirshak Building, belonging to the family of the same name. Like the Sobhanis, the Totounjis and the Masabnis, the Mirshaks were of Syrian stock (Syrian here refers to Greater Syria, including Lebanon and Palestine).

Relative latecomers to this corner of Giza, the Mirshaks built their post-war villa (designed by Antoine Nahas) on a plant nursery that separated the Sobhanis from their Mosseri neighbours. When, a few years later, the Mirshaks purchased Villa Sobhani they replaced it with a ten-storey apartment building. In view of its size, it meant sacrificing part of their garden.

Architectural historians will agree that the arrival of Immeuble Mirshak ushered in the first generation of high-rises on the previously pastoral riverside drive. As in Garden City, it was rich families from the Levant who set the precedent for high-rise structures in Giza. The Farid al Atrash and Abou al Fotouh Buildings followed in 1955 and 1959 respectively. Antoine Selim Nahas, who may have had some remorse regarding the rapidly changing skyline, having himself spent his formative years at the now extinct Villa Sobhani, designed all three.

For two decades the Fotouh building held the record as second tallest in Egypt. It also set a precedent when its owner, Hassan Abou al Fotouh, one of Cairo's eminent contractors, rather than lease his apartments sold them outright, thus circumventing the discouraging rent control laws that had just been implemented. The contiguous and much shorter building to the south belonging to the Arab World's acclaimed crooner-actor Farid al Atrash, intimidated by its soaring neighbour, would subsequently grow by a couple of floors.

The departure of the Mirshaks following the 1961 sequestrations by a state gone socialist signalled the gradual transformation of the riverfront's ethnic mix. For starters, the land which had accommodated Badia's casino in summer and a popular skating rink in winter, became in turn the property of King Faisal of Saudi Arabia and later the home to Cairo's first Sheraton Hotel. Ironically, none of the hotel's nightclubs, bars or cafés bears the name of Badia.

While a member of the Kuwaiti ruling family purchased Villa Mirshak, the Mirshak Building was sequestered by the State and partly 'squatted' on by a different set of tenants: an odd mélange of new bourgeoisie, Gulf money, plus the odd social climber and a well-known newspaper editor who pandered to the State and its president.

The Jewish quartet

What is today the Russian Embassy at No. 88 Al Nil Street, used to be the home of banker Joseph Nessim Mosseri from 1926 until he died in 1934. This large redbrick house, recognisable by its numerous pillars, pergolas, three-arched windows and stucco ornaments, was designed by architect Gaston Aghion, possibly a relation of Mosseri's wife.

A pious man, Mosseri Bey had his own place of worship at the south end of his garden. It was there, on January 14, 1934, that his eulogy was conducted by Egypt's Grand Rabbi Haim Nahum Effendi.

According to *Al Ahram*, Mosseri's funeral was very well attended. Prime Minister Abdel Fattah Yehia Pasha and his entire cabinet were there, as were other weighty mourners who enjoyed extensive credit at Banque Mosseri. Former and future prime ministers showed up including Ziwar, Sidki, Sabry, and Maher *frères*. The imposing funeral procession was lined with an honour guard up to the Zamalek side of the Pont des Anglais. From there, the coffin was carried by special car to the Mosseri vaults in Bassateen, south of Cairo.

The inconsolable widow, Jeanne Aghion, continued to live at Villa Mosseri until the mid-1950s. Residing with her was her eldest son Edgard 'Guido' and his wife Joyce, daughter of Alexandria's suburban developer Youssef Smouha. In a 1999 Paris encounter, Susan Mosseri (Mrs. René Danon) related how, when the US State Department declined to buy her grandfather's villa, Madame Aghion promptly sold it to the Soviet government. The new owners then turned Villa Joseph Mosseri into a residence for its ambassadors. Years later, the Soviets would amputate part of the garden to accommodate the embassy's obtrusive white chancellery.

Behind Joseph Mosseri's house, across the main street, one can still glimpse No. 60 Giza Avenue. This was where Joseph's learned cousin and brother-in-law, Victor Moussa Mosseri, lived. Even as it lies squashed between a tall building and the Pyramisa Hotel, its architecture is worth a second look, particularly its gothic arches, gargoyles and pointed chimneys. The adjoining homes of two of Joseph Mosseri Bey's brothers, Felix and Emile, are gone. What was their villa at No. 58 Giza Avenue has become a gaggle of high rises. Lionel Mosseri's villa survived, however, and is today the art deco Saudi Embassy near the University Bridge.

Across the narrow Joseph Mosseri Street (now Ibn al Ikshid), surrounded by palm and mango trees and facing the Nile, stand two identical apartment houses built in the 1930s for court jeweller Meyer Eliakim. For a time he lived in the one closer to the Nile with his wife and four daughters, Lili, Vicki, Jackie and Gabby. Surviving members of his family can still be sighted at Longchamps during the Paris racing season.

Among Eliakim's distinguished tenants at No. 86 were his son-in-law David Ades, businessman Ralph A. Harari (a nephew of next-door neighbour Mrs. Joseph Mosseri Bey) and bankers Abdullah and Maurice Zilkha of Banque Zilkha. Also in residence were Louis Van Damme, director of the Banque Belge; Jules Joseph Arnaud of the Anglo-Belgian Co.; Major William Roger Fanner, lawyer; and Julian May Wright, magistrate. Residents for a much shorter period were Egypt's ambassadors to London and Athens, Hassan Nachat Pasha and Ali Sirry Bey, respectively.

Contiguous to Eliakim's two buildings is Villa No. 84 built in 1925 for Mohammed Kamel al Bindari Pasha, Egypt's distinguished interwar diplomat and sometime minister of health. He is, however, best remembered as the 'Red Pasha', an allusion to the days when he was King Farouk's ambassador to Moscow. When serving abroad, the pasha leased his villa in turn to the legations of Sweden and the Netherlands. The pasha would later live on the former khedivial *dahabiah*, *Feirouz*, and sell his villa to Syrian businessman Fouad Matouk and his wife Odette de Freige. At the break-up of the Matouk marriage, the villa was leased out once again and is today occupied by a Saudi family. In view of its unkempt state and the overgrown vegetation that surrounds it, one can hardly tell that this art deco house (interior designed by Jansen and Krieger) is the work of architect Michel Liberman. Luckily, another one of his villas is in far better state further down the street.

Also destined never to return to Giza's riverside drive were several *dahabiahs*. The *Feirouz* that had served as a temporary home to businessman Gustave Heller and the Bindari Pasha family, sank to the bottom of the Nile, the result of a mid-river collision, taking with it several *objets d'art* and a lifetime collection of family mementos. There were other handsome *dahabiahs* moored along this portion of the Nile. These would eventually disappear making way for various rowing associations, yacht clubs and colourful speakeasies.

Presidential manor

Next to No. 84 Al Nil Street is a mansion whose various occupants do not want for celebrity status. While the identity of its original owner is unknown, its second owner acquired it in 1939. Its little-known saga resurfaced aboard the *Triton* during a 1996 New Year Nile cruise.

Somewhere between Luxor and Aswan, Egyptian-born international financier Gilbert de Botton recounted to Lord Rothschild and his other titled guests the happy months he spent at his aunt and uncle's house by the Nile in Giza. "Between the early 1940s until 1961, what became President Sadat's residence was the home of my aunt, Marguerite de Botton and her husband Charles Castro. It is there that I stayed when I attended Victoria College just before I left Egypt in 1954, never to return except nowadays."

The house of Charles Victor Castro was the scene of much entertaining, especially when his American suppliers were in town. Castro sold American agricultural pumps and Dodge cars. When summering, he, like most of his Giza neighbours, alternated between Alexandria and European resorts. "Our travelling through Europe was always without a driver. My father did the driving—he loved both travelling and driving. We once drove to Hotel Suvretta in St Moritz, the whole family plus governess, in one Dodge car," recalled Guido Castro at Le Doyen Restaurant in Paris, during a May 1998 gathering that brought together several former owners of Giza's Nile-front villas.

The Castros left Egypt in instalments, starting with their three children. Roland and Yolanda left in the late 1940s. Guido followed a decade later eventually settling in England. The senior Castros joined their children in 1960-1 never to return. Yolanda eventually became Lady Joseph—her husband, Sir Keith, was Margaret Thatcher's trusted minister for industry and later, education. In her book *The Downing Street Years,* Thatcher lauds the virtues of her minister recounting how he was one of her closest monetary advisors and mentors.

In view of its excellent location and priceless *savonneries,* stained-glass French window screens and other features left behind by the Castros, No. 82 Nile Street was soon occupied by one of the privileged members of the new oligarchy. President Nasser's daughter sojourned there while her own villa was being readied in Heliopolis. The next privileged occupant was President Anwar al Sadat. It was during his reign that fanciful photos and historic sound bites emanated from the villa, flashed via satellite around the globe on prime-time news especially when Nixon, Kissinger, Carter, Walter Cronkite and Barbara Walters came calling.

To accommodate Egypt's 'First House', so to speak, Villa Castro and its adjoining garden where Rajah, the Castros' Great Dane had once played unhindered, succumbed to major structural changes. Among them was the construction by Osman Ahmed Osman of an extra wing for Gladys Cotrell, Sadat's mother-in-law, and the extension of the first floor reception area so it now almost protrudes into the street. On the villa's Nile side a helipad was built to accommodate the president's American-made chopper.

Normally attired in Saville Row suits, President Anwar El Sadat was wearing a field marshal's uniform when he was assassinated on October 6, 1981. Leading statesmen and reigning princes filed through Villa Castro's massive iron gates as they paid their respects to the grieving widow. Arab dignitaries were conspicuously absent. To them, Sadat had been a traitor who preferred Israelis to Arabs.

Today, Sadat's helipad is unused. Dignitaries rarely call on the feebly guarded villa that looks abandoned unless Sadat's widow, Jehane Raouf, is in town. She now spends most of the year in the United States.

Giza's riverfront Jews may have left the country but standing as testament to their presence are their grand homes, now used as embassies, courtly homes of the rich and famous, or the official residence of the nation's president.

By grace of a woman's wrath

It was a happy day for Emilienne Hector Luce when she and her husband, Mohammed Mahmoud Khalil moved out of No. 11 Kasr al Nil Street and into their new Giza mansion at No.1 Kafour Street. The change of address was regarded as a major move up society's totem pole. In time, the dour-faced, monocle-sporting lawyer became a senior member of the Wafd Party and later President of the Senate.

Khalil Bey's high station gave Emilienne the endless pleasure of being one of Cairo's leading hostesses. Born into a modest French family, she revelled in the role of Grande Dame, a part that she played to perfection thanks to an earlier brush with the French stage—a fact that was not lost on Cairo's snobbish café society. According to those who knew her well, such as veteran boulevardier, Victor Semeika, Mrs. Mohammed Mahmoud Khalil was forever fond of frou-frou and *trompète* attire and had an obsession with jewels that she wore for the most trifling occasions. And occasions were plenty in both Cairo and Paris, for Khalil Bey was a millionaire businessman with a seat on several of Egypt's blue chip company boards.

It was no secret that Khalil Bey was enamoured with everything French. French wife, French cuisine, French shows, French culture, French architecture, not forgetting French art. In fact, Khalil Bey had successfully combined his sentimental and material urges. The house couldn't have been more Parisian in either style or taste, and the decor was of the finest quality.

Encouraged by his wife, Khalil Bey collected art compulsively. Together with Prince Youssef Kamal, Emile Miriel, Youssef Cattaui Pasha, Ali Ibrahim Pasha, Mohammed Taher Pasha, Henri Naus Bey, Sir John Home, Sir Robert Rolo, Aldo Ambron, Charles Boeglin, Ali Chamsi Pasha and G. Fouad Abdel Malek (who had created Le Salon du Caire), Khalil Bey founded La Societé des Amis de l'Art in 1924.

Years later, the French reciprocated Khalil Bey's love for France by awarding him with the title of Correspondant de l'Académie des Beaux Arts and the Grand Cordon de la Légion d'Honneur. The Italians followed suit with the Grand Cross of Maurice and Lazarre. Moreover, the huge success of the Exposition France-Egypt in 1937 earned Khalil Bey a sought-after seat in the Institut de France—naturally he was already a member of the Institut d'Egypte.

The Khalil art collection in Giza was rated as one of the best in Cairo, comparable in value to those belonging to the great private collectors of Alexandria, such as Sir Henry Barker, Alexandre Benachi, Emanuel Constanino, Jacques Matossian, Charles de Menasce, Max Rolo, Gregoire Sarkissian and Edwin Goar. Cairo too had its art-thirsty clique including Carlo Grassi, Mohammed Sultan, Levi de Benzion, Fortune Martino and Leon Rolin. Even though he was an absentee landlord, one must include Baron Empain in view of his exquisite collection of Gobelins tapestries adorning the walls of his Heliopolis Hindu Palace.

Khalil Bey prided himself on having Egypt's best collection of impressionist and modern paintings belonging to the French school: Champmartin, Daumier, Ricard, Delacroix and Toulouse-Lautrec. Number 1 Kafour Street was also home to several Renoirs, Pissaros, Trovons, Sisleys, Millets, Moticellis, Milots and Diaz de la Penas. Of course, one should not forget the *Fleurs* series of Van Gogh. The list goes on. Statuettes and marble busts included a work each by Rodin and Cajou, and there was the fabulous jade collection. All of these were listed in his 1933 inventory.

Plenty more art was forthcoming as European dealers hurriedly unloaded their treasures on the eve of the Second World War. Khalil Bey was a dependable taker. Each trip to Paris was a shopping extravaganza of French masters and *objects d'arts*. Khalil Bey's mansion was turning into the largest depository of French works this side of the Mediterranean. A curator was needed and one was quickly found in the person of international connoisseur Richard Mosseri, a distant relative of Joseph Mosseri Bey whom we met earlier.

Possessing such a fine collection boosted the couple's prestige in no small way. An Eliza-Doolittle-on-the-Nile, Emilienne could hardly believe her good fortune. She had made it to Grande Dame, which in Egypt had the Paris effect multiplied by four. Not only were the Khalils overlords of Giza's most famous mansion, but also as minister of agriculture and later as senate president, Khalil Bey entertained the best. Cairo's social calendar reserved the first day of the month for the Khalil's 'at home'. Entertainment during the war was even spicier than usual when Cairo, by bizarre circumstance, became home to both Vichy diplomats and those of the Free French.

During the Second World War's early years, Khalil Bey was recommended for high office. The idea was unthinkable to Sir Miles Lampson. The British ambassador harboured an intense dislike for the senator describing him as

"a poisonous snake who spreads enemy propaganda and defeatist talk."
The senior British diplomat went as far as to suggest that Prime Minister
Nahas Pasha place Khalil Bey under house arrest. Although he declined the
ambassador's recommendation, Nahas's rejoinder was most unflattering,
"Khalil is a senator and a completely worthless creature therefore not
deserving of incarceration."

Its opulence notwithstanding, one thing was lacking at the Giza palace.
Mohammed and Emilienne Khalil's marriage was childless. With such a
large fortune invested in art and no one to entrust it to, Khalil Bey drew up
a mammoth legal agreement. The surviving party to his marital union with
Emilienne would automatically come into legal possession of the Giza
mansion, its annexes and all of its art collection. The rest of the estate was
another matter and would be dealt with according to Shari'a (Islamic Law).

The ironclad agreement was irrevocable as would later be proven during
a protracted legal battle that erupted immediately after Khalil Bey's demise.

One day, to her absolute stupefaction, Emilienne ascertained for herself
what had been rumoured all around her. Smitten by a young Turko-
Circassian beauty, the ageing senator had secretly tied the knot. Not only
was the new bride Cairo's most beautiful catch but she also had the class to
match. The marriage lasted a very short time, yet long enough to produce
an heir.

Emilienne's subsequent wrath was only surpassed in its intensity by her
sense of revenge. She would contest the paternity. That failing, she made it
evidently clear no one was going to displace her from No. 1 Kafour Street
and no presumptive heir would enjoy or inherit the priceless wonders she
and her husband had collected since they were married in 1901.

Although in good health while enjoying his customary holiday in France,
Khalil died on December 28, 1953, after suffering from a massive heart
attack. Even France's leading cardiologist, Professor Mellies, could not save
him. Khalil Bey received his rites at the Paris Mosque with Egyptian and
Arab diplomats in attendance.

Grateful to its old friend, France gave Khalil Bey a state send-off. There
to do the honours were General Catroux, a friend from the old days; de la
Chavinière, Director of Protocol at Foreign Affairs; de Bourbon-Busset,
Director of Cultural Affairs representing the Quai d'Orsay; Charles Braibant,
Director of the National Archives; Hautecoeur and Dropsi, former members
of the French Academy; and Monsieur Cornu, secretary of the Beaux Arts
together with Frangoulis of the Diplomatic Academy. Even the Comédie

Française was represented with Mme. Jeanne Boitel. Khalil Bey's body was covered with Egypt's green flag on which rested his Academy costume, his bicorne (hat) and his decorations.

The French press, notably *Le Figaro*, ran an elaborate obituary. In Egypt, Ambassador (later Prime Minister) Couve de Murville eulogised Khalil Bey during the embassy's traditional New Year's address with these words: "France had lost its best friend ever in Egypt." Worth noting under the circumstances is how Sir Miles Lampson, now a retired peer in England, refrained from sending a note of sympathy to the deceased's wife.

Mohammed Mahmoud Khalil died never knowing his house and art collection would become a museum.

Having survived her husband, Emilienne drew up a new will, notarised in June 1954. The terms were crystal clear. Upon her death, the garden, the mansion and its annexes and all of the contents of No. 1 Kafour Street would go to the State. The house would become a museum to perpetuate her and her husband's memory to the exclusion of any other heirs. The State was more than happy to comply. It was, therefore, a woman's wrath and not Khalil Bey's generosity that allowed Egypt to legally acquire one of the finest museums of its kind.

Two decades later, it would require the highest authority in the land to temporarily bend Emilienne's ironclad codicils. Just before he succeeded Gamal Abdel Nasser, Anwar al Sadat had moved into the former house of Charles Castro directly opposite No. 1 Kafour Street. Once he became president, Sadat needed new space for his executive branch as well as a helipad for his frequent travels. In defiance of Emilienne's will, the Khalil Museum was expropriated to accommodate the president's men while the fronting river shore was asphalted, enabling the presidential chopper to take off and land.

Down came the paintings. Up came the credenzas, desks, telephone and telex machines. The art collection was relocated to No.16 Gezira Street in Zamalek, a confiscated palace belonging to a former member of the Mohammed Ali dynasty. There it would remain for twenty-odd years.

Sadat's sudden demise in October 1981 brought on a period of uncertainty. What would become of the former Khalil mansion? Would Emilienne's wishes be upheld or would they be ignored?

The answer came 14 years later.

On October 3, 1995, President Mubarak officially opened a refurbished Mr. and Mrs. Mohammed Mahmoud Khalil Museum in their former home.

Once again the museum's beautiful glass and steel pergola, its Doric arches and its symmetrical facade was open to the public. Art lovers could once more admire the museum's art treasures in their original setting. Not returned to the museum, however, is Khalil Bey's priceless jade collection.

In its time, No. 1 Kafour Street has been home to a senate president and his tenacious French wife, a private museum and offices for a president of the republic.

The house, built at the dawn of last century, is much more than a location on a Giza street map; it is an evocative address synonymous with history, culture and power.

A princess's palace

Next to the Mr. and Mrs. Mohammed Mahmoud Khalil Museum stands another palace with the misnomer of the 'Giza Palais.' This former royal residence was built in typical khedivial baroque-rococo revival style that characterised so many of Egypt's royal palaces. From 1919 the Giza Palais with its surrounding 2.5 feddans was the official residence and *daira* of Princess Fawkia, King Fouad's only daughter from the unhappy union with his cousin, the very rich Princess Shuvikar Ibrahim. When Princess Fawkia was not 'at home', it invariably meant she was in Europe where her husband, Mahmoud Fakhry Pasha, served as Egypt's first and long-time Egyptian envoy to France.

Once in Paris, and knowing that King Fouad was planning a state visit to France, the Fakhrys contemplated buying the Hotel Matignon. The deal, however, fell through when the legal heirs (the Austrian government) of that most famous of Parisian mansions reclaimed it in a lengthy legal battle. Unable to wait out the court's decision, the Fakhrys occupied a large suite at the Hotel Majestic on Rue la Perouse before moving into a handsome edifice (No. 2) overlooking the nearby Place des Etats-Unis. Not exactly the Matignon, the official residence of Egypt's ambassadors to France had been built and designed in 1886 by leading architect Paul-Ernest Sanson for Odessa-born magnate Jules Ephrussi, one of the more famous bankers and art collectors of his day.

Upon learning in 1949 that the newly created Egyptian *Majlis al Dawla*, a State Consultative Council patterned on the French model, was searching for temporary premises, Princess Fawkia offered her Giza palace for the sum of LE300 per month. Three years later the Princess decided to sell her palace to her favourite half-sister, the much younger Princess Faika. The understanding was that the council, headed by Sanhoury Pasha, would transfer to more permanent headquarters, thus enabling the new owner eventually to move in.

"But my mother never moved in," recalls Fouad Sadek, Princess Faika's eldest son, who lives in an apartment within walking distance of the Giza palace. "Very soon after the purchase my uncle abdicated the throne. It was the beginning of the end for the House of Mohammed Ali starting with my mother and the king's other [four] sisters. The Giza palace was summarily appropriated by the state." A related official document signed by the Cairo Court of First Instance is evidence that the sale did indeed take place on June 15, 1952, just five weeks before the king's abdication. The sum paid by the unfortunate new owner for the ephemeral palace amounted to LE205,290.

Now that the palace had become government property the sitting tenant saw no reason to move out. As the council slowly chipped away at the edges of the former royal residence, its original owner, a sensitive woman with a keen sense of humour and concealed literary talents, had long abandoned public life to become a semi-recluse. Widowed for the second time, the munificent ex-Princess Fawkia spent her remaining 20-odd years in a five-room suite at the Dolder Hotel in Zurich. On February 9, 1974, the hotel's room service discovered the aged princess stone dead in an armchair surrounded by countless unopened parcels and a collection of jewels. As her only heir took stock, he was at a loss over the disposal of Comte d'Adix, the princess's long-departed White Russian companion. His body was lying in state in a memorial park in Schwamendingen outside Zurich. Fawkia's visits to the mummified Comte were reportedly her only sorties from her fashionable hotel suite.

The palace's second owner died of cancer on January 7, 1983, in far less extravagant circumstances. Princess Faika, who for a time after 1952 lived in a villa off Pyramids Avenue, spent her last years in a Giza apartment in an unpretentious building owned by her husband's family.

Meanwhile, the state council's supposed temporary location became permanent, since it is still there today. The garden, however, is not. It was replaced by a massive granite and marble office building needed to accommodate an expanding bureaucracy. In its haste to expand, the council did not see fit to leave a respectful distance between the new structure and the palace.

Originally set up as a quasi-judicial body with the authority to order compensation and abolish illegitimate rulings or decrees found to violate citizens' rights and public law, it is up to the council today to adjudicate singular petitions from surviving members of the ex-royal family. Half a century after King Farouk's abdication, Fouad Sadek and his stalwart relations have yet to receive compensation for any of the personal family assets unjustly confiscated by the Nasser regime after 1952.

The field marshal's fort

A couple of blocks south from the Giza Palais-turned-*Majlis al Dawla* stands another famous mansion that bears the name of a more recent ruler.

If you were to ask anyone at the Mubarak Public Library who built the mansion in which the library is domiciled, the answer is always Tahawi Pasha. This conviction has its roots in the name of the adjacent side street: Al Tahawia Street. Unfortunately, this kind of simplistic deduction often leads to self-perpetuated historical inaccuracies that are unforgivable if the object happens to be a centre for learning.

As it turns out this superb redbrick art deco house on No. 4 Tahawia Street was built by and belonged to the Credit Foncier bank of Egypt. The mansion consisted of two palatial apartments; Marcel Vincenot Bey, the last French director of the bank, occupied the upper floor and fellow countryman and colleague, Emile Minost, occupied the ground floor. The design of the mansion is attributed to yet another Frenchman, Georges Parcq. His works are all over Garden City and downtown Cairo in addition to that famous Zamalek architectural milestone, 'Nile View' on Saray al Gezira Street where, by agreement with the owner, Parcq had the lifetime benefit of the penthouse (today the residence of the Portuguese ambassador).

To the credit of Nasser's socialist era, houses of the stature of No. 4 Tahawia Street were not destroyed. In fact, many became headquarters of the Socialist Union Party, government offices or homes of the party faithful. The grandest among them were allocated free of charge to Nasser's ruling elite, which is how the Credit Foncier villa overlooking the Nile became home to Abdel Hakim Amer, Egypt's much-decorated republican *Mushir* (Field Marshal).

It was during the Mushir's financially unencumbered tenancy that the two sumptuous apartments were merged into one. The *immeuble de rapport* was turned into a *hôtel particulier*. For several years, No. 4 Tahawia Street was home to Nasser's closest sidekick. Related by marriage, the two men enjoyed a special relationship envied by the rest of the junta. But the special rapport eventually turned into enmity. And with good reason, the Mushir failed to deliver the promised victory during the June 1967 war.

The year 1967 should have been the 'Year of the Mushir' but instead of defeating Israel, Egypt lost its air force and the Sinai peninsula in a matter of hours. All that remained intact of Egypt's arsenal was the field marshal's baton. For some within the rancorous junta this was their opportunity to shower Nasser's confidant with shame and injury.

At first, Abdel Hakim Amer was put under surveillance, with State Security surrounding No. 4 Tahawia Street. Then, in July 1967, orders came that the defrocked Mushir was under house arrest. Many within the dispirited army who still believed in their fallen commander flocked to the Mushir's house in a show of support. Fretful that Amer may have been hatching a putsch, Nasser ordered a state of siege, calling in several armoured trucks. The mansion was now sealed. No one could step in or out. The surrounding area turned into an urban war zone.

A few days later, Amer was forcibly removed from his house to an undisclosed location. His death was announced soon after. It was not long before Egypt was once more rife with rumours. Had the Mushir taken his life or was life taken out of the Mushir? The autopsy reports stated suicide but in a country that had become used to writing and reading between the lines, the consensus in the street was that the former Free Officer had been liquidated. An already demoralised Egypt was the unwitting spectator of a unique show where the 1952 'revolution' was devouring itself.

With the demise of Abdel Hakim Amer, the former Villa Credit Foncier went from state of siege to the house of wounded pride. In an effort to compensate the memory of the fallen general—after all, he had been a founding Free Officer—Amer's family was allowed to remain free of charge at No. 4 Tahawia Street for as long as the *first* Madame Amer remained alive. No provisions were made for the other Madame Amer. Renowned for his salacious escapades and hashish sessions, the Mushir, shortly before the 1967 defeat, had found time to take on an additional wife, the rousing starlet Berlanti Abdel Hamid.

It was only after the first Madame Amer's death in the 1980s that the house reverted to the State, at which time discussions were initiated with Germany's Bertelsmann's Foundation to turn it into a public library.

Throughout the first half of the 1990s, Villa Credit Foncier received a much-needed face-lift when architects Mamdouh al Habashi and Achim Krekeler, both under contract from Germany's Bertelsmann Foundation, turned the former *hôtel particulier* into a state-of-the-art library. Instead of the demolition ball, the house was given a new lease on life. Scaffoldings were erected and very slowly, cornices, balustrades and high reliefs depicting tropical vegetation were restored.

On March 21, 1995, President Mubarak inaugurated a completely restored Villa Credit Foncier as the Mubarak Public Library. With him to mark the occasion were German Minister of Foreign Affairs, Klaus Kinkel and the Bundestag's President, Rita Susmuth.

Once the emblem of Franco-Egyptian co-operation, this *belle époque* landmark is today a symbol of collaboration between Egypt and Germany. Thankfully, no one wants to remember how No. 4 Tahawia was so closely connected to Egypt's hour of shame. Maybe this is why they would rather tell you it belonged to a fictitious Tahawi Pasha.

Another house of wounded pride lies just behind No. 4 Tahawia. Its last Egyptian owner was Ali Maher Pasha, a director of the Credit Foncier Egyptien. It was to Maher Pasha that the Free Officer's entrusted the first post-Farouk government. Relegated to a mere yes-man, the warrior-politician went into self-imposed confinement and died in August 1960, a despondent, forgotten man. His house and award-winning garden at No. 2 Sharia Tahawia were subsequently sold for LE75,000 to the Embassy of the Kingdom of Cambodia. This would later transmute into the embassy of the reprehensible Khmer Rouge. Today, the former prime minister's house lies abandoned, its garden reduced to a pitiful dump yard.

Sugar king and
department store baron

South of the Credit Foncier villa is the Giza Public Water Works Authority, almost as old as the district itself. Once upon a time, the water works were considered the unofficial demarcation line separating the lands of Prince Hussein Kamel to the north, from the Zervudachi estates extending south to the Giza Bridge.

On the south side of the water works, across Yemen Street (ex-Souq al Ahad), stood 'Les Flamboyants', the villa of Henri Naus Bey, the Belgian director of the Sucreries Egyptiennes. Naus Bey, regarded by many as the father of Egypt's sugar industry, was the head of the Industrial Federation of Egypt. The story goes that because his name 'Naus,' means 'half' in Arabic, Henri Naus Bey never made it to pasha. It would have sounded odd to have someone call His Excellency Half-Pasha! Half-Bey was the limit propriety could go.

Although the much older Villa Naus disappeared, until recently Naguib Salha's Mediterranean-style villa, designed in the early 1950s by Sabet Barsoum, stood on the Nile-front property (No. 66 Nile Street).

The son of an Ottoman Pasha from the Levant, Salha reportedly quadrupled his fortune in the Gulf long before the oil rush and is often described by envious contemporaries as Lebanon's first *nouveau riche*. Besides owning four imposing buildings on Cairo's Cherif Pasha Street (at the intersection with 26th of July) and a much talked-about villa in the centre of Beirut, he is also credited with building the Phoenicia, Lebanon's first glitzy hotel rivalling the legendary St Georges, in which he also held shares. According to his son Mazen, Salha came to Egypt from Saudi Arabia in 1948, "with the objective of starting up a business enterprise in what was then the commercial centre of the Middle East. He invested in several trading enterprises and purchased several prime properties in and around Cairo."

As Salha lived in the Hadayek al Koubbeh district, he leased his Giza villa to a variety of people. Notable among them was a senior American attaché, Jefferson Patterson. He was followed by a string of polo-playing Argentine diplomats. Today the land on which the villa stood lies abandoned, used mostly as a depot for rusty old cars strewn on the once elegant driveway.

On the south side of Al Ramah Street is Cairo University's School of

Oriental Studies, once the Cairo residence of Auguste Luzatto Pasha. An Italian Jew, he was the director of the Banque d'Egypte before it went bankrupt. It is said that Luzatto was Alexandria's earliest slum baron, whereas in Cairo he reportedly owned several important buildings including No. 36 26th of July Street. It was following Luzatto Pasha's death in Alexandria on February 19, 1909, that his heirs sold the Giza house.

A subsequent owner of Villa Luzatto was Solomon Moreno Cicurel, co-proprietor of the famous department store of the same name.

Ever since Raya and Sikina (Egypt's answer to Jack the Ripper) nothing had captured society's imagination like the brutal Hollywood-style murder of Solomon Cicurel. Cairo talked about little else during March 1927. This real-life drama had all the trappings of a fantastic spectacle: famous household name, money, exclusive address, politics and death row. Because radio was still making its debut, information-seekers were once again relying on broadsheets and gossip, with a heavier emphasis on the latter.

If everyone anticipated a sensationalised spin to the celebrity murder, none was forthcoming in the press. *La Bourse Egyptienne,* like other leading publications, reported an 'open and shut' case. Sir Thomas Russell, Cairo's Chief of Police, and Mahmoud Fahmi Keissy Pasha, the Director-General of Public Security, led a team of investigators that included Chief Public Prosecutor Taher Noor Pasha, the Governor of Giza, Sadek Kholoussi Bey, and Inspectors Mustafa Hanafi and Chams al Din Abdel Gaffar. Cicurel's murder was Cairo's most talked-about event, and because it was under the glare of the general public, no one was going to accuse the legal system of cheese-paring.

The only witness was Cicurel's wife, Elvire Toriel, but her husband's assailants had chloroformed her before they committed the crime. Cicurel's children, Rosie, 10, and Raymond, 6, also had nothing to say since they slept in another part of the house under the watchful eye of their English governess, Miss Williams. At the time of the crime, Cicurel's other daughter, Lili, was in France studying art. As for the servants, they were quartered in a different part of the large house.

The findings showed that what started out as a poorly planned burglary had deteriorated into a bloody murder. Within hours of their apprehension, the four criminals sang like canaries. Seemingly, the victim and his wife were asleep in their upstairs master bedroom when the men stormed in. Forced to inhale ether, Madame Cicurel was rendered unconscious, whereupon the assailants bludgeoned her resisting husband, making off with the jewellery. By the time the wife came to, it was all over. Next to her, in the blood-drenched marital bed, lay the corpse of her husband.

Even though the motive of the heinous crime was portrayed as a burglary at the home of Cairo's richest merchant, the Giza homicide department kept everyone on edge. Notwithstanding the fact that Egypt's top investigators were assigned to the case, crime-watchers claimed their findings were all too pat, refusing to settle for anything less than sex and scandal. And if some bemoaned how the inquest had been sanitised, the majority agreed it had been inexorably politicised both inside and outside parliament.

To begin with, under the regime of Capitulations, foreigners in Egypt were exempt from local laws and taxes. The direct linkage of this system to the question of sovereignty had therefore re-surfaced in the Cicurel murder trial. "How," cried the daily *Al Ahram*, "could it be that both Italian defendants—Edouardo Moramarco and Grimaldi Dagaro—are tried in Ancona, Italy; their Greek accomplice—Anesthi Christo—appears before a judge and jury sitting in the Greek Court at Alexandria; and the fourth criminal, Dario Jacoel, shows up in an indigenous Egyptian court?"

"By distinguishing between criminals according to their nationalities and not according to their deeds, Capitulations was making a mockery of the justice system," exclaimed the *Egyptian Gazette*.

Because the death penalty was not applicable in Italy or Greece, the stateless Jacoel, 21 years old, faced the hangman alone. He was buried in a corner of the Jewish cemetery of Bassateen, not far from where his co-religionist, Solomon Cicurel, rested in a palatial crypt.

Rumors and innuendo persisted after the trial, fuelled by new evidence that Solomon Cicurel's disgruntled ex-chauffeur—Anesthi Christo—had publicly sworn vengeance against his former employer following his summary dismissal. "More humbuggery," decried those who whispered of a sex cover-up. They pointed out how Cairo's leading department store only hired dazzling females. When one of the shop girls caught the simultaneous fancy of the big boss and a panting subordinate, the dumped employee settled the score his own way.

Eventually the scalding homicide was buried in *Al Ahram*'s page eight, so that readers and everyone else could get on with their lives. The wealthy Madame Cicurel would endure another family tragedy when her daughter, Rosie, died relatively young. Her only son Raymond moved to France where his sister, Lili Cicurel, married the future socialist Prime Minister, Pierre Mendes-France.

Understandably, Villa Cicurel was sold. Within two years it was the official address of Cairo University (ex-Fouad al Awal) later to become its School of Oriental Studies. Today, situated behind the Swissair Building, the villa stands opposite Giza's *Mudireyet Amn*—Security Station—and the Missaha Survey Department.

If little or nothing is known today of the three foreign defendants, the legend of Dario Jacoel lives on. Consider the following communication from another Dario Jacoel in Houston, Texas, dated March 2000.

> My great-uncle was the Dario who killed Salomon Cicurel. My father Leo Jacoel told me a very different story than what I read in *Ahram Weekly* (December 15, 1994), Dario was having an affair with the wife of Salomon. When she tried to break it off he became very angry. My hot-blooded great-uncle told her he would have her in the presence of her husband. Which is why Dario went over to the house to rape her in front of Salomon. With his friends to help him they restrained the husband while Dario assaulted the wife. One of the other men stabbed Salomon with a screwdriver several times. The blood that was on Dario however was that of Mrs. Cicurel. She had been menstruating during the rape.

Midway

On the block south of Villa Cicurel (behind the Swissair Building) stood Villa Elhamieh, the residence of Princess Hourieh Mahmoud Hamdi and her stepdaughter, Princess Mounira. The intolerance of the latter was matched only by her peculiar physique, for Mounira was short, squat and a hunchback.

It is said that during one of the frequent parties given by a well-to-do neighbour at the Ganage Building, the princess picked up her gun, nipped over to the clamorous party and took a potshot at the host. Luckily for him, she was a poor markswoman. But unlucky for her the intended victim was the distinguished Member of Parliament for Minya and a nephew of Egypt's leading feminist, Mme. Hoda Shaarawi. Furthermore, Mohammed Sultan Pasha was also president of the Royal Automobile Club whose principle patron was King Farouk. And the king only liked beautiful women.

Aziza Sabit, a distant relation of the two princesses, remembers how the gun-totting Mounira was said to have been equally alert during the Second World War. Passers-by occasionally glimpsed her squatting in her balcony, shotgun in hand, waiting for the enemy to arrive.

In the end, the princess had her revenge, in a way, as Villa Elhamieh still exists, in fairly decent condition in its new role as a Secondary School— complete with ugly additions to house an ever-increasing student population. As for the home of her neighbour of the noisy parties, it was recently replaced by a multi-million pound semi-circular, glass and concrete apartment building.

Almost bordering University Bridge's northern side is Villa de Saab (No. 3 Ahmed Nessim Street), which was originally surrounded by several plant nurseries. Although one knows little of the Saab family lifestyle, it is credited for producing the renowned French-language author Andrée Chedid. Villa Saab was reportedly sold to Naguib Salha whom we met earlier. For three decades ending in the late 1990s, Villa Saab was leased to the Embassy of Lebanon.

University Bridge, built by Germany's Fried Krupp-Stahlbau conglomerate, was completed in the final days of 1957. On hand to observe the mid-Nile meeting of the east-west steel spans was the then Transport Minister Mustafa Khalil accompanied by the constructor's representatives, Walter Becker and Max Buchinger.

In a recent e-mail to the author, Solomon Green, grandson of that other Solomon Green mentioned earlier in this chapter, gives a brief description of what was on the Giza riverfront before the bridge was built.

> My father's villa, built about 1930 by the French architect Max Edrei fronted the Nile alongside that of Sir Robert Greg, until it was bought by the government in July 1956 to allow for the bridge from Rhoda Island to Giza to be built. Before that there was a very successful ferry run by a small felucca that took students who did not wish to take the tram. Our own road was called Sharia Ibn Malek and at one time ours was the only house there. In fact, our garden went as far as Giza Avenue and the land between us and the Saabs was farmed for flowers by a peasant family living in an extended mud hut. The land fronting the avenue, also farmed by the peasant, was owned by my other grandfather and after the war was sold to Anis Serageddin, who put up a block of flats. I knew some of the peasant children quite well and sometimes played with them but I can no longer remember their names.

Heading south

On the south side of University Bridge stood the villa of Sir Robert H. Greg (No. 8 Ibn Bakil Street). He was the British Commissioner at the *Caisse de la Dette*, a financial organisation set up by European creditors soon after Khedive Ismail went bankrupt. Although Egypt's financial situation had long since improved the *Caisse* lived on, providing a welcome sinecure for retired senior civil servants.

Next to Sir Robert was the villa of Wissa Wassef Bey. The Wassefs may have left but the street bordering their now defunct villa bears their prominent name. In the 1920s, the Wassefs played an important role in the creation of the Wafd Party, described in those days as the repository of bourgeois Egyptian nationalism. Skyscrapers, including Borg al Riyadh, which houses Alfa supermarket, replaced the villas of Greg and Wassef.

Parallel to Wissa Wassef Street and perpendicular to the Nile is Ibn Arhab Street, on which the mansion of Dr. Ahmed Shafik Pasha still stands. The adjoining garden that had seen better days when the entire estate belonged to the Riaz Pasha family was gradually eradicated by a collection of tall buildings, the last one appearing in the 1970s practically atop the Shafik villa. The contiguous villa, once belonging to Shafik Pasha's neighbour, Naguib Youssef, has been replaced by the Embassy of the United Arab Emirates.

On the next block stands the beautiful redbrick mansion built for Princess Kazima, daughter of Sultan Hussein Kamel. When Kazima died childless in 1921, her house passed on to her brother, Prince Kamal al Din Hussein, who also died childless. The Republic of Turkey subsequently acquired the mansion but with a considerably reduced garden.

In the late 1940s and early 1950s, the Turkish Embassy residence was home to Ambassador and Madame Fouat Tugay. Through her mother, Princess Nimet Mokhtar, Amina Tugay was a granddaughter of Khedive Ismail and therefore a direct cousin of both King Farouk and the late Princess Kazima. In a sense, the house had reconnected with Egyptian royalty. But not for long, for the Tugays were the dejected witnesses to the toppling of King Farouk before being thrown out of Egypt themselves. Nasser had taken a distinct dislike to the patronising Turkish Ambassador and his outspoken wife.

Relations with Turkey remained at an all-time low several years thereafter.

On the other hand, an all-time high was reached during the ambassadorship of Yasar Yakis or 'Yashar Bey', as he was known in Cairo circles. One of Turkey's ablest envoys to Egypt, he took great pride in Kazima *Saray* especially its inimitable marble *éscalier d'honneur* which is indeed second to none. He eventually returned to Ankara to co-launch a progressive political party and became his country's foreign minister.

Across from the Turkish Embassy is an empty tract of land, so far. It was there that two large landowners from Upper Egypt kept separate homes. Mohammed and Abdel Hakim Marzouk were married to Aicha and Mounira, the daughters of Ali Shaarawi Pasha, the long-time senator from Minya. The two clans produced several senators and deputies who represented Minya in the Egyptian parliament, all claiming direct ancestral lineage to the Prophet's tribe in the Hejaz.

While Mohammed Marzouk's redbrick villa disappeared in the 1980s, following its sale to Sheikha Moody al Ankari from Saudi Arabia, his brother's three-story apartment house, No. 36 Al Nil Street fronting Ibn Nouf Street was purchased by the United Arab Emirates government. It stands out as a resounding example of 1930s art deco architecture with its interiors designed and decorated by Armando Centofanti.

Francophile Copts

Right across Ibn Nouf Street, perpendicular to Al Nil, lived one of Egypt's leading Coptic politicians. This was the residence of Wafdist Foreign Minister Wassef Boutros Ghali (son of a former prime minister and uncle of a future UN secretary-general) and his French wife. Known in those days to society as *Tante* Louise, she was actually born Louise Majorelle, a name wrongly associated with the Majorelle furniture design. In fact, Louise Ghali belonged to the silk Majorelles of Lyons.

When Wassef and Louise Ghali purchased this piece of prime Giza property in 1919, Egypt, then a British Protectorate, was in a state of fiery political upheaval. Amongst those the British jailed in 1919 were the nuclei of the future Wafd Party, including Ghali. That is perhaps why the property was registered by default in Louise Majorelle's name and why, 45 years later, it was her heirs and not her late husband's, who inherited the property. The Wassef-Ghalis had no children.

It was Louise who picked her new home's designer-architect, Signor Domenico Limongelli. Through his wife Kitty, a daughter of Artin Pasha, an Armenian-Egyptian with considerable connections, Limongelli landed himself several contracts with the extended Ghali family, one of whom had also married a high-born Armenian. Another Limongelli creation in Giza is the twin set of elegant apartment buildings on Bahy al Din Barakat Street that intersects with Avenue al Nil at its southernmost tip.

A frequent visitor to his uncle's home, Michel Boutros-Ghali describes it as a low-lying structure consisting of one floor and an elevated basement. "While the roof harboured a tiny room for Mémé Majorelle [Louise's mother], the basement was where my uncle and aunt kept a valuable collection of carpets along with two relic *Taxis de la Marne*." The latter were imported leftovers from the Great War when the French army found it necessary to requisition taxis to transport troops from Paris to the frontline on the Marne.

Several historic meetings took place at the Ghali House during the interwar period, dealing with the formation of the nationalist Wafd Party, in which the Copts played such a prominent and constructive role. Understandably, it was in Ghali's Giza residence where, in January 1928, the Wafd caucus endorsed Mustafa al Nahas Pasha as the new party boss following the unexpected death of Saad Zaghloul Pasha the previous summer.

"The Wassef Ghalis liked to summer in France where they owned a house at La Prieuré near St. Rémy-les-Chevreuses," says their nephew Michel, an estimable Francophile who is equally conversant in English. "It was also in France that Wassef Ghali Pasha died in November 1957. Tante Louise followed him a few years later, about the time when the assets of Egypt's landed aristocracy were being sequestered and their property confiscated."

As predators from the new regime were already circling around the Wassef Ghali property, Louise Majorelle's heirs heeded the advice of their counsel, Maitre Platon Valaskakis, and sold the Giza property to the first cash-ready buyer. The French government having exercised its right of first refusal, the choice fell on the American State Department's offer of about LE235,000.

It was a decade later, during Nixon's epic June 1974 visit to Egypt, that the American administration, in an act of largesse, offered the former Ghali property to President Anwar al Sadat along with a $2 million helicopter. When Congress raised angry objections, the Americans withdrew their real estate offer, leaving Sadat the chopper for his frequent travels. The Egyptian president's elaborate blueprints for the new house were reluctantly shelved.

The Americans then proceeded to replace Ghali's arabesque house with a colonial-style villa designed by Washington's Meltcalf & Associates under the supervision of Federal Buildings Bureau. The local contractor was Galal al Abd. The ambassadorial villa was to become the home of Alfred Leroy Atherton, the then US envoy to Egypt. But if one believes Washington buzz, the intended Nile-side residence became enmeshed in a network of dubious financial deals.

The official version for not moving in was that the house was faulty and fell short of security requirements. Those were the days when America was recovering from Watergate. To avoid additional scandals, the house and land were put up for sale and the whole caboodle swept under Foggy Bottom's (US Department of State) carpet with a profit to boot. These were the speculative economic open door-*infitah* days when the price of Cairo's real estate started its dizzying upward spin.

The land stood empty for quite a while with a bilingual sign proclaiming this was US government property. The neighbouring French embassy, although very interested, failed for the second time to come up with the asking price, so it was finally eager Gulf-moneyed developers who picked up the entire block at a US government-sponsored auction in the 1980s. They anticipated building a multi-million dollar complex with the expectation of it becoming Cairo's most expensive address. In addition to luxury apartments rumoured to house a number of famous actors, megabuck belly dancers and the pashas of the new era, the twin towers of this new complex called the First Residence also house a five-star Four Seasons Hotel complete with swimming pool and casino.

Ambassade de France

At every July 14 garden party, self-congratulating ambassadors, Cairo's bold and beautiful, survivors of the *ancien regime* and some disdainful pseudo-royalty, agree that elegance and chic still reign at No. 29 Giza Avenue (renamed Avenue Charles de Gaulle).

Although diplomatic relations between France and Egypt go back several centuries, the first French legation opened in Cairo in the nineteenth century and even then it was subordinate to the one in Alexandria. The first French Agency (or Consulate) was located diagonally opposite the old Shepheard's

Hotel on Kantaret al Dekka Street (later Naguib al Rihani), before moving in 1887 to the European district of Ismailia, opposite the old hippodrome. For the sum of one million francs the French Diplomatic Agency took over the amazing *okel* (a corruption of the Arabic word *wekala*—agency) of antique collector Charles Gaston de Saint-Maurice along with its priceless artefacts.

Saint-Maurice served under General Fleury before becoming Khedive Ismail's Master of the Horse. It was Saint-Maurice who fitted Ismail with magnificent stables, copying those of Napoleon III. His neo-Mamluke okel, decorated with *mashrabiya* windows and a façade painted in broad bands of pink and orange, was built by French architect Ambroise Baudry. Bordering Kasr al Nil, Chawarby and Madabegh (now Cherif) Streets, the okel was contiguous to the Aero and Royal Automobile Clubs, and to the British Benevolent Society. Across from it on Kasr al Nil Street stood the National Bank (today the Central Bank). One of the better-known consuls who lived and worked there at the turn of the century was de la Boulinière.

As for the French Consulate-General or Maison de France as it was then called, it moved in November 1925 from Djelal Street in Ezbekiya to its present day location No. 5 Al Fadl Street, near Midan Talaat Harb. The land was purchased through public subscription from among Cairo's French residents. Paul Conin Pastour, Director of Public Buildings in the Egyptian government, designed the ornate premises. The groundbreaking ceremony took place on March 13, 1925, in the presence of the French Minister M. Gaillard.

By the mid-1930s, it was the turn of the French Legation to look for appropriate quarters away from the city's bustle. Preferably, a location fronting the Nile in Giza since Garden City and Zamalek were already spoken for.

Up until 1936, No. 29 Giza Avenue belonged to the Sinnot Hanna family. A Wafdist senator from the city of Assiut, Sinnot Bey died on July 23, 1933, leaving behind a widow and an only daughter, Camille. Far too big for the Hanna ladies, they sold their homestead to the French government, which proceeded to refurbish it *à la française*. Thankfully, the two-acre garden needed no improvements. Khedive Ismail's trees, a legacy from his famous botanical parks were still very much in evidence. All that was missing was a chancellery.

In 1937, architects Georges Parcq and Jacques Hardy designed the new French chancellery taking into account that the building would house antique pieces from the old legation. Hence the colossal door, the great hall's wall and the exquisite ceiling woodwork. There were also the mosaics, the fountain, the marble columns and arches, and the pottery and statuettes to be considered. The result was the resounding masterpiece located in the south-west corner of the garden. For a few years, at least, the ensemble would serve to remind visitors of the old legation's arabesque character. The latter had meanwhile been sold and replaced by four giant apartment blocks collectively known as the Immobilia Buildings, designed by architects Max Edrei and Gaston Rossi, and completed in 1940.

In 1938, the French Agency, headed by Baron Pierre de Witasse transferred to the new premises. According to an embassy source, Witasse celebrated the move with an extravagant gala reception on February 19, which coincided with King Farouk's week-long birthday celebrations.

A year later, Witasse, who as a young diplomat had served in Alexandria on the eve of the Great War, announced the mobilisation of all able-bodied Frenchmen in Egypt. And just as *Les Poilus* were getting ready for the Second World War, Baron Pierre was replaced by Jean Pozzi, a familiar figure in Cairene society. His wife was sniped at as 'la Greque d'Egypte' as though that meant she was inferior to a Greek from Athens!

The Pozzis' tour of duty ended in shame and recrimination, for not only were they socially and politically ostracised by half of the French living in Egypt, but they were declared *persona non grata* and asked to leave Egypt because of their Vichy connections. Against advice from his peers, the unfortunate Jean had thrown in his lot with the reviled Pétain government that had signed the June 22, 1940, Franco-German armistice. As the dejected diplomat and *la greque* departed for Vichy-controlled Syria (via Palestine) on March 31, 1942, the Swiss flag was hoisted above No. 29 Giza Avenue.

Although France was no longer directly represented in Egypt, during the first part of the war the French had had the benefit of two bitterly opposed legations operating simultaneously in Cairo. While Pozzi represented Vichy from his Giza Chancery, Baron Louis de Benoist, president of the *Anciens Combattants*, stood in for General de Gaulle's *France Libre* from his unofficial headquarters (today the Banque du Caire et de Paris) in Garden City, right across from the British Embassy.

In 1944, French diplomat Jean Lescuyer retook possession of the Giza premises on behalf of the Free French. From then on, successive French ambassadors and their wives are remembered in Egypt either as footnotes to history or because they left their personal mark on the Giza residence.

The de Murvilles, who replaced Gilbert Arvengas in 1950, are remembered for both. De Murville's wife, Jacqueline Schweisguth, a.k.a. Vera Fabre in artistic circles and Couvette to intimate friends, was no wallflower. Marie-Alice Leclercq, a sparkling hostess herself and a latter-day contributor to this famous dwelling, had this to say about her predecessor. "It was Couvette and Couvette alone, who was responsible for introducing the Salon Bleu at No. 29 Giza Avenue. And contrary to current belief, she did *not* paint its famous ornamented panels. These were ordered directly from Atelier Zuber de Mulhouse in Alsace."

Maurice Couve de Murville witnessed first-hand Egypt's transition from monarchy to republic. Shortly after returning to France in 1954, he became his country's minister of foreign affairs and later its prime minister under Charles de Gaulle and George Pompidou. Connoisseurs of good fare and vintage wines will tell you de Murville's passage in Egypt was enhanced by his embassy's chef, whose *haute cuisine* was the talk of the town. Many years later Chef Christian Carnec would author *De Palais en Palais* where he recounts his sojourns in Cairo and other world capitals observing the different culinary customs and traditions. "*Chacune de ses recettes est une alchimie qui se nourrit de toutes ses expériences.*"

Murville's successor was the courtly Comte Armand du Chayla. He watched in alarm as France's relations with Egypt took a free-fall. His agony was cut short when, immediately following the October 1956 Tripartite Aggression, his deputy Guy Dorget handed the embassy keys to Max Koenig the Swiss diplomat who, for the next few years, would become custodian of Franco-British interests in Egypt.

Seven years passed before the Tricolour flapped once more above No. 29 Giza Avenue. The first post-1956 French ambassador to Egypt was Jacques Roux. It was Consuelo, his rich and flamboyant Latin American consort, who was responsible for the chancellery's pink colour. Somehow a *Casa Rosada* reminded her of South America's stately colonial government houses. Francois Puaux, who had in his younger days worked in the French Section of the Swiss Embassy in 1943-44, succeeded Roux in 1968. Then came in succession, Baron Bruno de Leusse de Syon (1972); Comte Jacques Senard (1976); Jacques Andreani (1979); Philippe Cuvillier (1981); Pierre Hunt (1985) and Alain Dujamet (1989).

From autumn 1991 to 1996, No. 29 Giza Avenue was home to the highly successful duo, Patrick and Marie-Alice Leclercq, along with their children Victor and Benjamin, and Loukoum, their white French poodle.

During the early part of their sojourn, Giza's most beautiful residence received a sweeping face-lift with its interior refurbished in a chic and unapologetic way as though echoing the character of Egypt's First French Lady. To be seen at the Leclercq's parties, in the company of witty politicians, international couturiers and prime-time celebrities, was to be at the heart of Cairo's swinging society of that period.

For those who haven't visited it, No. 29 Av. Charles de Gaulle is not just a dwelling; it's a point of view and a statement where many consequential political, cultural and financial resolutions were instigated. On a social level, it embodies a sense of audacity, spontaneity and *savoir* only the French know.

End of the line

Right across narrow Abou Shamar Street, overlooking the Nile and across the French embassy's southern perimeter stood the home of another Coptic Wafdist, this time, lawyer and former Finance Minister Kamel Sidki Pasha. Behind him lived Court Master of Ceremonies, Ali Rachid Pasha. Unlike Sidki's villa that is now an apartment building, Rachid's house has survived, if in a somewhat forlorn and neglected manner.

Owning the dahabiah *Aida* moored opposite Abou Shamar Street was Ragheb Hanna Bey, yet another Coptic Wafdist politician and former minister of state. Together with several other prominent politicians, he later left the party, joining a splinter group formed by dissident Wafdists.

One of the last survivors of this block, until it was pulled down in 2000, was Villa Alhambra, the redbrick house of the much-decorated Dr. Mohammed Sobhi Pasha, a prominent optometrist in his day. His former house at No. 6 Dr. Sobhi Street is today the property of the Kuwait Real Estate Investment Consortium (KREIC). With long-standing plans to build a new chancery for the Embassy of Kuwait, KREIC purposefully left the property to decay, inducing the collapse of its stately royal palms and other rare flora.

Across Dr. Sobhi Street (No. 1 ex-Zi Osbaa street) is a beautifully restored art deco villa built by Michel Liberman. This house, which was once occupied by a Doctor Ahmed Deif, has extraordinary high reliefs alternating with *trompe l'oeil* windows, true masterpieces in themselves. They depict a mixture of pharaonic motifs with a Mayan touch. The house was the scene of many a colourful reception when it was leased to the Brazilian embassy in the 1980s. Today it is used as offices for an Egyptian association.

Next door to the art deco villa, is 'Karma Ibn Hani', the recently restored villa of court Poet Laureate Ahmed Shawki. The character is typically pasha-style—a rich blend of baroque with columns, thick cornices, balustrades and a main entrance with twin stairs. Sometimes, this type of staircase would be substituted with a ramp so that the pasha could be driven right up to his front door. In this case, however, the poet laureate preferred to walk.

Although a low-lying house, the Giza pyramids could still be seen long after Shawki was gone. Everyone knew of Shawki's long-standing affair with the pyramids. When he lived in downtown Cairo, unable to spot the peaks of Chefren, Cheops and Mykerinos, Shawki would picnic on the Giza plateau almost every other week. By relocating to Giza in the mid-1920s, he no longer needed to travel up Pyramids Avenue. All it took was to open his upstairs windows to view the three massive tombs in all their glory.

Another villa in the same style stands behind the Shawki Museum. No. 6 Ahmed Shawki Street belonged to the poet's relatives the Alailis and, up until 1999, housed the offices of the Mexican Embassy.

Across the street and facing the Nile, stands an art deco building built by the Elmi family, who were related to the poet laureate through his wife. Either in this building or the one down from it at No. 12, lived pioneer movie director Togo Mizrahi and his wife, Myriam Donato. Behind No. 12 is yet another art deco building built in 1931 by Italian architect Guido Gavassi. Today it is the Côte d'Ivoire Embassy. And right next door to it, at No. 8 Al Hasn Street, is the former home of banker Levo Perez.

At No. 3 Al Hasn (now Pakistan Street) stood the *saray* of Princess Khadiga. A daughter of Khedive Tewfik, she was the next to youngest sister of Khedive Abbas Hilmi, in whose honour the nearby bridge was named. Married to Prince Mohammed Abbas Halim, both a cousin and former governor of Turkey's ancient capital of Borsa, Princess Khadiga had six daughters and endless royal relations in both Egypt and Turkey, so that her Giza residence never lacked for wedding celebrations. One of the last ones was that of Ottoman Princess Seljuk to the debonair dandy Gazouli Rateb Bey. In the wake of the 1952 coup, the palace was transformed into a school and subsequently pulled down. All that remains of the palace today is the old coach house and a few thirsty palm trees.

Closer to Abbas Bridge, is 'Ghaliland', so named because the Ghali family, whom we met earlier, owned a sizeable portion of this Nile frontage. They could have owned it all had it not been for the two arabesque villas standing in the core. The architect of both these interesting villas was Mario Rossi, whose other works include the mosques of Sidi Morsi Abou al Abbas in Alexandria and Omar Makram in Cairo. The first villa, coming from the south, belonged to Atta Afifi Bey and his Spanish wife, Isabelita Casanova— reportedly a former paramour of King Alfonso of Spain. The second belonged to Afifi Bey's sister, Hedayat Hanem, wife of Wafdist Minister of Education Bahy al Din Barakat Pasha. It was no coincidence that the Afifis chose Giza's riverside drive as a place of residence, for their mother, Nefissa Khalil Hanem, was a sister of Mohammed Mahmoud Khalil Bey. Giza was certainly not foreign to them.

Aside from its remarkable architecture and its thematic salons, Villa Barakat should have been listed in the historical register. It was in its inner courtyard, probably around the fountain, that Egypt's intelligentsia debated the early drafts of Egypt's landmark Anglo-Egyptian Treaty before its 1936 ratification in both London and Abdin Palace.

In its last years, before it transmogrified into a skyscraper, Villa Barakat was leased to a director of the Chase Manhattan Bank. Knowing it would someday go, one wonders if the banker kept as a souvenir the stylised eyes of Horus, which were used as door handles to the pharaonic salon?

Although squashed between two apartment blocks, Villa Afifi, on the other hand, was spared destruction. Its wonderful ceramic interiors and its imposing arabesque portal are still there, gasping for light. Serving as a residence for Dutch ambassadors in the 1960s and 1970s, it is presently leased by Nasser Bank to the producers of Vitrac jams and other such edible preserves.

At the tip of Giza's riverside drive, just before you come to the ex-Abbas Bridge underpass, stands an imposing modern building with wrap-around balconies. This is one of two modern Ghali Buildings in the area. This one was designed by one of its current owners, Michel Boutros Ghali, who lives there, as do his brothers Raouf and Boutros. The latter is the beneficiary of the penthouse, which despite defensive *mashrabiya* barriers, looks like a cat copulating with a giraffe. The former UN secretary-general's terrace is literally wedged into a towering glass and aluminium complex belonging to the Ministry of Foreign Affairs Housing Association.

This too-close-for-comfort situation prompted many unsympathetic remarks from environmentalists and preservationists, along the lines of, "Et tu, Boutros?" Did the former UN secretary-general, who would one day head the Rio Summit on Environment, really need to sanction the sale of the tiny Ghali-owned plot of land on which the high-rise was built? Does profit always have to come before other considerations?

Lesser homes have been classified or listed elsewhere in the world, yet in Egypt we are first-hand witnesses to the wanton destruction of irreplaceable edifices, mansions and statues built for and by our former leaders and notables. Thank God, therefore, for the three villas on Giza's riverside that have received a new lease on life: Karma Ibn Hani (the Shawki museum), the Villa Credit Foncier (Mubarak Public Library) and the Mohammed Mahmoud Khalil Museum. They may be all that is left as we burrow into the new century—three lonely testimonials of what was once Giza's elegant riverside drive.

6. Palaces and pavilions

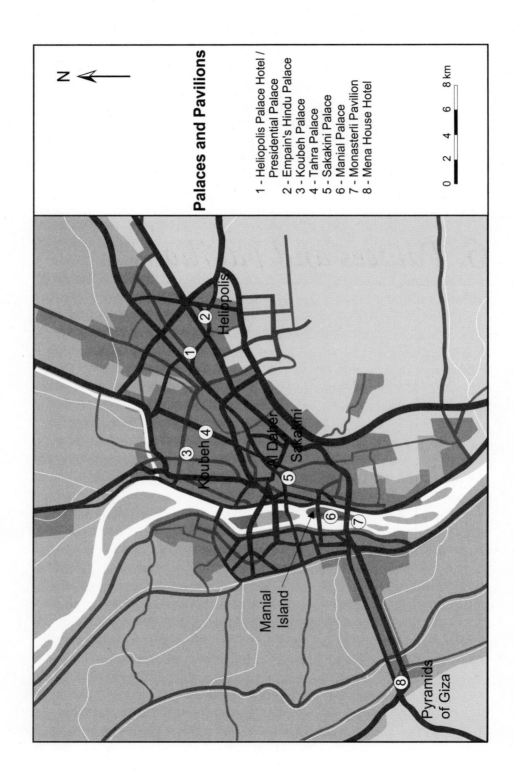

Palaces and Pavilions

1 - Heliopolis Palace Hotel /
    Presidential Palace
2 - Empain's Hindu Palace
3 - Koubeh Palace
4 - Tahra Palace
5 - Sakakini Palace
6 - Manial Palace
7 - Monasterli Pavilion
8 - Mena House Hotel

0   2   4   6   8 km

N

Heliopolis

Koubeh

Al Daher

Sakakini

Manial
Island

Pyramids
of Giza

Desert Taj Mahal

Thanks to transparency, electronic media, sex scandals and UN resolutions, the world's presidential haunts are accessible to television viewers around the globe. But unlike the Elysée, the White House and now, Saddam's Shangri-Las, Egypt's presidential palaces remain a conundrum to the people of this country.

More than half a century after Nasser's Free Officers vowed to turn this nation into a republic 'by the people and for the people', its citizenry is as removed from the temples of power as they were millennia ago when Pharaoh ruled the land and high priests prohibited access to temples. Except for a very few halls in Abdin, few Egyptian citizens have ever seen the gilded interiors of the former royal palaces of Tahra, Koubbeh and Ras al Tin. And unless plans to turn them into public historic sites ever surface, there is no chance they ever will.

Not so the Kasr al Ittihadiya, now perhaps the most august and restricted of them all. While few other than national leaders and journalists can visit it these days, there are still some around who remember having frequented it as the Heliopolis Palace Hotel.

International conferences, weddings and honeymoons took place there as did the coveted *après courses* celebrations—the races at the nearby Heliopolis Sporting Club were second to none. Although veterans are probably not around anymore to remind us, during the First World War the hotel was requisitioned and turned into a British military hospital.

Like Heliopolis itself, the grandiose Palace Hotel rose out of the desert wastes in 1908-10 when lengthy sojourns in Egypt were a social ritual, and the hotel's register resembled a leaf out of Burke's Peerage. Its first proprietor was Monsieur Marquet. Its inaugural director Herr Doerhoefer had been with the Mena House, and its first food and beverage manager was Monsieur Bedard, assisted by Chef Gouin. They had come from the Paillard Restaurant in Paris.

On December 1, 1910, all four were on hand to greet Egypt's best as they celebrated the official launch of Africa's most luxurious hotel.

Conceived by Belgian architect Ernest Jaspar, the hotel boasted 400 rooms including 55 private apartments. Its banquet halls were amongst the biggest anywhere. The utilities were the most modern of their day. All had been constructed and put together by the contracting firms Leon Rolin & Co.

and Padova, Dentamaro & Ferro, the two biggest civil contractors in Egypt. Messrs. Siemens & Schuepert of Berlin fitted the hotel's web of electric cables and installations.

As though intentional, its severe, almost forbidding exterior contrasted sharply with the sumptuousness of the interior. A 1912 visitor recounts:

> Beyond the reception offices are two lavishly decorated rooms, in the Louis XIV and Louis XV styles respectively and then comes the central hall, which is a dream of beauty and symmetry. Here the architecture, which is responsible for so many wonderful effects in Heliopolis, reaches its artistic zenith. From every nook and cranny hang, suspended like stalactite pendants, Damascus-made Oriental lamps of fantastic loveliness.

To give us a sense of the central hall's monumental dimensions the overwhelmed visitor carries on:

> Above soars the dome rising upward in a bold scheme of frolicsome fancy with all the involved convulsions of Oriental ornamentation. No photograph or description could do justice to the wondrous and elusive loveliness of the scene, which is baffling to the language as it is to the lens.

"C'est une merveille!" exclaimed the King of Belgium in 1911 when he entered the main hall accompanied by his consort. The royal couple spent an entire month at the Heliopolis Palace Hotel during which time Queen Elizabeth, who was recovering from typhoid, slowly regained her health. The dry air of Heliopolis had been strongly recommended by her doctors in Brussels.

The height of the central hall's dome measures 55 metres from floor to ceiling. The 589 square metre hall, designed by Alexander Marcel of the French Institute and decorated by Georges-Louis Claude, was carpeted with the finest oriental rugs and fitted with large floor-to-ceiling mirrors, draperies and a large marble fireplace. Twenty-two Italian marble columns connect the parquet to the ceiling. To one side of the hall there was the grillroom, which seated 150 guests, and to the other was the billiard hall with two full-sized Thurston tables, as well as a priceless French one. The mahogany furniture was ordered from Maple's of London. The upper gallery contained oak-panelled reading and card rooms furnished by Krieger of Paris.

The basement and staff area was so large that a narrow gauge railway was installed running the length of the hotel, passing by offices, kitchens, pantries, refrigerators, storerooms and the staff mess.

Two wars interrupted the hotel's hospitality activities, and on both occasions the Heliopolis Palace Hotel was transformed into a hospital for British and Dominion soldiers, who became the largest single category of tourists to visit Egypt.

Following the Second World War, air travel reduced the average tourist stay to a few days. Mass production and consumption introduced the era of the camera-clicking crowds. As tourism became a mega-industry, massive vertical hotels cropped up along the Nile with interiors calculated on the basis of return per square metre. Unable to compete, the Heliopolis Palace became a dinosaur.

In the 1960s, the abandoned hotel became the headquarters of various government departments. One by one, an untutored public chipped its inimitable artefacts away. It was all over. The dustbin of history was waiting; perhaps the bulldozer and a demolition ball were not far behind.

We shall never know.

Whether by divine or temporal intervention, the Palace Hotel was granted a new lease on life. Situated within earshot of where President Mubarak lives, the former hotel was given a thorough facelift in the 1980s and declared the headquarters of the new presidential administration. Once again, the Taj Mahal of the desert became the focus of international attention.

So will we lesser mortals ever get a virtual gape at its eye-popping interiors? Don't hold your breath.

Royal lodge

One of Cairo's most famous and spectacular hotels began its life, not surprisingly, as the personal property of one of Egypt's famous leaders. The Mena House at the pyramids was originally Khedive Ismail's rest house and hunting lodge, and its core became what is today the Oberoi Hotel's arabesque dining room.

The first international celebrity to visit the lodge was Empress Eugenie of France when she attended the November 17, 1869, opening celebrations of the Suez Canal. Pyramids Avenue was created specifically for her sojourn. The grateful empress offered her munificent host acacia trees, which he later planted on either side of the avenue.

When she revisited the site in 1909, Eugenie was no longer empress of France and a hotel had replaced the khedivial lodge, while eucalyptus trees were now bordering the avenue. Unchanged, however, was the setting that remained just as sensationally beautiful. The gardens of the lodge-turned-hotel still burst with roses, oleanders and magnolias, all of them looking out towards the pyramids.

Between Eugenie's two visits, France had abandoned Emperor Napoleon and Khedive Ismail had lost Egypt. The latter's Giza hunting lodge had been picked up by the Englishman Frederick Head and his wife Mary, the Australian daughter of Queensland treasurer John Donald McLean. They named their new hotel Mena House in honour of King Mena, who is listed on the tablet of Abydos as the Great Unifier.

After the death of Mr. Head, the Mena House became home to Hugh and Ethel Locke-King. Ethel also knew Australia well, for her father, Sir Thomas Gore Brown, had been Tasmania's governor during the 1860s. The Locke-Kings undertook major structural changes such as installing fireplaces and giving the place a more English look—sharply deviating from the prevailing Ottoman decor characterised by mother-of-pearl inlays and *mashrabiya*. Large public rooms, terraces and verandahs were also added. As car racing fanatics, the Locke-Kings added motorcar gymkhanas to the hotel's social calendar of events. Managing the hotel on their behalf was Baron de Radokawsky.

The Locke-Kings left a robust well-established Mena House to be managed in turn by a Mr. Klinger and then by Emil Weckel, whose annual fancy dress ball and Sunday and Wednesday concerts were novel attractions to the already popular hotel. Others amenities included a golf course, two croquet lawns and horses and donkeys for hire. A pre-First World War description of the hotel sums it up in the following terms:

> At the foot of the Pyramids, on the borders of the desert, is one of the finest hotels in Egypt, Mena House. At tea-hour its terraces are crowded with a gay and brilliant throng. The large and comfortable salons, the delicious Moorish dining room, the excellent food, the open air-swimming bath, the golf course, the tennis courts, the croquet lawns all go to make a stay at Mena House one of the most pleasant incidents of a trip to Egypt.

A sporting event near the Mena House Hotel that fascinated the First Australian Division camping nearby during the war was the camel race. The highpoint was when a camel, furious at being passed, would sink his teeth in the leg of his rival's jockey. If the poor rider were lucky, he would be taken to the Mena House, which had become a hospital during most of the war, staffed by Anzac nurses.

During the interwar period, the 150-room Mena House was managed by the Egyptian Hotels Company (EHC), which succeeded the George Nungovich Co. Under the directorship of its veteran Swiss hotelier, Charles Baehler, EHC multiplied the rooms, added a swimming pool and extended the overall facilities.

Cairo's Mena House was the only hotel in the vicinity of the pyramids up until the 1960s and hosted every emperor, king, president, general, business tycoon and megastar who visited Egypt. Enemies-to-the-death and wartime allies stayed there between 1939-45 including Josef Goebbels, Generalissimo Chiang Kai Chek, Franklin D. Roosevelt and Winston Churchill.

Even as Roosevelt and Churchill deliberated final plans for a wholesale victory over Germany and Italy, the British RAF was taking no chances. Security around the Mena House had never been tighter. A picture and newspaper clipping of that historic event says it all:

> During the Allied conferences at the Mena House all possible precautions were taken to prevent interference by enemy aircraft. The picture shows an observation post above the Cheops pyramid. The airmen carried all the equipment 500 feet up to the summit and completed the installation in one day.

According to Julian Eley, the son of one of the airmen in question, when asked to put a mobile installation on top of the pyramid:

> The RAF personnel had to make it out of spare parts, as there was no mobile unit available. Later, when asked by a senior officer which model the unit was, they had to say there was, of course, no model number. Not having any rank, no credit was given. Apparently it was usual to get a mobile unit with a team dispatched from base and it could be that noses were "put out of joint" by a field crew who "knocked" one up on the spot.

Exiled kings also made Mena House their temporary home including King George of the Hellenes, who stayed there with his English mistress.

After the Second World War, the EHC resolved to give its five-star properties a much overdue overhaul. Supervising the decoration of two of them—Cairo's Mena House and Jerusalem's King David—was hotel consultant, Denise Dreyfus, daughter of Cairo financier Elie Mosseri who held considerable interest in EHC.

Both hotels, each set in a historically dramatic location, were ultimately confiscated. The first was taken over by the post-1952 government of Egypt when private companies were axed under the new socialist laws, and the second when the government of Israel expropriated all Egyptian-owned assets.

Perhaps appropriately enough, the first Egyptian-Israeli peace talks were held at the Mena House in the late 1970s. By then, the much-transformed hotel had become a member of a leading Indian hotel chain. The Bombay-based Oberoi Hotels Group manages the Mena House to this day.

The garden palace

Situated several kilometres north of downtown Cairo, Koubbeh Palace—so named in reference to the dome (*koubbeh*) of a nearby mosque—was once surrounded by agricultural fields and rural villages to one side and the desert on the other. Access to and from the city was along a cobbled carriage road that passed through the sprawling suburb of Shubra.

According to unpublished jottings by Prince Mohammed Ali Tewfik, who was born there in 1875, the main building of the 400-room Italianate palace, the Haramlek, overlooked 70 acres of gardens filled with tropical plants. Part of the garden was used as an acclimatisation centre for flowers, shrubs and trees brought from all over the globe. Pavilions and jasmine-covered kiosks were everywhere. While some of these were built with sliding *mashrabiya* screens ensuring the privacy of princesses and palace maidens, others had copper roofs that gleamed like jewels in the sunshine and under the full moon. All had rich cushions of silk and satin strewn with seed pearls so that residents and guests alike could play *shatarang, dameh* and *tawlah* in absolute comfort.

"The palace was originally the property of the Fazil branch of the House of Mohammed Ali," explains Princess Ulvia Halim, the daughter of the 'blue collar' prince we met earlier. She is also the granddaughter of Princess Ulfet Fazil. "Subsequently enlarged by Khedive Mohammed Tewfik, it was the venue for many One Thousand and One Night celebrations, royal weddings, and a place where visiting dignitaries admired the magnificent gardens." Having attended several royal weddings at Koubbeh, Princess Halim, who now resides in a small Zamalek apartment, is a member of that privileged group of people who entered the forbidden realm.

During Khedive Abbas Hilmi's rule, the garden palace gradually came to be regarded as complementary to Cairo's Abdin Palace in terms of officialdom. When King Fouad ascended Egypt's throne in 1917, Koubbeh became the official royal residence. By then a royal train station had been added to the palace complex whereby visiting dignitaries arrived by special carriage directly from Alexandria or from Cairo's main railway station. During his reign, King Fouad ordered numerous enhancements and extensions to Koubbeh including a six metre wall around the 75 acre premises, as well as a new gate and an external garden. In his chronicle of court life, historian Shafik Pasha describes how the wall's construction supposedly caused a major shortage of bricks in the country.

It was a few days after King Fouad died that his 16-year-old son Farouk greeted his subjects during a momentous inaugural radio broadcast on May 8, 1936. Now that wireless technology had become an established means of interacting with the public at large, a special radio transmitter was installed in Koubbeh. This turning point in communications was echoed 40 years later when Egypt's first ever live satellite transmission went out from Koubbeh Palace during US President Richard Nixon's state visit.

Considering it his private residence, King Farouk kept his personal collections at Koubbeh. These priceless treasures encompassed a precious stamp collection, an 8,500-piece coin and medals collection, studded clocks and watches, in addition to many other beautiful antiquities including a pure gold coffee set and a 1906 Fabergé egg that belonged to the last Russian czar. Much of these were auctioned off in 1954 as shown by front-page advertisements placed in most of the contemporary newspapers.

The worth of the coin collection alone was substantial. In 1954 a certain John Jay Pittman bought four rare coins for $454 and another three for $514. These seven coins were then sold in an auction in the United States 25 years later for a staggering $224,950.

After the toppling of the monarchy in 1952, Koubbeh Palace was earmarked as one of three official presidential palaces, the other two being Abdin in downtown Cairo and Ras al Tin in Alexandria. If Koubbeh came third in terms of opulence, it was nevertheless there that Gamal Abdel Nasser preferred to host his official guests. It was also there that his body lay in state prior to his historic funeral in September 1970.

To this day Koubbeh remains Egypt's principal guesthouse. African chiefs have stayed there, Chinese leaders helped themselves to cuttings from the gardens, Arab potentates admired and later copied the staterooms, and European prime ministers including Britain's Tony Blair found time to enjoy the sun on one of the numerous palace balconies.

But according to accompanying diplomats who have stayed there, it is not always the most comfortable of abodes. One Nordic envoy accompanying his president on a state visit to Egypt during the winter complained that hot water was only available at night and there were no electric outlets for heaters or hair dryers.

The only potentate to visit the palace both when it was royal and later, when it was presidential, was the Shah of Iran, for it was there that he had once stayed and later sipped tea with Egypt's Queen Mother when he celebrated his March 1939 wedding to Farouk's sister, the Princess Fawzia. He would return to Koubbeh Palace during a state visit in 1974 and again in 1979 on his way to a very painful exile.

Palace of the English patient

Attributed to Italian court architect Antonio Lasciac, Tahra Palace was built early in the twentieth century for Mohammed Taher Pasha's mother, the Princess Amina. "The fact that the palace is called Tahra and its original occupant Taher is purely coincidental," says palace researcher Amr Talaat. "In effect it was named after (Baba) Taher, an eleventh century Persian poet."

The style is pure Italianate *palazzo*, a fact accentuated by its inimitable marble stairways and fantastic alabaster ceilings. Another reminder of Italy is the exquisite water fountain fronting the palace. To many connoisseurs its design clearly evokes the architectural marvel gracing Rome's Piazza Barberini.

Once surrounded by green fields and palm groves, this palace's only neighbour of consequence was Taher Pasha's maternal uncle, King Fouad, who resided in the nearby Koubbeh palace.

Taher Pasha's brief marriage to one of his royal cousins notwithstanding, this particular grandson of Khedive Ismail was a virtual bachelor for most of his life. An unassuming member of the Egyptian ruling family, he was nevertheless an avid sportsman. He was the first president of the Egyptian Olympic Committee and his patronage of other sporting activities extended to the presidencies of the Mohammed Ali Club, the Royal Automobile Club, the Feroussia Club and, closest to the pasha's heart, the Aero Club. It was Taher Pasha's keen interest in the latter that brought him together with Ladislas 'Lazlo' Almazy who became a permanent houseguest at Tahra.

Of limited fame at the time, the Hungarian-born Almazy—sometimes referred to as Count Almazy—would, many decades later, be portrayed by Hollywood as the celebrated daredevil pilot and desert explorer in the 1996 blockbuster *The English Patient*. Indeed, it was under the royal patronage of Taher Pasha and Prince Youssef Kamal that Almazy, flying his Gypsy Moth, criss-crossed the Libyan Desert in search of the legendary lost oasis of Zarzoura.

A few years later, the Magyar aristocrat, who had forfeited an existence of leisure in Austria's Castle Berstein for a life of adventure at Cairo's Tahra Palace, allegedly ferried German spy John Eppler across the Libyan Desert and into the Nile valley during the Second World War. This amazing feat is well described in Ken Follett's bestseller *Key to Rebecca*.

But what Follett fails to mention in his thriller is how the pro-German Taher Pasha was himself placed, by order of the British, under house arrest for part of the war, first in a house near Wasta south of Helwan, and later in Sinai. Did Taher Pasha miss the comforts of Tahra? Not really, for it was no longer his to miss. Just before the war King Farouk had purchased the palace for LE40,000 and offered it to his bride, Queen Farida. Taher Pasha relocated to No. 5 Amir Fouad Street (now Dr. Mahmoud Azmi), Gezira, opposite Villa Yildiz belonging to the very wealthy Khayatt family from Upper Egypt. The latter having arrived in Zamalek in the early 1920s, were considered 'old establishment' by the rest of the island. (Villa Yildiz was pulled down in the 1980s to make way for a large US embassy housing unit.)

The new owner of Tahra Palace meanwhile proceeded to embellish it with priceless *objets d'arts* collected from other palaces and from the plenteous royal *garde-meubles*. For a more detailed perspective of what was in the palace let's refer to Amr Talaat's account:

The King added a large hall to the Palace, which he named after his great-grandfather. Therein he brought from Shubra Palace an ebonite billiard table inlaid with gold and a large Roman mosaic tableau—both items were gifts to Mohammed Ali from the King of France and the Pope respectively. Also in the Mohammed Ali Hall, King Farouk ordered the placement of a piano made of ebony and inlaid with ivory that had belonged to Khedive Ismail. Hanging on one of the walls was a large clock, modelled on the original of Strasbourg city fame. And somewhere, also on the first floor, was a marble statue of Khedive Ismail and a grand humidor.

In 1953, Tahra Palace was confiscated, along with the rest of the palaces belonging to the House of Mohammed Ali. Much of Tahra's precious heirlooms would soon reappear at state-sponsored auctions as the government attempted to replenish its emptying coffers.

New plans were being drawn up for Tahra. It would henceforth serve the dual purpose of presidential palace and official guesthouse—paradoxically becoming home to exiled members of other toppled monarchies.

Among the palace's first republican-era guests was a humble shop girl from one of Cairo's department stores who made it big when she wed Ghana's independence leader, Kwame Nkrumah. Along with Yugoslavia's Tito, Indonesia's Sukarno, and Egypt's Nasser, Nkrumah founded the Non-Aligned Movement. For a while, it was Fathia Nkrumah, her mother and several members of her Coptic family who resided in the palace where Taher Pasha and Lazlo Almazy had once held separate courts.

Other state guests and heads of liberation movements followed. Yet in 1973, during the run-up to the October War, there was activity of a different kind at Tahra. Very discreetly, parts of the palace were being transformed into makeshift 'situation rooms.' Huge maps of Sinai covered Belgian mirrors and where *savonneries* and *gobelins* had once decorated walls, larger-than-life pictures of the Suez Canal area were plastered. It was from Tahra that Sadat directed his celebrated October canal crossing.

By the time the Shah of Iran's widow occupied the premises free of charge in 1980, Tahra Palace was already in a sorry state of decline. The long-term effects of neglect and pilfering had started to show. Which is perhaps why Farah Diba together with her extended Iranian family preferred rented villas in the south of France and stately homes off New England's Long Island Sound. Such was her hurry to vacate Tahra, the ex-empress forgot to tip the personnel. Similarly, Egypt has nothing to show for the gracious hospitality extended to the exiled shah, whom only Anwar al Sadat wanted to host.

In May 1999, France's Prime Minister Lionel Jospin was another notable guest at Tahra, around the time when there was talk of the palace being immortalised in a splendid European-made documentary on the life of Lazlo Almazy. If the required filming permits had been forthcoming, Tahra Palace might perhaps have been shunted into the bracket of other illustrious homes such as Rambouillet, Balmoral and Blair House. Alas, no permits.

Palace of the problem-solver

In *Al Lata'ef al Masreya's* (Variety Magazine) June 18, 1923, issue Tewfik Moufarej reproached his recently departed co-religionist, Count Gabriel Habib Sakakini Pasha, for having been a skinflint. "Why hadn't the eccentric pasha been more generous towards his community? All he left behind was a church. Where then, are the Sakakini hospitals, Sakakini Orphanages and Sakakini Schools?" laments the editor of the popular Egyptian magazine. But as though contradicting himself, Moufarej goes on to describe how Sakakini had become a household name sported on tramways running through Fagallah and Daher on their way to the residential district bearing the pasha's name. And how the same tramways passed through Midan Sakakini clanking away beneath the inimitable Sakakini Palace.

While some of his descendants claim that Sakakini came to Egypt for health reasons, according to Moufarej, this rags to riches saga started when 16-year-old Gabriel Habib Sakakini arrived from Damascus in 1857 to take on a job with the nascent Suez Canal Company in Port Said. For the next four years the Syrian worked for the paltry sum of 3-4 French francs per month, which leads one to believe that Sakakini's eventual move to Cairo was more for economic rather than any other reasons. Otherwise, why did he sojourn in the city's north-western outskirts, an abandoned area known for its mosquito-infested marshlands?

It was precisely at the centre of this wretched area that Sakakini would later erect his rococo-pastry palace. Having become a rich contractor, he transformed part of the area between Abbassia and Ghamra from swampy mire into an upmarket residential district (subsequently named after him). Somewhere along the way he developed his distinctive attention-getting style that would stay with him well into the after life.

When it came to selecting a site for his home, Sakakini Pasha chose the convergence of eight important roadways. Henceforth, all roads led to Sakakini Palace.

Seen from above, the pasha's Disney-esque abode looks like the sun with roads radiating outwards in all directions. The lord of the manor liked to be at the centre of things. This is quite evident at the Malachite Cemetery in Old Cairo. It was, after all, Sakakini Pasha who had donated the large chunk of property contiguous to the Hanging Church in 1896 for the new Greek-Catholic cemetery. It came as no surprise, therefore, that the central plot was set aside for his family mausoleum.

Upon his death, Sakakini was buried smack dab in the middle of the cemetery, inside the crypt of his own Byzantium-styled Mar Elias Church. First among equals, Sakakini Pasha, lies in state surrounded by the leading members of his community including the Zananiris, Nahas, Matouks, Sednaouis, Eids, Khers, Pharaons, Aswads, Ganages, etc., all buried in no less handsome mausoleums. Even in 1923, the overall setting must have awed Sakakini's critics starting with Moufarej.

But what happened between the destitute young man's arrival from Port Said and his meteoric rise to fame and fortune, earning him the lofty titles of Papal 'count' and Ottoman 'pasha?'

Legend has it that Habib Sakakini attracted Khedive Ismail's attention when he exported, by Camel Express, sacks full of famished cats to the rat-infested Suez Canal Zone. Within days, a nasty rodent epidemic was halted. Quick to recognise inventiveness and initiative, the khedive made good use of the shrewd Syrian, giving him the daunting task of completing the Khedivial Opera House designed by Pietro Avoscani.

Working under the Italian architect Avoscani, Sakakini installed a round-the-clock triple shift work system for the next 90 days. It worked, and the Opera House was completed in time for the arrival of visiting European monarchs for the lavish festivities celebrating the opening of the Suez Canal on November 17, 1869. The munificent khedive's gratification was boundless and henceforth building and public works contracts did not fail to come Sakakini's way.

At 39 years of age, Habib Sakakini was elevated to the Ottoman title of bey, confirmed in Constantinople by Ismail's suzerain, Sultan Abdel Hamid.

A decade later, Rome's Leon XIII conferred upon Sakakini the Papal title of count for services to his community. Le Comte de Sakakini had donated the former palace of Saint Simonian architect Linant de Bellefonds to the Greek-Catholic community for the construction of a cathedral.

Unlike the staid cathedral (located behind the Jesuit School in Fagallah), Sakakini's circular palace is another story. With its many turrets, conical and onion-shaped domes, medieval gargoyles and steeples, it looks more like a child's dream castle than a pasha's mansion. All it lacks to complete the fantasy are a moat and drawbridge. The palace's 50 rooms and halls have more than 400 windows and doors, and the conspicuous decor includes over 300 busts and statues, many of them quite risqué. All in all, this is one of the best examples of a khedivial architectural folly.

According to the inscription above the western entrance, the palace was built in 1897, making it more than a century old—one wonders therefore, why such a rare piece of architectural kitsch is in such an advanced state of neglect? In Miami, Florida, or any other place, the Sakakini palace would have become a shrine. Here, it is a dumping ground.

After becoming government property in 1961, the palace fell into chronic disrepair, not unlike the condition of the surrounding neighbourhoods of Daher and Fagallah. It seems as only yesterday however, that several ministers surrounded by fawning aides and a panel of conservation 'experts' paused next to it for some eye-catching photo-ops.

That 'yesterday' was actually back in April 1991. The deteriorated palace had just been featured in a popular TV program *Ahawi wa Hakawi* (Coffee Shop Tales), catching President Hosni Mubarak's attention. Overnight, there was the predictable surge of Potemkinesque interest by the concerned cabinet members. As if by magic, a seven-digit sum was whipped out of the state treasury and allocated for its restoration.

More than a decade later, there is still no evidence of these restoration works. Did the related funds evaporate along with the feigned enthusiasm? When was the last time a concerned minister dropped by for another publicised photo-op?

Whether Count Habib Sakakini was a miser or not, the man was a problem-solver, who could be counted upon by his community and sovereign. Despite what Moufarej had to say about him, had Sakakini Pasha been alive today, he would have found the right type of cats to rid this country of the plethora of self-interested and deceiving rats. Small wonder they ignore his palace.

Palace of rumours

Ever since thousands of bats moved into Heliopolis's most famous landmark, Baron Empain's Hindu Palace has been the subject of innumerable reports, some of them stranger than the building itself. Quibbling Gulf heirs are supposedly talking of transmogrifying the pseudo-Cambodian temple into a Caesar's Palace complete with gambling casino, Liberace-style performers, and who knows what else.

Meanwhile Brussels-based Eurocrats deliberate the merits of turning the Belgian baron's heirloom into a spectacular EuroMed centre. Back in Cairo, the Egyptian government is still undecided whether it should turn the palace into a desert museum or better still, a pantheon for Egypt's Greats. But the reports which get highest marks are the headlines claiming that the palace dungeon—formerly the baron's servants quarters—is where Cairo's black-clad, tattooed devil-worshipping youth hold lusty orgies, skin cats and draw rats' blood. Makes you wonder whether Baron Empain or Count Dracula built the palace.

Undoubtedly turning in his black granite crypt beneath the nearby Byzantine-style basilica is the palace's creator, the Belgian-born industrialist, Baron-General Edouard Louis Joseph Empain, the visionary creator of Heliopolis. It was shortly after he ordered the construction of Heliopolis in 1907 that he commissioned French architect Alexander Marcel, a member of the prestigious French Institute, to build him a Hindu palace on an artificial elevation. From his terrace, the Baron could watch the rising of Heliopolis against the dramatic backdrop of the 4,000 plus-year-old Giza pyramids, far to the west.

Shielding the baron from lesser mortals were aristocratic neighbours. To his left facing Avenue Baron, which stretches southwards towards the pious baron's basilica, was the arabesque palace of Boghos and Marie Nubar Pasha (now a military HQ). He was the son of Nubar Nubarian, the wily Armenian who served several khedives as chief minister and was often referred to as Egypt's Bismarck. Well-connected, Nubar *fils* facilitated Empain's acquisition of 6,000 acres of empty desert at LE1 per acre. In return, he was appointed a director of Empain's budding Egypto-Belgian empire.

Diagonally opposite the Hindu palace, stands the former compound (today, a presidential guesthouse) of Sultan Hussein Kamel, who reigned over Egypt between 1914 and 1917. A childhood friend of Boghos Nubar

Pasha, he was the only Egyptian monarch ever to live in Heliopolis. His widow, Sultana Malek, occupied the palace until the 1950s.

The Hindu palace's exterior was the responsibility of Marcel. Influenced by a Cambodian temple, he reproduced a motley crew of busts, statues, elephants, and snakes, Shivas and Krishnas. The elaborate interior meanwhile was the responsibility of his French associate, Georges-Louis Claude. They had previously constructed and decorated the Oriental Pavilion attached to the Royal Palace of Laeken in Belgium. Later they created an entire Far Eastern complex at the Paris Exhibition.

Although dwindling in numbers, there are those who still remember when the landscape surrounding the palace was a wonderland festooned with ascending green terraces each with its own set of erotic marble statues and exotic vegetation. As guests negotiated the terraces on their way to the grand steps leading into the awesome palace foyer, they felt as though some mythical *Deus* was watching from the palace's interior. These theatrics pleased the Baron no end. In a letter to his mother, Georges-Louis Claude relates how the marvelled Baron, "had no criticism in store when we last met." Known to be a stickler for details, Empain had given his workers, employees and advisors, a hard time.

Three generations of Empains occupied the premises. The austere first Baron Empain entertained all of Egypt's *hôtes de marques* including King Albert and Queen Elizabeth of the Belgians during their pre-First World War visit to Egypt. The last to live there were Janine and Huguette Empain, who much preferred the lounges of the trendy Heliopolis Sporting Club or the roof garden of the old Semiramis Hotel to the sepulchral halls of their grandfather's palace. In between there was the playboy son, Baron Jean Empain. He took to entertaining his guests either at the Heliopolis races or at his innumerable palace balls where he cut a dashing figure with his multiple consorts. It was an American cabaret dancer Rozell Rowland, a.k.a. Goldie, who finally nailed him to the altar. The baron and the showgirl had met in a Cairo nightclub where she performed painted entirely in gold.

The heirs sold the palace in 1957. The sheen of this inimitable structure has since evaporated. It hasn't just faded; it's been stripped away. Gone are the mural frescos and massive gilded doors. Gone also are the balustrades, the beautifully designed parquet floors and the gold-plated doorknobs. Even the famed Belgian mirrors were wrenched from their sockets. Instead of gilded ceilings, bat droppings are everywhere, making it impossible to believe that this was once the nexus of economic power and the toast of international café society.

No doubt incredible stories will continue to come out of this palace and its lost fortunes. None, however, will be more unbelievable than the one about the priceless architectural treasure left to decay and crumble in full view of every minister, VIP, tourist and airline passenger as they motor up the airport road on their way in or out of Cairo.

Ottoman pavilion

The three kilometre-long island of Rhoda is unofficially divided into a northern and southern section with the Manial Palace in the middle. The name of the island reportedly derives from a residence that once stood in the south, belonging to Prince Manial of the Bahari Mamlukes.

Two historic landmarks are in the southern section. The older by far is the *Mikyas al Nil* (nilometer) used since civilization began to measure the progress of the Nile flood, thus predicting the resulting harvest and taxation. With the Nile now ensnared behind Aswan's High Dam, the retired nilometer serves as a reminder that for 7,000 years of recorded history the annual floods had religiously synchronized the entire nation's psyche.

The first recorded evidence of the present nilometer goes back to the year 715 during the reign of Omayad Caliph Sulayman Abdel Malek. Restored in 815 by Caliph Al Mamoun, it toppled over during an exceptionally high flood in 850. Rebuilt by Caliph Al Motawakil and subsequently restored by Fatimid Caliph Al Mostanssir in 1092, the Nilometre survived albeit in a poor state up until the arrival of the French Expedition under Napoleon Bonaparte in 1798.

Plans and drawings by Bonaparte's scholars show the nilometer with a bubble dome. At its next rebuilding this dome was replaced by a pointed vault inspired by an eighteenth-century painting by Danish traveller Fredrik Ludvig Norden. Accidentally destroyed in 1825 following an explosion in the nearby *barood-khana* (powder factory), the vault was refitted using Norden's painting as a reference for a second time.

The other important landmark at the island's southern tip is the Manasterli Pavilion. This delightful nineteenth-century structure was actually the Salamlek section of a much larger complex that included a

Haramlek and an adjoining garden. In its entirety the Manasterli complex, rich in Islamic design, was known as the Red Palace. The surviving riverside pavilion reflects the character of some of the showy halls on the Bosphorus with its deep curved cornice, wood bracing, inlaid windows, terrace and undulating arches.

The Haramlek, built *circa* 1846, and its bordering garden disappeared in the 1950s to make way for a water treatment plant completed in 1961. With regards to these radical changes an ongoing litigation 'Manasterli Estate vs. Ministry of Public Works' emerged and is still pending a final court decision. Asserting that they were never properly compensated, claimants are countering the government's April 24, 1943, decision to appropriate the Red Palace and some of its annexes.

The acknowledged owner of the complex was Hassan Fouad al Manasterli Pasha, who, according to one of his descendants, hailed from Manastir, an area on the Macedonian-Greek border. He held several important posts during the short reign of Abbas I including that of Governor of Cairo in 1854 and Head of Interior in 1857. It was at the Manasterli pavilion that the Pasha held his *diwania* (meetings). It was also during that time that he was proclaimed custodian of the nearby nilometer.

Having rebuilt the neighbouring mosque of *Game'a al Mikyas*, the Pasha was buried in the newer nearby version on September 30, 1859. For several generations thereafter the Manasterli Pavilion was the official launch pad for the *Wafaa al Nil* (Indebtedness to the Nile) celebrations over which the Manasterli family proudly presided.

Manasterli Pavilion made history once more, this time after the Second World War when King Farouk, along with several Arab monarchs and leaders met there in 1947 to discuss final arrangements regarding the creation of an Arab League.

Spared the demolition ball, the nilometer, the Manasterli mosque, the Manasterli Pavilion and its annexes are now under the aegis of the ministry of culture. Part of the surviving complex has been transformed into a cultural centre and most recently into the Umm Kulthum Museum. The pavilion itself is home to the newly-created International Music Centre where concerts, recitals and other cultural manifestations are held.

Turkish delight

When he commissioned Sheikh Mohammed Afifi to create his magnificent oriental *alcazar*, Prince Mohammed Ali Tewfik chose the island of Rhoda. Not only was it, back then, safe from the dust and turmoil of modern Cairo, it also housed the remains of the *Bostan al Kebir* (Big Gardens) started in 1829 by the Prince's great-grandfather, Viceroy Ibrahim Pasha. The silt-laden island was still home to banyans, cedars, royal palms and Indian rubber trees.

A modern-day Ibn Battuta, the well-travelled and European-educated prince was bent on reviving what remained of the fabled gardens in a large dedicated enclosure henceforth known as the Manial Palace. Born in the palace of Koubbeh north of Cairo, then on the edge of the desert, Mohammed Ali Tewfik retained vivid recollections of its "garden of a thousand delights," as he described it in his unpublished journal.

With Manial Palace nearing completion in 1900, the prince and his head gardener took off for the four corners of the globe in search of saplings and one-of-a-kind floral species with which to enrich the palace gardens. The pride of the collection consisted of several cacti acquisitions from Mexico.

It was therefore against a background of luxuriant tropical and desert plants that the five detached palace buildings formed the ensemble of Manial Palace with a prevailing Turco-Islamic aesthetic. Whether in the Salamlek (reception and public halls), the Haramlek (private quarters), the Throne Room, the Golden Hall or the palace mosque, Turkish ceramics from Iznik and Kutahaya adorned the walls.

The palace's plaster and wooden ceilings were decorated with intricate designs and works of art from which hung giant Turkish chandeliers and glass *mishkas*. And if the darkened and confined arabesque living quarters and salons abounded with Turkish jades, Persian opals and inestimable ceramics, the palace's marble and wooden floors were covered with priceless oriental carpets. The walls, meanwhile, were graced by *sermas* and portraits of Egyptian and Turkish royals, some of them painted especially by court favourite Hedayat.

While it is difficult to distinguish between the private and public areas of the Haramlek, the fanciful Diwan with its lookout tower is probably where the prince wrote the polished publications describing his travels. Housed somewhere by the southern corner of the palace gardens was a collection of stuffed sub-Saharan fauna, many of which had been personally hunted by the Prince. Situated nearby were the royal stables stocked with pure-bred Arabians.

Having spent a substantial part of his life as monarch-in-waiting, Prince Mohammed Ali Tewfik never made it to the throne yet it appears he was prepared for such an eventuality. Tucked away in his palace gardens is a facsimile throne room. Whether out of design and ambition, or simply another fetish with which to embellish his wondrous environment, the purpose of this unique hall remains a riddle.

In *A King Betrayed*, self-styled royal biographer Adel Sabit describes the prince as "a harmless, colourless and uncontroversial snob devoid of any ambition save that formalities be observed at all times". On the other hand, Mohammed Ali Tewfik's grandnephew, Prince Abbas A. Hilmi, currently an investment banker in London and Cairo, remembers him as a devout and cultured man. "He was so aloof it was almost impossible to break through the immaculate façade."

Twice Egypt's Heir Presumptive (1892-99 and 1936-52) and for a short while Head of the Regency Council, the throne-hall-that-never-was became the venue where the tidily attired prince—best known for his precariously slanted tarboush—held virtual court directing etiquette and protocol.

Several contemporaries attest the palace salons were never without grace. "Privileged friends and select members within the royal entourage were sporadically invited to a variety of genteel lectures, concerts and poetry readings," remarks Aziza Sabit, one of his younger relations. "These were elaborate affairs where Turkish Delight was served next to French pastries and *petit-fours*." It appears that at these selective encounters, conversation was conducted in a simultaneous hushed babble of Turkish, French and English, for although the prince spoke excellent Arabic, it was a tongue alien to most of his high born peers.

For other kinds of entertainment, there were music, billiard, fencing and reading rooms situated directly above the movie-set throne hall.

It was at Manial Palace that the prince's houseguest, Camille Saint-Saens, gave private recitals and composed certain pieces, including 'Piano Concerto no. 5' and 'The Egyptian'.

With the birth of King Farouk's only son in January 1952, the thought of reigning over Egypt was forever erased from the septuagenarian prince's mind. In any case, Mohammed Ali's dynasty would rendezvous with a fatal blow the following July when the Free Officers did away with Egypt's tottering monarchy.

Like his older brother, Khedive Abbas Hilmi, who died in exile in Geneva in 1944, Prince Mohammed Ali Tewfik also expired in Switzerland, not far from Chateau de Lancy where he had studied as a schoolboy. And despite his having prepared an elaborate marble mausoleum in Cairo for his final resting-place, his remains were never returned to Egypt. "Perhaps it had something to do with the fact that the mausoleum was dismantled and the marble used for President Gamal Abdel Nasser's own tomb," remarks a younger member of his family.

Just as he had planned his final resting-place, Prince Mohammed Ali Tewfik left specific instructions regarding Manial Palace. In the 1940s, the childless prince decreed that the palace and its newly added private museum were to be turned into a *waqf*—trust— with the intention that after his death its entirety should serve as a museum of antiquities. Similarly, the garden would become a public park.

But before the Prince's wishes could be honoured, a turbulent interim period intruded with dire consequences. Exactly when is difficult to say, yet it was during the second decade of the republic that the palace gardens succumbed to the first post-monarchy attempts at tourism promotion. For starters, rudimentary wooden cabanas were potted between the park's magnificent trees so that libidinous Club Med holiday makers could frolic freely with the consent of palace's new caretaker—the newly formed ministry of tourism.

Then came the winding cement alleys carved out of the floral base and a large swimming pool dug where unique tropical trees had once stood. What escaped the Rothschilds-owned holiday chain went to a mélange of government departments so that an army of futile bureaucrats and civil servants, most of them insensitive to their unique surroundings, replaced what had formerly been the exclusive preserve of royal guards, black eunuchs and trained palace personnel.

The Golden Hall meanwhile became the scene of sundry Sadat-era mega-weddings. And where poetry readings and piano recitals had once filled the rarefied palace halls, belly dancers and gawking commoners were pounding the floor to the sounds of disco music. Such festive occasions were alien in the prince's days. His 1941 marriage to his French companion of many years, Suzanne Hemon, had been such a private affair that few realised

Prince Mohammed Ali Tewfik was no longer a bachelor. When in September 1940 a few privileged Egyptian and Ottoman royals attended the wedding of the prince's nephew to the beautiful Neslishah, a granddaughter of Turkey's last sultan, not even the tiniest *zagroota* (ululation) had been allowed. All one ever heard coming out of the palace was the occasional drawn out cry of a *karawan* (stone curlew) going to sleep or the chirp of some migratory species in blissful transit.

Nowadays, thanks to a government decree to conserve and restore all former royal palaces, the Manial Palace and its botanical gardens have a new lease on life. Plans to further transform the palace into a five-star hotel have been scrapped and the century old complex will revert to what it was originally destined to be: a museum and botanical garden.

Amen.

7. Appendices

Pre-1950 architects
Garden City, Zamalek, Giza

Adolfo Brandani (Erfan Seif al Nasr Villa, now Greek Embassy, Zamalek)
Albert Zananiri (various)
Ali Labib Gabr (various & Indian Embassy residence)
Angelo Ercolani (Gezira Palace Hotel)
Antoine Selim Nahas (various)
Antonio Lasciac (various)
Ara Charakian (Harari Building)
Auguste Perret (Elias Awad Pasha residence, Zamalek, pulled down)
C. Calligopoulo (Avramoussi Building, Zamalek)
Carlo Prampolini (Chalres Beyerle Palace, GC)
Charles Ayrout (various)
Ciro Pantanelli (Kasr al Nil Palace, pulled down)
Domenico Limongelli (various)
Edward Matasek (various)
Ernest Jaspar (Gezira Mansion)
Ernest Richmond (government villas, Zamalek)
Ferdinand Debanne (Boulad Building, Corniche, GC)
Florestano di Fausto (Italian Embassy)
G. Scognamiglio (No. 8 Brazil Street)
Garo Balian (various)
Gaston Aghion (Villa Mosseri, now Russian Embassy residence)
George Parcq (various)
George Philipous (Phillipous Building, Zamalek)
Giacomo Alessandro Loria (Smouha Buildings, GC)
Giuseppe Tavarelli (Ali Ibrahim Pasha Villa, GC; Awqaf Building, Midan Falaki)
Giussepe Mazza (various)
Guido Gavassi (Zamalek Building; Alaili Villa, Giza)
Hardy, Jacques (French Embassy)
Henri Fresco (Philippe Drakidis Building, Zamalek)
Julius Franz (Gezira Palace)
Luigi Manham (Ali Mahmoud Bey Palace, now Russian Embassy, Zamalek)
Mahmoud Riad (various)
Marco Olivetti (various)
Mario Rossi (Gabalaya House, Zamalek; various)

Maurice Menasche (Villa Leon Regenstreif, Giza)
Max Edrei (various)
Michel Liberman (various)
Mustafa Fahmi Pasha (numerous)
Nubar Kevorkian (Sapriel Building, GC)
Paolo Caccia Dominioni (various)
Raoul Zeheri (various)
Raymond Antonious (various)
Romollo Gilardini (Ali Sadek Bey Villa, now Wafd Party HQ, Giza)
Tuilo Parvis (Semiramis Hotel)
V. Tragni (Zamalek Mansion Building)
Ramses Wissa Waasef
Zulke (Villa Abdel Baki al Kocheri, Zamalek)

Some works by the more prolific architects mentioned

Albert Zananiri

Auberge des Pyramides, Avenue des Pyramides
Auberge du Lac, Lake Karoun, Fayoum; inaugurated by Winston Churchill
Chourbagi textile factories
Dar al Chifaa Hospital, Abassia
Dar al Hilal printing & publishing house (founded by George Zaidan), Lazoghli
Elie Sedanoui Villa, Ruffer Street, Ruchdi Pasha, Alexandria
Elie Sednaoui Building, 6 Adly Pasha Street
Freda Court, 10 Montaza Street, Zamalek
Ismail Sidky Pasha Building, Maa'had al Swissri Street (now Aziz Abaza), Zamalek,
Osman Abdel Gaffar (ex-Mahran) Villa (Embassy of Kuwait Residence), Dokki
Paul Rostom Building, Hadika Street, Garden City
Saad al Abdallah al Sabbah (Kuwait) Building (ex-Zananiri), 7 Hassan Sabri, Zamalek
Wadie Saad Building, Salah al Din Street, Zamalek
Zaidan (Emil & Shoukri) Building, Abdel-Khalek Sarwat Street
Zaidan (Emil & Shoukri) Building, Midan al Tahrir

Antoine Selim Nahas

Al Chams Building, Midan Kasr al Dubara
Al Chams Building, Mubtadayan
Al Mukawlun al Arab Building, Adly Street
Aziz Abdel Malek Hanna Building, Midan Sheraton, Giza
Aziz Bahari Building I & II, Midan al Tahrir
Aziz Bahari Building, Midan Moustafa Kamel (ex-Suares)
Aziza Abdel Malek Building, Midan Sheraton, Giza
Badrawi Building, Bab al Louk
Baehler Building
Bissada Building
Borg al Giza (Abou al Fotouh) Building, Nile Street, Giza
Choucha Building, 26th of July Avenue
College Des Freres, Daher
Doss Building, Soliman Pasha/Fouad Avenue
Farid al Atrash Building, Nile Street, Giza
Francois Tager Building, Corniche al Nil, Kasr al Dubara
Inji Zadeh Building, Ramses Street
Lebon Building, Gabalaya Street, Zamalek
Leon Chaldjian Building, Blocks A & B, Soliman Pasha and Baehler Streets
(participation L. Nafilyan)
Lewa Building, facing Waqf Institution
Mirshak Building, Giza
Mirshak Villa, Nile Street, Giza
Mitry Buildings, 14 & 16 Nabatat Street, Garden City
Naus-Eid Building, Kasr al Nil Street (opposite Automobile Club)
Nitocrise Building, 26th of July Avenue
Paul Lifschitz Villa, Midan Mosseri, Maadi
Protestant Church (behind Mogamaa), Kasr al Dubara
Sabet Apartment Building, Corniche, Garden City
Shooting Club, Dokki
Shoucair Building, 13 Cherif Street
Soussa Building, corner Tahrir Street and Soliman Pasha
Taleb Building, Fouad Avenue
Tawil Building
Wahba-Choucha Building, Cherif Pasha Street opposite ex-Al Ahram

Antonio Lasciac

Adly Yeken/Sherif Sabri Palace, Garden City (demolished)
Asicurazione de Trieste Building, Kasr al Nil Street

Banque Misr, Mohammed Farid Street
Khedivial Buildings, Emad al Din Street
Mazloum Pasha Palace, 13 Mazloum Pasha Street (pulled down in 1935 after serving as a Lycée Français)
Omar Sultan Pasha Palace, Bab al Louk
Prince Youssef Kamal Palace
Princess Amina Palace (Tahra), Koubbeh
Princess Nimet Kamal al Din Palace (Foreign Affairs), Kasr al Dubara
Said Halim Palace (Nasriya School), Maarouf, Cairo
Suares Palace (non-extant)
Zafaraan Palace (later Ein-Shams University)

Domenico Limongelli

French Embassy Residence (ex-Villa Sinot Hanna), Giza
Wassef Boutros-Ghali Pasha Villa, Giza
Building on Kasr al Nil Street atop Cinema Kasr al Nil
Limongelli Building, 4 Hod al Laban, Garden City
Sobhani Villa, (replaced by Giza Sheraton)
Sacred Hearts Church, Abdel Khalek Sarwat Street (corner Ramses Street)
Salesian Institute, Rod al Farag
Philomene Villa
University Music Academy, Shagaret al Durr Street, Zamalek
Church of St. Mary, Zeitun, Cairo

Georges Parcq

Cassab Building, 14 Saray al Kobra, Garden City
Credit Foncier Egyptien Villa (Mubarak Public Library), Nile Street, Giza
Emile Jacob Villa, Corniche al Nil, Garden City
French Embassy Chancery, Giza (participation Jacques Hardy)
Martatos Building, 6 Walda Pasha, Garden City
Elias Sednaoui Villa, 13 Ahmed Pasha Street, Garden City
Joseph Simon Sednaoui Villa, 13 Tolombat Street, Garden City
Sednaoui Department Store, Midan Khazindar
Setton (or Sabet) Building, 2 & 3 Ismail Pasha Street, Garden City
Shahin Pasha (Hassan) Building "Nile View" 18 Saray al Gezira Street, Zamalek
Shahin (Negm al Din) Building, Hoda Sha'raawy Street
National Insurance Building, Midan Moustafa Kamel (ex-Suares)
Union Vie de Paris Building, Avenue Fouad
Demerdash Building, corner Emad al Din, Alfy, Saray al Azbakia & Bustan al Dikka Streets

Giuseppe Mazza

Airways Building, Midan Tahrir
Agababa Building, Soliman Pasha Street
Apartment Building (Banque du Caire), Adly Street
Elhamy Hussein Building(s), Garden City
Muscat Gobran Building, Ibrahim Naguib Street, Garden City
Groppi's Building (Razouk Homsi), Midan Soliman Pasha
Sednaoui Building, Midan Soliman Pasha
Menasce-Mayer Villa, Garden City

Giuseppe Tavarelli

Ali Ibrahim Pasha Villa, Garden City
Ismail Sidki Pasha, Zamalek
Ariditi Building, Zamalek
Mahmoud Tayar Bey Building(s), Zamalek
Mahmoud al Meski Building, Zamalek

Gaston Rossi

Cinema Metro, Cairo and Alexandria
Cinema Kasr al Nil, Kasr al Nil Street
Kom-Ombo Mosque, Kom-Ombo
Hotel Continental Galleries, Opera Square
Chester Beatty Villa, Pyramids Avenue
Hanan Villa, Zamalek
Victor Salama Villa, Dokki
Cerva Factory, Heliopolis
S.E.P. Offices, Dokki
Immobilia Building (participation Max Edrei), Cherif Street, Cairo
Automobile Club, Kasr al Nil Street
Elie Mosseri Mausoleum, Bassateen
Bajocchi (Albert) Villa, Road 17, Maadi

Henri Fresco

Philippe Drakidis Building, Midan Sidky, Zamalek
Embassy Court, Gabalaya Street, Zamalek
Building No. 18 Aziz Osman, Zamalek
Building No. 36 Mansour Mohammed, Zamalek
Emmanuel Appel Building, Tantah Street, Heliopolis

Marco Olivetti (partner with Maurice Cattaui & Edward Matasek)

Continental Hotel transformation works, Opera Square
Homsi Building, Tewfikieh
Lloyds Bank, Cairo
Mausoleum Ades, Bassateen
Mausoleum Marzouk Family
Palais Abdel Khalek Sarwat Pasha, Giza
Palais Clemente Antonio, Cairo
Palais Del'Mar, Kasr al Dubara
Palais Dr. E. Herdan Bey
Palais Mansour & Ades
Palais Taverna-Bertolissi, Soliman Pasha Street
Villa Abdel Hakim Marzouk, Giza
Villa Emil Ades, Kasr al Dubara
Villa Leon Suares, Kasr al Dubara
Villa Mohammed Marzouk, Giza
Villa Youssef Cattaui Pasha, Garden City

Max Edrei

Cinema Radio (participation Garo Balian), Soliman Pasha Street
F. Nahas vaults, Melchite Cemetery, Old Cairo (collaboration with Jacques Hardy & Leon Azema)
Green Villa, replaced by University Bridge, Giza
Hettena Buildings, Abdel Khalek Sarwat Street
Immobilia Building, Cherif Pasha/Kasr al Nil Street
Court Buildings, 26th of July Street
Khayatt Buildings, Adil Abou Bakr Street, Zamalek
Mohammed Shahin Pasha Building, Sheik Hamza Street, Cairo
Union Building, Zamalek (participation Garo Balian)

Michel Liberman

Alaili Villa, 10 Taha Hussein Street, Zamalek (US Embassy property)
Bindari Villa, Nile Street, Giza,
Clouet Villa, Shagaret al Durr, Zamalek (Ministry of Culture)
Ex-Brazil Embassy Residence, Nile Street (corner Sobhi Pasha) Street, Giza
Hamed al Lozi Building, 5 Mohammed Saqib Pasha Street
Khalifa Villa (Embassy of Bahrain), 15 Brazil Street, Zamalek
Matattia Apartment Building, 5 Taha Hussein Street, Zamalek
Sarruf-Shoucair Villa (Citibank), Ahmed Pasha Street, Garden City

Raymond Antonius

Ahmed Hamdi Villa, Giza
Anderson Villa, Giza
Cassab Villa, Giza
Elias Ghadban Building, 11 Nabatat Street, Garden City (participation Aklimandos)
Elie Curiel Building (sold in 1949 to Dr. Mohammed Reda), 15 Nabatat, Garden City
Debbané Villa, Heliopolis
Emil Kahil Villa, Heliopolis
Farid Saad Building, Misr Street, Heliopolis
Hatwell Villa, Heliopolis
Khouri Building, Maarouf
Tamraz (Edouard) Building, 20 Saray al Gezira, Zamalek
Tamraz (Edouard) Villa, 5 Mohammed Mazhar, Zamalek

Mustafa Mahmoud Fahmi Pasha

Better-known works

Cairo University
Numerous Primary & Secondary Schools
Mausoleum of Prime Minister Saad Zaghloul
Mausoleum of Prime Minister Adly Yeken Pasha
Mausoleum of Prime Minister Ismail Sidki Pasha
Mausoleum of Prime Minister Mohammed Mahmoud Pasha
Mausoleum of Minister Aziz Izzet Pasha
Mausoleum of Senator Ali Shaarawi Pasha
Church and mausoleum of Minister Naguib Mahfouz Pasha
Medical Society "Dar al Hikma" Headquarters on Kasr al Aini Street
Engineering & Architectural Society Building on Ramses Street
Young Muslim Association Building
Benevolent Muslim Society Hospital
Egyptian Women Union Building on Kasr al Aini Street
Agouza Hospital
Bridge at Montazah Palace in Alexandria
Exhibition Buildings (Grand & Petit Palais) in Exhibition Grounds, Zamalek
Residence of Dr. Naguib Mahfouz Pasha, Garden City
Mansion of Justice Minister Mahmoud Ghaleb Pasha, Pyramids Road
His own villa, No. 1 Said Zulfikar Street, Manial al Rhoda.
Numerous villas and apartment blocks

Manufacturing plant at Ghamrah for account of United Yeast Co. LTD., Manchester

Annexes of Haram al Sharif, Mecca, Saudi Arabia

Mosque in Medina, Saudi Arabia

Three royal palaces in Riyadh, Saudi Arabia

Positions held

Chief Architect of Royal Palaces 1930-52

Director General of the State Buildings Department 1926-39

Director General of Cairo Town Service 1939-45

Director General of Alexandria Municipality 1945-49

Minister of Public Works 1949-50

Director General of Cairo Municipality 1950-52

Decorations received

Title of pasha in 1946

Grand Officer of the Cordon of the Nile

Commander of the Legion d'honneur, France

Grand Officer of the Order of the King of Greece

Grand Officer of the Order of the King of Albania

Grand Officer of the Order of Humayun, Iran

Grand Officer of the Crown of Italy

The House of Mohammed Aly

1805-1953

Viceroy Mohammed Aly	1805-48
Viceroy Ibrahim	1848-48
Viceroy Abbas	1848-54
Viceroy Said	1854-63
Viceroy/Khedive Ismail	1863-79
Khedive Tewfik	1879-92
Khedive Abbas Hilmi	1892-1914
Sultan Hussein Kamel	1914-17
Sultan/King Fouad	1917-36
King Farouk	1936-52
Regency Council	1952-June 1953

Prime Ministers of Egypt

1892-1953

Mustafa Fahmy Pasha	1892-93	1895-1908		
Hussein Fakhry Pasha	1893-93			
Mustafa Riaz Pasha	1893-94			
Nubar Nubarian Pasha	1894-95			
Boutros Ghali Pasha	1908-10			
Mohammed Said Pasha	1910-14	1919-19		
Hussein Rouchdi Pasha	1914-19			
Youssef Wahba Pasha	1919-20			
Adly Yeken Pasha	1921-21	1926-27	1929-30	
Abdel Khalek Sarwat	1922-22	1927-28		
Mohammed Tewfik Nessim	1922-23	1934-36		
Yehya Ibrahim Pasha	1923-24			
Saad Zaghloul Pasha	1924-24			
Ahmed Ziwar Pasha	1924-25			
Mustafa al Nahas Pasha	1928-28	1930-30	1936-38	1942-44 1950-52
Mohammed Mahmoud Pasha	1928-29	1937-39		

Ismail Sidki Pasha	1930-33	1946-46	
Abdel Fattah Yehya Pasha	1933-34		
Ali Maher Pasha	1939-40	1952-52	
Hassan Sabry	1940-40		
Hussein Sirry Pasha	1940-42	1949-50	1952-52
Ahmed Maher Pasha	1944-45		
Mahmoud F. Nokrashy Pasha	1945-46	1946-48	
Ibrahim Abdelhadi Pasha	1948-49		
Naguib Al Hilali Pasha	1952-52		
General Mohammed Naguib	1952-June 1953		

General chronology

1868	King Fouad born in Giza Palace
1869	Inauguration of Suez Canal
1872	Statue of Mohammed Ali designed by Jacquemart erected in Alexandria
1874	Statue of Soliman Pasha designed by Jacquemart erected in Cairo's new Ismailia quarter
1880	Inauguration of Credit Foncier Egyptien
1882	British occupation of Egypt
1891	Giza Palace park home to Egypt's first zoo
1893	Inauguration of British Embassy in Kasr al Dubara
1896	Creation of Greek Catholic Cemetery
1897	Construction of Sakakini Palace in Daher
1897	Inauguration of Giza Zoo in former Giza palace gardens
1898	Inauguration of National Bank of Egypt
1899	Inauguration of Gates of Heaven Synagogue
1902	Inauguration of Antiquities Museum by Khedive Abbas Hilmi
1903	Inauguration of Credit Foncier Egyptien building in Cairo
1905	Garden City created
1906	Creation of the Heliopolis Oasis Company; birth of new town
1907	Financial crash
1907	Inauguration of Semiramis Hotel
1907	Construction of Hindu-style palace begins in Heliopolis
1908	Inauguration of Abbas and Malek al Saleh Bridges
1909	Inauguration of Maison Groppi
1910	Construction of Tiring Department store on Ataba Square
1910	Inauguration of St. David Building downtown Cairo
1910	Inauguration of Heliopolis Palace Hotel
1911	Inauguration of Heliopolis Mosque
1912	Inauguration of Bab al Louk indoor market
1913	Inauguration of Sednaoui department store at Midan Khazindar
1914	Inauguration of Café Riche
1914	Britain proclaims protectorate over Egypt.
1914	Groundbreaking of Cairo University complex by Khedive Abbas Hilmi
1914	Inaugural Sultanic cortege departs Kamal al Din Palace for Abdin
1922	British Protectorate over Egypt ends
1924	Inauguration of Societe des Amis de l'Art
1925	Groundbreaking of new French consulate downtown cairo

1925   Inauguration of Groppi Soliman Pasha branch
1925   Egypt Awakening statue by Mahmoud Mokhtar unveiled at Bab al
        Hadid
1927   Saad Zaghloul dies
1927   Murder of Solomon Cicurel
1928   Groundbreaking of Fouad al Awal University designed by Eric
        Newnum
1929   Inauguration of new Italian Embassy building
1929   Founder of Heliopolis dies; Baron Empain buried in Heliopolis
        Basilica
1931   Inauguration by King Fouad of Modern Arts Museum
1934   Inauguration of Justice Palace
1934   Military Museum opens in Kasr al Dubara on Sheikh Barakat Street
1936   Saad Zaghloul Pasha's remains laid in former Pantheon
1936   Inauguration of Desert Highway between Cairo and Alexandria
1937   Exposition France-Egypte in Paris
1938   Giza home to new French Embassy
1938   Ministry of Foreign Affairs moves to Kemal al Din Palace by the Nile
1940   Mustafa Kamel statue designed in 1910 by L. Savine unveiled by
        King Farouk
1941   Gray Pillars seat of British Minister of State
1947   British military evacuate Kasr al Nil Barracks
1947   Bomb in Cinema Metro
1947   Midan Suares renamed Midan Mustafa Kamel
1947   US purchases embassy property in Kasr al Dubara
1947   Kasr al Walda Pasha torn down
1949   Mixed Courts abolished
1951   Beba Izzedine dies in car crash
1951   Inauguration by King Farouk of Desert Institute
1952   Burning of Cairo
1952   King Farouk abdicates
1953   Republic of Egypt declared
1954   Bomb placed in Groppi
1954   Name changes of Cairo streets
1954   British Embassy cedes grounds for construction of Nile corniche
1955   Statue of Ramses transferred from Mit Rihan to Midan Bab al Hadid
1955   Egypt Awakening statue moved to Giza
1955   Groundbreaking of Nile Hilton Hotel attended by President Nasser
1956   Tri-partite invasion of Egypt (Suez War)
1957   University Bridge completed by Germany's Krupp
1958   Completion of Cairo's tallest building nicknamed "Imarat Belmont"

1959	Inauguration of Nile Hilton designed by Santa Monica's Wilton Becket
1960	Inauguration of Arab League building designed by Mahmoud Riad
1961	Inauguration of Egypt's first Sound and Light Show at Giza
1964	Statue of Talaat Harb replaces Soliman Pasha
1966	Inauguration of Kasr al Nil Bridge "Kamal al Din Salah" ramp
1971	Cairo Opera House burns to the ground
1979	Statue of Simon Bolivar unveiled
1995	Inauguration of Mubarak Public Library in Giza
1995	Inauguration of renovated Mr & Mrs Mohammed Mahmoud Khalil Museum

Chronology of Gezira/Zamalek

1864	Construction of Gezira Palace in several stages
1869	Empress of France and Emperor of Austria-Hungary stay at Gezira Palace
1869	Prince and Princess of Wales stay at Gezira Palace
1872	Inauguration of first Kasr al Nil Bridge and placement of four lions designed by Jacquemart
1873	Princes' wedding (40 days)
1876	Construction of Khedive Ismail Mosque on Gezira Island
1883	Gezira island home to Khedivial Club (Gezira Sporting Club)
1888	African Mission sets up school, church and farm on Gezira island
1899	Inauguration of Cotton Museum
1902	Inauguration of aquarium
1903	Inauguration of Anglo-American Hospital
1906	Construction of 19 villas in Gezira
1907	Inauguration of the National Club (Nadi al Ahli)
1907	Gezira welcomes first apartment building "Gezira House"
1907	Inauguration of neo-Gothic Villa Hug
1910	Agatha Christie spends month at Gezira Hotel
1912	Inauguration of Boulak (Abu Ela) Bridge
1912	First diplomatic agency moves to Gezira
1915	Inauguration of Zohria Garden
1919	Gezira Hotel purchased by Habib Lutfallah Pasha
1924	Assassination of Sirdar Sir Lee Stack
1930	Polo stand burns to ground at Gezira Sporting Club
1933	Inauguration by King Fouad of new Kasr al Nil Bridge
1933	Inauguration of Andalusian Garden

1936	Inauguration of Museum of Civilization; Grand & Petit Palais designed by M. Fahmy Pasha
1937	New St. Joseph Church designed by Bantarle-Guarienti of Verona; supervised by Gnatta & Tonazzolli
1938	Statue of Saad Zaghloul by Mokhtar unveiled
1939	New St. Joseph Church consecrated; old church becomes ad hoc parish theatre
1940	Hassan Sabry Pasha dies while reading Speech from the Throne
1941	Gabalaya Street renamed Hassan Sabry Street
1942	Inauguration of Nachat Pasha Mosque on Bahgat Ali Street; contractor Ibrahim Rabie
1944	Assassination of Lord Moyne on Hassan Sabry Street
1945	Inauguration by King Farouk of restored Gezira Mosque
1945	Gezira's Kamel Mohammed Street zionist wedding
1949	Inauguration of new race stand at Gezira Sporting Club
1950	Ahmed Maher Pasha statue unveiled by Mother Nature
1951	Gezira Sporting Club taken over by state
1952	Vatican declares Zamalek separate parish detached from Boulak, Agouza and Imbaba.
1955	Gezira Casino gutted by fire
1955	Inauguration of Zamalek Mosque designed by Mario Rossi; contractor Abdel Khalek Mustafa
1958	Ramses II obelisk brought from Tanis to Zamalek's Andalus Garden
1960	Groundbreaking of Mar'ashly Church designed by Ramses Wissa Wassef
1961	Inauguration of Cairo Tower designed by Naum Shebib
1963	Inauguration of Mokhtar Museum designed by Ramses Wissa Wassef
1969	Inauguration of Moheb Pasha Mosque on Hassan Sabry Street
1972	Construction of the 6th of October flyover begins
1977	Groundbreaking of All Saint's Cathedral; Awad & Selim Kamel architects
1982	Inauguration of Marriott Hotel
1982	Gezira Sheraton designed by Alan Steiner, Hussein Mohana & Ahmad Fathi
1988	All Saints Cathedral consecrated
1988	Inauguration of new Opera House designed by Nieken Sikkei of Japan
1991	Opening of AUC Hostel; Architects P.S. Sabour & Amr Al Alfy
1995	Inauguration of Greater Cairo Library
2001	Inauguration of Hadikat al Horreya wa al Sakkafa

Glossary

Bowwab	doorman/caretaker
Ciftlik	extensive agricultural domain
Dahabiah	house boat
Daira	privy council offices
Dameh	checkers
Dawwar	folksy country house
Diwania	reunion
Emaret	building
Feddan	roughly one acre
Hanem	lady
Hara	alley
Haramlek	private quarters
Infitah	economic liberalism
Karawan	stone curlew
Kasr	palace
Khawaga	foreigner
Khediva-Mother	Queen Mother
Kobri	bridge
Manshar	clothesline
Mashrabiya	wooden latticework, often covering windows
Midan	square, roundabout, traffic circle
Mishka	glass chandelier
Okel	house containing commercial, storage and lodging space
Qassaba	midpoint
Salamlek	official quarters
Saray	palace
Serma	silk embroidery
Sharia	street
Shatarang	chess
Shisha	water pipe for smoking tobacco
Sitt	woman
Tawlah	backgammon
Waqf	endowment or trust
Willaya	Ottoman province
Zagroota	ululation
Zar	spiritual dance

Bibliography and sources

Newspapers & periodicals

Al Ahram
Ahram Weekly
The American Architect
La Bourse Egyptienne,
Bulletin de L'Union Syndicale des Agriculteurs d'Egypte
Egypte Nouvelle
Egyptian Gazette
Al-Emara.
Le Figaro
Ha'aretz
Le Journal du Caire
Al Lata'ef al Masreya
Le Mondain Egyptien
Al Mussawar
Le Progrés Egyptien.
The Zionist Review

History & literature

Agstner, Rudolf - *Matrikel Buch*, Austrian Cultural Institute, Cairo, 1994

Carman, Barry & McPherson, John - *The Man Who Loved Egypt: Bimbashi McPherson*, BBC Publications, London, 1987

Carnec, Christian - *De Palais en Palais*, Publibook, Paris

Cooper, Artemis - *Cairo in the War 1939-45*, Hamish Hamilton, London, 1989

Copeland, Miles - *A Game of Nations*, Weindefeld & Nicholson, London, 1969

Fargeon, Maurice - *Silhouettes d'Egypte,* Editions Orient, Cairo, 1931

Follett, Ken - *The Key to Rebecca*, William Morrow, New York, 1980

Guerville, Amédée Baillot de - *New Egypt*, Heinemann, London, 1905

Hassan, Hassan Aziz - *In the House of Muhammad Ali*, AUC Press, Cairo, 2000

Kober, Marc et al - *Entre Nil et sable: écrivains d'Égypte d'expression française (1920-1960)*, Montrouge, CNDP, 1999

Lançon, Daniel - *Edmond Jabes l'Egyptien*, Jean Michel Place, Paris, 1997

Leprette, Fernand - *Egypte: Terre du Nil*, Paris, 1939

Lively, Penelope - *Oleander Jacaranda*, Viking, London, 1994

Manning, Olivia - *The Levant Trilogy*, Penguin, London, 1977

Mansfield, Peter - *The British in Egypt*, Holt, Rinehart & Winston, New York, 1971

Martin, Percy F. - *Egypt–Old and New*, George Allen & Unwin, London, 1923

McEwan, Dorothea - *A Catholic Sudan; Dream, Mission, Reality*, Rome, 1987

Mynti, Cynthia - *Paris along the Nile*, AUC Press, Cairo, 1999

Sabit, Adel - *A King Betrayed*, Quartet, London,1989

Shafik, Ahmed Pasha - *Muzakeratee fee noss qarn* (My diaries of a half century), 1934, Egyptian General Book Authority, Cairo, 1994

Sladen, Douglas - *Egypt and the English*, London, Hurst and Blackett, 1908

Stadiem, William - *Too Rich: the High Life and Tragic Death of King Farouk*, Robson Books, London 1992

Storrs, Sir Ronald - *Orientations*, Nicholson & Watson, London, 1943

Thatcher, Margaret - *The Downing Street Years*, HarperCollins, London, 1995

Wavell, Archibald P. - *Allenby in Egypt*, Harrap & Co., London, 1943

Worsfold, W. Basil - *The Redemption of Egypt*, George Allen & Unwin, London, 1899

Wright, A. (ed.), - *Twentieth Century Impressions of Egypt*, Lloyds Publishing Company, London, 1909

Acknowledgements

I have to thank all those who are directly quoted in this book for the kind interest they have shown in my research, and for the encouragement they have given me all along.

To the late Cai Vera Ortiz I am beholden for his insistence that I write this book, otherwise I would be written off as a one trick pony.

To Kadria Foda endless appreciation for sharing a reservoir of information and chronicles that have to do with the Second World War years and beyond.

To Nelly al Alfy and her mother Mrs. Bouthaina Younes, I am indebted for the cover photo, which in a way got me going on this project. Also to Injy Sirry and Mona Samy for photographs of their ancestral homes.

To Luciano Prinzivalli, Marco Olivetti, Selim Nahas, Diego Kuzmin, Myrna and Nevine Zananiri, Mireille and Arlette N. Shebib, Giuseppe Dana, Victor Salama and Kadria Zaki for supplying information on Cairo's interwar and post-Second World War architects.

To May al Gindi for accepting to proof-read the final draft and suggesting changes here and there.

To Karima Khalil for a "fresh pair of eyes".

To Hisham Kassem, publisher of the *Cairo Times*, for his kind permission to reproduce certain articles.

To the proprietors of Lehnert & Landrock for their kind permission to reproduce the photographs appearing on pages 111, 118 and 119.

Index of people mentioned in the text